PENGUIN BOOKS

An Introduction to the Bible

J. W. Rogerson was born in London in 1935 and studied Theology in Manchester, and Semitic Languages in Oxford and Jerusalem. From 1979 to 1994 he was Professor and Head of Department of Biblical Studies at Sheffield University, and he retired in 1996. He is also an Anglican clergyman and a Canon Emeritus of Sheffield Cathedral. His many books and articles cover the historical and social background to the Old Testament, the history of biblical interpretation and the use of the Bible in relation to social, moral, political and environmental issues.

John Hinnells is Advisory Editor for Religious Studies and Non-Western Classics in Penguin. His speciality for over thirty years has been the study of Zoroastrianism, particularly the modern Parsis. In the course of this study he has undertaken overseas fieldwork in fourteen countries, and published several books and numerous scholarly articles. After holding professorships at the University of Manchester and the School of Oriental Studies in London he is now Research Professor in Comparative Religion at the University of Derby. He is the editor of many books, including *Who's Who of Religions* (1996), *The Penguin Dictionary of Religions* (second edition, 1997) and *A New Handbook of Living Religions* (1997), all of which are published in Penguin.

An Introduction to
the Bible

J. W. ROGERSON

PENGUIN BOOKS

PENGUIN BOOKS

Published by the Penguin Group
Penguin Books Ltd, 27 Wrights Lane, London w8 5tz, England
Penguin Putnam Inc., 375 Hudson Street, New York, New York 10014, USA
Penguin Books Australia Ltd, Ringwood, Victoria, Australia
Penguin Books Canada Ltd, 10 Alcorn Avenue, Toronto, Ontario, Canada m4v 3b2
Penguin Books (NZ) Ltd, Private Bag 102902, NSMC, Auckland, New Zealand

Penguin Books Ltd, Registered Offices: Harmondsworth, Middlesex, England

First published by Penguin Books 1999
10 9 8 7 6 5 4 3 2

Set in 10/12.5 pt Monotype Garamond
Typeset by Rowland Phototypesetting Ltd, Bury St Edmunds, Suffolk
Made and printed in Great Britain by Clays Ltd, St Ives plc

For Merab

Contents

Preface

No work has been more intensely studied than the Bible. This is true of its 2,000-year history, and especially of the last 200 years. Yet few members of the general public, and this includes regular church-goers, are aware of the nature or results of this intensive study. Although the present work is an introduction to the Bible rather than to the academic study of the Bible, the one cannot be divorced from the other. Questions such as, 'What is the Bible?', 'Who wrote it, where, when and why?', 'How close are our translations to what the biblical writers wrote?', 'Who decided what would be included and what would be left out?', 'How is the Bible being used today?' can only be answered on the basis of a great deal of technical study; and it is the aim of the present work to try to deal with such questions. Because the technical nature of the material necessitates the use of a certain amount of scholarly jargon, there is a Glossary of important terms and names. Words given in the Glossary are marked *.

Two matters of some importance need to be addressed before the main text begins, and these concern the title of the book and the use of the term 'Old Testament'. The title, 'An Introduction to the Bible', deliberately repeats that used by Stanley A. Cook for his Pelican book published by Penguin in 1945, and the present work was conceived as a replacement for that book and an attempt to emulate Cook's aims as summed up in his sub-title: 'A survey of the history and composition of the books of the Old and New Testaments in the light of modern knowledge, and a discussion of their meaning for the twentieth century'. Among the many changes that have occurred since Cook wrote is a sensitivity among biblical scholars to the anti-Judaism that has historically been implicit in some Christian biblical scholarship, and this has led, in some circles, to the abandonment of the title 'Old Testament', in favour of 'Hebrew Bible' and even to a questioning of the appropriateness of the term 'Bible' without qualification when used in a 'Christian' context. It has been seriously and plausibly suggested that a better title for this book would be 'An Introduction to the Christian Bible'.

In what follows, 'Bible' and 'Old Testament' have been retained for the following reasons. First, although the Bible in the sense of the Old and New Testaments and the Apocrypha would not exist in its present form or forms (see the first chapter) without its conservation by the churches, it has become, at least since the invention of printing, more than simply the property of the churches. A title such as 'An Introduction to the Christian Bible' would give the impression that this was a book about Christianity, which is not the case. On the other hand, I believe that any general reader looking at a book which claimed to be an Introduction to the Bible would be extremely surprised if it contained nothing on the New Testament.

The main reason why some circles have dropped the title 'Old Testament' is because it is an explicitly Christian term which also implies that its content is in some way inferior to or superseded by the New Testament; and it cannot be denied that this is the view of the Old Testament held by many church-goers. That there is also an element of anti-Judaism in this attitude cannot be denied. However, it is easier to sympathize with these difficulties than to find a satisfactory solution. 'Hebrew Bible' has the difficulty, on analogy with 'English Bible', that it is the Bible in Hebrew that is being referred to. 'First' or 'Older Testament', two other suggested titles, do not seem to me to avoid the difficulty that something is being referred to that has been superseded. There is also another major difficulty, and this is that for the early Church, and for the majority of churches since the Reformation in the 16th century, the Old Testament was not simply the twenty-four books of the Hebrew canon, but the larger, Greek, canon including the books that Protestant churches call the Apocrypha. These matters are discussed fully in chapter 1 and cannot be elaborated here. They do, however, lead me to conclude that 'Old Testament' is a title that can be retained, as long as there is sensitivity to the reasons why it has been called into question.

Except where indicated otherwise, quotations are from the Revised Standard Version (RSV). A convention that has become commonplace in recent biblical scholarship is to use the terms BCE (Before the Common Era) and CE (Common Era) instead of BC and AD, and this is followed in the present work.

Among those to whom I wish to express my thanks are Miss Mary Hodge and Professors Philip Davies and John Hinnells who have made constructive comments on the drafts, and my wife Rosalind who has word-processed the text from my longhand. The dedicatee is Merab Lavinia Cracknell.

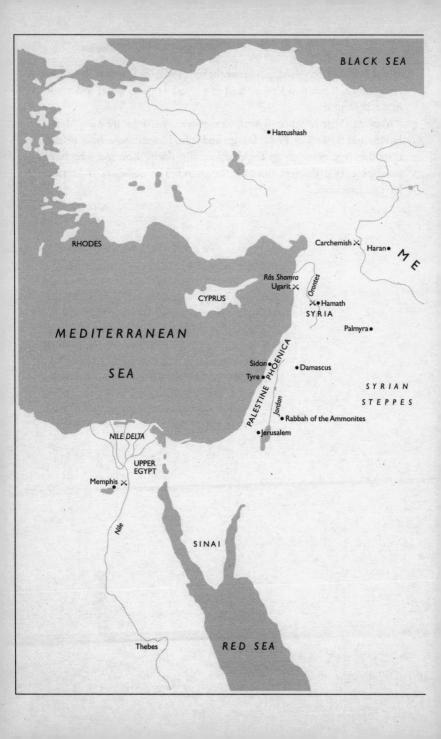

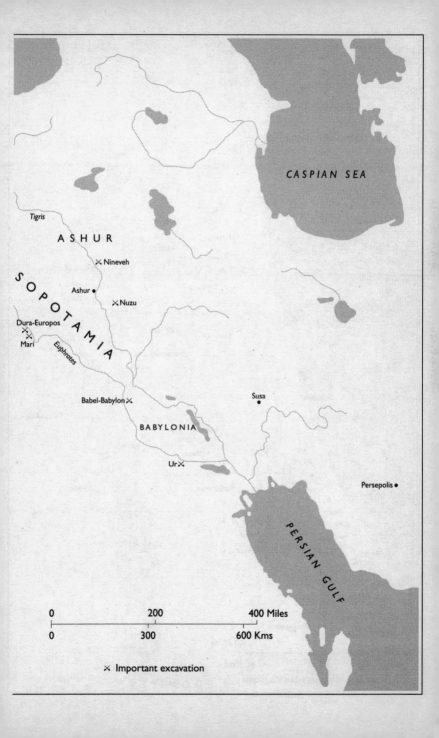

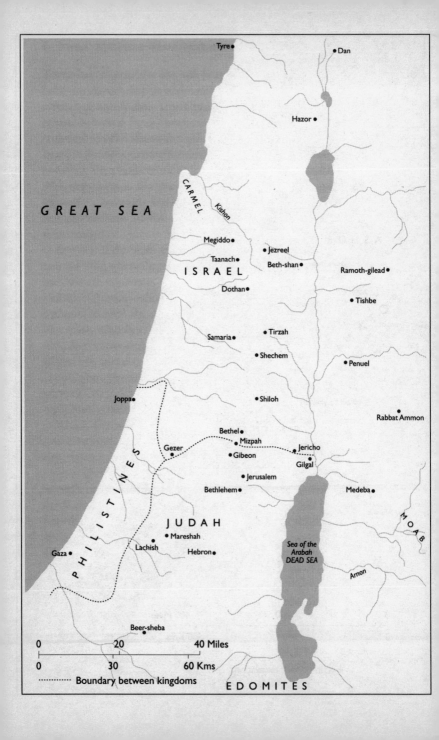

Tyre•   • Dan

Hazor •

GREAT SEA   CARMEL   Kishon

Megiddo •
        • Jezreel
Taanach •   Beth-shan •   Ramoth-gilead •
ISRAEL
        Dothan •   • Tishbe

Samaria •   • Tirzah
        • Shechem   • Penuel

        • Shiloh
                                Rabbat Ammon •
Joppa •
        Bethel •
Gezer •   Mizpah •   Jericho •
        • Gibeon   Gilgal •
        • Jerusalem
Bethlehem •   Medeba •

JUDAH

        • Mareshah
Gaza •   Lachish •
        Hebron •   Sea of the
                             Arabah
                             DEAD SEA   M
                                          O
                                          A
                                          B
                                  Arnon

PHILISTINES

Beer-sheba •

0   20   40 Miles
0   30   60 Kms
••••••••• Boundary between kingdoms

EDOMITES

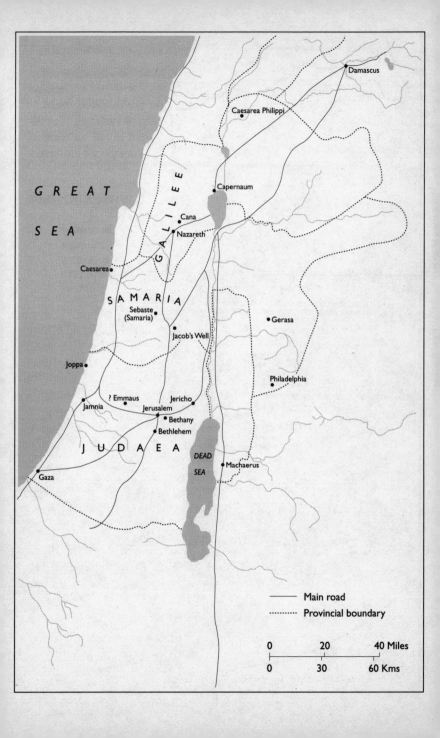

GREAT

SEA

GALILEE

SAMARIA

JUDAEA

Damascus

Caesarea Philippi

Capernaum

Cana

Nazareth

Caesarea

Sebaste
(Samaria)

Jacob's Well

Gerasa

Joppa

Philadelphia

? Emmaus

Jericho

Jamnia

Jerusalem

Bethany

Bethlehem

DEAD

Machaerus

SEA

Gaza

— Main road

········· Provincial boundary

0   20   40 Miles

0   30   60 Kms

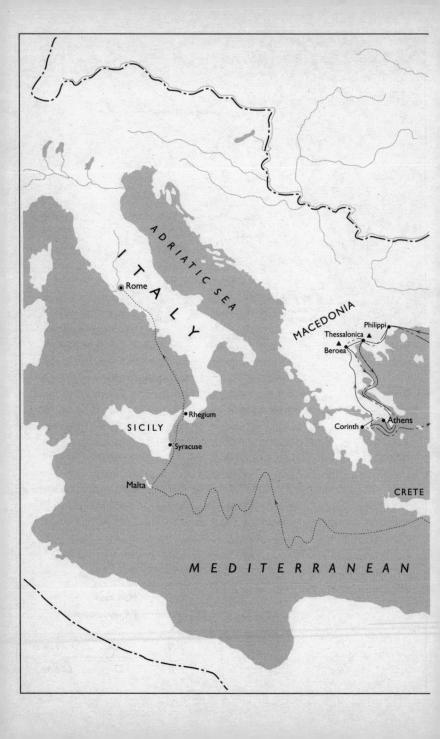

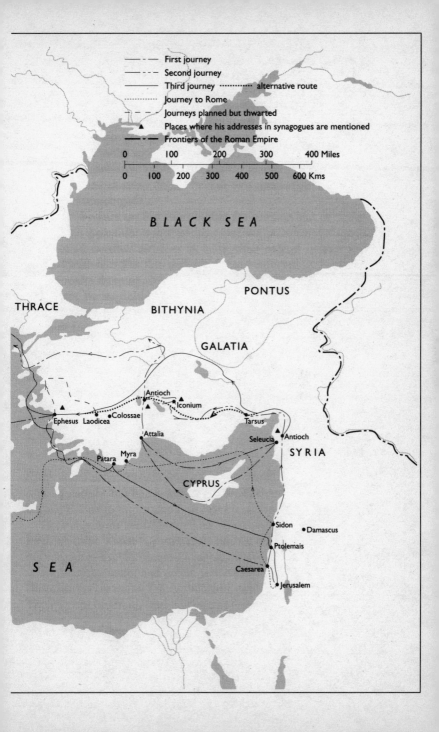

First journey
Second journey
Third journey .... alternative route
Journey to Rome
Journeys planned but thwarted
▲ Places where his addresses in synagogues are mentioned
Frontiers of the Roman Empire

0   100   200   300   400 Miles
0   100   200   300   400   500   600 Kms

BLACK SEA

THRACE

BITHYNIA

PONTUS

GALATIA

Antioch
▲ Iconium

Ephesus Laodicea ● Colossae

Tarsus ▲

Attalia

Seleucia ● Antioch

SYRIA

Patara ● Myra

CYPRUS

Sidon ● Damascus

Ptolemais

Caesarea

SEA

Jerusalem

What is the Bible?

'The English word Bible derives ultimately from the Greek word *biblia* meaning "books".' An opening sentence such as this can be found in more than one introduction to the Bible, and such an opening sentence, having established that 'Bible' means 'a collection of books', prefaces a treatment that begins in the ancient world and works its way forwards in time. Rarely do such works start where people are today, and recognize that while most people connect the Bible with the Christian churches (less often with Judaism), they soon become aware, if they begin to take an interest in the Bible, that it exists in English in a bewildering variety of translations, and that even the contents can vary from one translation to another.

If we follow an imaginary inquirer, who has no particular religious affiliation, into an academic bookshop where she intends to purchase a copy of the Bible, she will find herself spoiled for choice. In addition to the Authorized or King James Version of 1611 (AV), she will probably find the Revised English Bible (REB), the New Jerusalem Bible (NJB), the New Revised Standard Version (NRSV), the New International Version (NIV) and the Good News Bible (GNB), the prevalence of the adjective 'new' witnessing to the considerable effort expended in recent years on the revision or provision of translations of the Bible.[1]

The first thing that will strike our inquirer is that some Bibles contain more books than others, in that some will have a longer Old Testament section than others and some will have a section headed 'Apocrypha'. The New Jerusalem Bible will certainly be longer than the Authorized Version and the New International Version. Depending on what the bookshop stocks, longer or shorter editions may be available of the Revised English Bible and the New Revised Standard Version. Assuming that the longer REB and NRSV are available, our inquirer will find that

Authorized Version	New Jerusalem Bible	Revised English Bible	New Revised Standard Version
Genesis	Genesis	Genesis	Genesis
Exodus	Exodus	Exodus	Exodus
Leviticus	Leviticus	Leviticus	Leviticus
Numbers	Numbers	Numbers	Numbers
Deuteronomy	Deuteronomy	Deuteronomy	Deuteronomy
Joshua	Joshua	Joshua	Joshua
Judges	Judges	Judges	Judges
Ruth	Ruth	Ruth	Ruth
1 & 2 Samuel	1 & 2 Samuel	1 & 2 Samuel	1 & 2 Samuel
1 & 2 Kings	1 & 2 Kings	1 & 2 Kings	1 & 2 Kings
1 & 2 Chronicles	1 & 2 Chronicles	1 & 2 Chronicles	1 & 2 Chronicles
Ezra	Ezra	Ezra	Ezra
Nehemiah	Nehemiah	Nehemiah	Nehemiah
Esther	Tobit	Esther	Esther
Job	Judith	Job	Job
Psalms	Esther	Psalms	Psalms
Proverbs	1 & 2 Maccabees	Proverbs	Proverbs
Ecclesiastes	Job	Ecclesiastes	Ecclesiastes
Song of Solomon	Psalms	Song of Solomon	Song of Solomon
Isaiah	Proverbs	Isaiah	Isaiah
Jeremiah	Ecclesiastes	Jeremiah	Jeremiah
Lamentations	Song of Solomon	Lamentations	Lamentations
Ezekiel	Wisdom of Solomon	Ezekiel	Ezekiel
Daniel	Ecclesiasticus	Daniel	Daniel
Hosea	Isaiah	Hosea	Hosea
Joel	Jeremiah	Joel	Joel
Amos	Lamentations	Amos	Amos
Obadiah	Baruch	Obadiah	Obadiah
Jonah	Ezekiel	Jonah	Jonah
Micah	Daniel	Micah	Micah
Nahum	Hosea	Nahum	Nahum
Habakkuk	Joel	Habakkuk	Habakkuk

Authorized Version	New Jerusalem Bible	Revised English Bible	New Revised Standard Version
Zephaniah	Amos	Zephaniah	Zephaniah
Haggai	Obadiah	Haggai	Haggai
Zechariah	Jonah	Zechariah	Zechariah
Malachi	Micah	Malachi	Malachi
	Nahum	1 Esdras	Tobit
	Habakkuk	2 Esdras	Judith
	Zephaniah	Tobit	Additions to Esther
	Haggai	Judith	Wisdom of Solomon
	Zechariah	Additions to Esther	Ecclesiasticus
	Malachi	Wisdom of Solomon	Baruch
		Ecclesiasticus	Letter of Jeremiah
		Baruch	Song of the Three
		Letter of Jeremiah	Daniel and Susanna
		Song of the Three	Bel and the Dragon
		Daniel and Susanna	1 & 2 Maccabees
		Daniel, Bel and the snake	1 Esdras
		Prayer of Manasseh	Prayer of Manasseh
		1 & 2 Maccabees	Psalm 151
			3 Maccabees
			2 Esdras
			4 Maccabees

she has no fewer than four options when she compares the Old Testament sections of these versions. The differences are set out in the table on pp. 2–3.

It must be added that our inquirer has been lucky to be presented with only four options. Had she also found on the shelves the special edition of the Good News Bible designed for Catholic readers and a Jewish translation of the Hebrew Bible such as that issued by the Jewish Publication Society of America, she would have been faced with six options. The most striking would be the Jewish translation, with the same number of Old Testament books as the Authorized Version, but with these books in a different order from 2 Kings onwards. In order to explain this apparent chaos to our inquirer it will be necessary to outline the difference between the Old Testament and the Apocrypha and to sketch how this has affected English versions of the Bible since the Reformation.

The distinction between the Old Testament and the Apocrypha goes back to the dispute in the early Church as to whether the Hebrew or the Greek canon of the Old Testament was to be accepted as authoritative.[2] The Hebrew canon consists of the books found in Protestant Bibles today as the Old Testament. (They are in a different order in the Hebrew Bible, but that is not an issue here.) The Greek canon, found in the ancient Greek version known as the Septuagint*, is longer than the Hebrew canon, its additional material consisting of books that were either not originally written in Hebrew, or whose original Hebrew has not survived. Preference for the Greek canon prevailed, and the Latin Vulgate*, which became the standard Bible for the Western Church until the Reformation, contained the larger, Greek canon, in the content and order to be found today in the New Jerusalem Bible (see table above).

Because the Reformation included a revival of Hebrew and Greek, and the resolve to translate the Bible from its original languages into vernaculars such as German and English, the issue of the status of those Old Testament books for which no Hebrew existed, became contentious. In 1520 Andreas Karlstadt argued that only the works that existed in Hebrew were canonical, and he designated the rest as Apocrypha.[3] This was put into practice by Luther in his Bible of 1534, in which the

Apocryphal books were placed after the Old Testament and prefaced by the comment that these books were not on the same level as Holy Scripture but were useful and good for reading. The first complete Bible in English was produced by Myles Coverdale and printed probably in Cologne in 1535. It was based largely upon William Tyndale's* translations of the New Testament and parts of the Old Testament, as well as the German work of Luther. Coverdale followed Luther in placing the Apocrypha in a separate section after the Old Testament, although he employed a different order. He did not include the Prayer of Manasseh, which was the final book in Luther's Apocrypha.[4]

The first English Bible to include the Prayer of Manasseh was Matthew's Bible of 1537,[5] a Bible which was largely based upon Tyndale's work and produced by John Rogers working under the pseudonym of Thomas Matthew.[6] With the work of Coverdale and Rogers the content and order of books of Protestant Bibles in English were laid down, and were followed by the Great Bible (1539), the Geneva Bible (1560), the Bishops' Bible (1568) and the Authorized Version (1611). However, in the 17th century the Apocrypha came under attack, and the practice began of producing Bibles without the Apocrypha. Thus, an edition of the Geneva Bible without Apocrypha was published in Amsterdam in 1640, while in 1648 the Westminster Confession of Faith* decreed that the books of the Apocrypha were no more to be used in the Church of God than other human writings.

This view of the Apocrypha prevailed in the Church of Scotland and among Non-conformist churches in Britain, and in 1827 it became the policy of the British and Foreign Bible Society to print Bibles without the Apocrypha. A similar attitude prevailed in the United States of America, and it is noteworthy that when companies were set up in Britain and America in the 19th century to revise the AV and to produce respectively the Revised Version (complete edition 1896) and the American Standard Version (1901) the former included the Apocrypha while the latter did not.

What has been said so far concerns Protestant Bibles in English. While the Reformation was relegating the Apocrypha to a subordinate status the Roman Catholic Church, at the Council of Trent in 1546, was affirming the equal status of the Apocryphal books with those of the

Old Testament. However, the books so defined did not include the Prayer of Manasseh and 1 and 2 Esdras (called 3 and 4 Ezra). Roman Catholic usage regarded what Protestants called the Old Testament as proto-canonical*, and what Protestants called the Apocrypha as deuterocanonical*, without implying thereby any distinction of rank. Catholics reserved the term Apocrypha for the Prayer of Manasseh and 1 and 2 Esdras only. The Douay*-Rheims Bible of 1609–10 and its various 18th-century revisions by Richard Challenor was based upon the Latin Vulgate, and thus followed the content and order of books found today in the New Jerusalem Bible. In what follows in the present work, 'Apocrypha' and 'Old Testament' will be used in their Protestant senses.[7]

This brief outline should serve to explain to our inquirer why she has found at least four differing types of Bible. The AV is the Bible preferred by some Protestant groups verging on fundamentalism, as well as by some devotees of the English language. Although the AV originally included the Apocrypha, the Protestant groups that espouse the AV reject the Apocrypha, and thus demand for the AV has been a demand for the Old and New Testaments only. It was difficult to purchase a copy of the AV with Apocrypha until Oxford University Press recently reissued the AV with Apocrypha.[8] Because the New International Version is used by mainly conservative churches with their traditional rejection of the Apocrypha, this version was, until recently only available without the Apocrypha. The New Jerusalem Bible, on the other hand, is a Roman Catholic Bible, with the Apocrypha integrated into the Old Testament rather than segregated into an appendix.

The REB and NRSV both stand within the mainstream Protestant tradition of British and American Bible translation, even though they included Catholic scholars among their panels, and are thus available in two editions – one with and one without the Apocrypha. Where they include the Apocrypha they differ with regard to the number and order of the books. The REB follows the order that goes back to Matthew's Bible of 1537. The NRSV embodies a development that occurred in 1977, when its predecessor, the Revised Standard Version (RSV), expanded its coverage of the Apocrypha to include 3 and 4 Maccabees and Psalm 151, texts recognized as sacred by the Eastern Orthodox churches. At this point, the RSV could claim to be officially authorized for use by the Eastern Orthodox churches as well as the Roman Catholic Church, the Protestant churches and the Anglican communion. The NRSV repeated this position.

Our inquirer now has some idea why she is confronted by different Bibles, and has discovered that there are Protestant Bibles, Catholic Bibles, and at least one Bible that claims to represent Protestants, Catholics and the Eastern Orthodox churches. But are these differences simply that some churches include more books in their canon than others? The answer is no. There are other differences, some of which are textual, some of which are linguistic, and some of which are doctrinal. Although these topics will now be addressed separately, they are often interconnected.

TEXTUAL QUESTIONS

So far the discussion has been concerned with translations of the Bible that can be purchased today. From what texts are they translated, and how close are these texts to what the biblical writers wrote? For the moment the brief answer will be given that the Old Testament is translated mainly from a medieval Hebrew text form of the 10th century CE, that the Apocrypha is based mainly on medieval Greek manuscripts of the Septuagint and that the New Testament has such a wealth of manuscripts* and papyri* available, some as early as the 2nd century CE, that the registration of their various readings and the decision as to which are closest to what the biblical writers wrote is a branch of study in its own right. For present purposes, in order to explain to our inquirer why she will find differences between translations, the discussion will concentrate on the New Testament.

When the New Testament part of the Revised Version was published in 1881 there was an outcry because readers discovered that passages familiar to them from the Authorized Version were missing! For example, the version of the Lord's Prayer in Luke 11:2–4 was much shorter in the RV:

AV	RV
Our Father which art in heaven, Hallowed be thy name. Thy kingdom come. Thy will be done, as in heaven, so in earth. Give us day by day our daily bread. And forgive us our sins; for we also forgive every one that is indebted to us. And lead us not into temptation; but deliver us from evil.	Father, Hallowed be thy name. Thy kingdom come. Give us day by day our daily bread. And forgive us our sins; for we ourselves also forgive every one that is indebted to us. And bring us not into temptation.

In John's Gospel a short section was missing at 5:3–5

AV	RV
In these lay a great multitude of impotent folk, of blind, halt, withered, waiting for the moving of the water. For an angel went down at a certain season into the pool, and troubled the water: whosoever then first after the troubling of the water stepped in was made whole of whatsoever disease he had. And a certain man was there ...	In these lay a multitude of them that were sick, blind, halt, withered. And a certain man was there ...

Material was also missing from the account of Paul's conversion in Acts 9:5–6

AV	RV
And he said, Who art thou, Lord? And the Lord said, I am Jesus whom thou persecutest: *it is* hard for thee to kick against the pricks.	And he said, Who art thou, Lord? And he *said*, I am Jesus whom thou persecutest:

And he trembling and astonished said, Lord, what wilt thou have me to do? And the Lord *said* unto him, Arise, and go into the city, and it shall be told thee what thou must do.

but rise and enter into the city, and it shall be told thee what thou must do.

Some omissions seemed to weaken the doctrinal content of the New Testament. Thus, as against the AV of Galatians 6:15, 'For in Christ Jesus neither circumcision availeth any thing, nor uncircumcision, but a new creature', the RV simply had 'For neither is circumcision any thing nor uncircumcision, but a new creature'. Again, the RV at 1 Corinthians 6:20, 'for ye were bought with a price: glorify God therefore in your body' seemed tame compared with the AV: 'For ye are bought with a price: therefore glorify God in your body, and in your spirit, which are God's.'

The most notorious difference occurred at 1 John 5, where, for verse 7 the AV had 'For there are three that bear record in heaven, the Father, the Word and the Holy Ghost: and these three are one.' In the RV this verse is numbered verse 8 and reads 'For there are three who bear witness, the Spirit, and the water, and the blood: and the three agree in one.'

The reason for these differences is that the AV is a translation of a printed edition of the Greek New Testament that first appeared in Paris in 1550. In 1633 an edition of this text was published by Elzevir in Leyden which claimed that it was 'the text which is now received by all'. This led to it being known as the Textus Receptus or Received Text.[9] In fact, it was based upon comparatively late manuscripts of the New Testament and in between the AV (1611) and the New Testament part of the RV (1881) the much earlier Codex* Sinaiticus was discovered in 1844 by Tischendorf in the Monastery of St Catherine on Mount Sinai, and scholars gained access to Codex Vaticanus in the Vatican library. Two of the translators of the RV, B. F. Westcott and F. J. A. Hort, were also collaborating on a new edition of the Greek New Testament and the revisers largely accepted their advice as to what readings to follow. Since 1881 manuscripts and papyri older than Sinaiticus and Vaticanus have been discovered, and the science of how different readings should be evaluated has been refined. The REB New Testament is based largely upon the 26th edition of the so-called Nestle-Aland Greek Testament published by the German Bible Societies in 1977, while the NRSV depends on the 3rd edition of the United Bible Societies text of 1983.

There are, in fact, several thousand handwritten witnesses to the books of the New Testament, although in most cases their differences are very small. Several of the larger differences have been referred to above. Another interesting difference occurs in the so-called longer and shorter texts of Luke's account of the institution of the Last Supper (Luke 22:17–20) and provides possible evidence for how what were perceived to be mistakes in manuscripts were corrected. The longer and shorter readings are given in the AV and RSV.

AV	*RSV*
And he took the cup, and gave thanks, and said, Take this, and divide it among yourselves: For I say unto you, I will not drink of the fruit of the vine, until the kingdom of God shall come. And he took bread, and gave thanks, and brake it, and gave unto them, saying, This is my body which is given for you: this do in remembrance of me. Likewise also the cup after supper, saying, This cup is the new testament in my blood, which is shed for you.	And he took a cup, and when he had given thanks he said, 'Take this, and divide it among yourselves; for I tell you that from now on I shall not drink of the fruit of the vine until the kingdom of God comes. And he took bread, and when he had given thanks he broke it and gave it to them, saying, 'This is my body.'

Although there are defenders of the longer reading as most accurately representing what Luke wrote (e.g. the NIV and NJB), it can be argued that Luke's unusual order of cup and bread in the shorter text is more likely to be original and that the longer text has made it conform to liturgical practice and the other Gospels by adding a cup after the bread.

Whether or not it is possible to speak of a Received Text today is a matter of opinion; but sufficient progress has been made for even a conservative translation such as the NIV to accept all the readings quoted above from the RV as against the AV. None the less, churches or readers who continue to use the AV use a version of the New Testament that often differs quite widely from translations from the RV onwards.

LINGUISTIC DIFFERENCES

The AV has come to be regarded as one of the great achievements of the English language and thus it is not surprising that some revisions have sought to remain within the literary tradition of the AV. Revision has become necessary because many words in the AV have become obsolete in modern English,[10] quite apart from the fact that many discoveries have enabled scholars to understand the biblical languages much better than in the time of the AV, and to get closer to what the biblical authors wrote. Among the directives given to the translators of the NRSV by the National Council of Churches of Christ in the USA in 1980 was that they should 'continue in the tradition of the King James Bible' (i.e. the AV), 'but to introduce such changes as are warranted on the basis of accuracy, clarity, euphony, and current English usage'. The NRSV is thus a self-confessedly literal translation in the tradition of the AV.

A totally different approach has been adopted in the Good News Bible. Based upon Noam Chomsky's theory of transformational grammar* as worked out by Eugene Nida,[11] the GNB aims to be a 'dynamic equivalence' translation whose aim is to make upon modern readers the impact made upon the original readers. This aim raises many questions that cannot be pursued here, such as whether anything about the original impact can be known today, or whether there was or is one impact that is common to all readers. These questions aside, the translation theory underlying the GNB gives priority to the culture of the target language (the language into which the Bible is being translated) over the source language, and to direct speech over reported speech. It is also based upon research into the target language, and into the particular level to be used. Putting it another way, is a translation to use the English of *The Times* and the *Washington Post* or of a popular tabloid newspaper such as the *Daily Mirror* or the *National Inquirer*? In fact the GNB is part of a programme of producing Common Language translations, that is, translations into languages such as English, French, Spanish and Chinese which are widely known and used as second languages in various parts of the world. The result of dynamic equivalence translation can be readily appreciated if three renderings of Mark 1:4 are compared.

NRSV	*REB*	*GNB*
John the baptizer appeared in the wilderness, proclaiming a baptism of repentance for the remission of sins.	John the Baptist appeared in the wilderness proclaiming a baptism in token of repentance, for the remission of sins.	So John appeared in the desert, baptizing and preaching. 'Turn away from your sins and be baptized,' he told the people, 'and God will forgive your sins.'

Leaving aside the fact that the GNB follows the Received Text (compare the AV, 'John did baptize in the wilderness, and preach . . .') while the others do not, the striking difference lies in the use of direct speech and the unpacking of the dense 'baptism of repentance for the remission of sins'. It would be tempting to call the GNB a paraphrase and not a translation, a view that would be resisted by the GNB translators. The substantive point, however, is that the GNB is strikingly different from the other versions because of decisions taken by its translators about the theory and practice of translation.

One linguistic factor that has affected all recent translations is the matter of gender-free language. Versions such as GNB, REB and NRSV have tried to avoid the third person masculine 'he', 'his' and 'him' wherever possible, as well as 'man' and 'men', with the NRSV doing this most consistently. Psalm 1 in the RSV is a fairly literal rendering of the Hebrew,

> Blessed is the man
> who walks not in the counsel of the wicked,
> nor stands in the way of sinners . . .

The GNB and NRSV try in different ways to eliminate the 'sexist' language.

GNB	*NRSV*
Happy are those	Happy are those
who reject the advice of evil men,	who do not follow the advice of the wicked,
who do not follow the example of sinners . . .	or take the path that sinners tread . . .

with the GNB introducing 'men' in a context unlikely to offend women readers! The REB prefers

> Happy is the one
> who does not take the counsel of the wicked for a guide . . .

but soon introduces 'his' at verse 2. The use of gender-free language is a sincere attempt to be sensitive to the culture of the target language. It is arguable, however, that it sometimes obscures the sense and crosses the admittedly hazy boundary between translation and commentary, since the original Hebrew is certainly not gender free. The substantive point for present purposes is that, depending on what Bible our inquirer has chosen, she will get either a literal (formal equivalence) translation or a dynamic equivalence translation, and a version with or without gender-free language.

DOCTRINAL ISSUES

The New International Version makes no secret of the fact that, while
not the official version of any denomination, it represents those churches
that are committed 'to the authority and infallibility of the Bible as God's
Word in written form'. Part of the not-too-hidden agenda of the NIV
is to be a translation that accords with certain doctrinal understandings
of the Bible. Several examples illustrate this.

It has long been accepted in critical biblical scholarship that Genesis
1 – 2:4a and 2:4b–25 are two distinct accounts of the creation of the
world. The differences between them have been pointed out many times,
and scholarly orthodoxy teaches that they come from two originally
separate literary sources.[12] The constituency represented by the NIV
has been reluctant to accept the two-source theory, and in any case is
unwilling to admit that there are discrepancies in the Bible. Accordingly,
the NIV translates Genesis 2:19 in such a way as to minimize the
differences between the two opening chapters of Genesis. The AV
rendering of Genesis 2:19 is, 'And out of the ground the LORD God
formed every beast of the field . . .', a translation followed by all major
versions in English, but giving rise to the problem that, according to
chapter 1, God has already created the various types of animal. The
NIV harmonizes chapters 1 and 2 with its rendering, 'Now the LORD
God had formed out of the ground all the beasts of the field . . .'

Another controversy caused by the advent of biblical criticism in the
19th century was how to translate and interpret texts in the Old Testament
that were understood in the New Testament as prophecies of the birth
and death of Jesus Christ. In Matthew 1:22–3, Isaiah 7:14 is cited as
follows:

> All this took place to fulfil what the Lord had spoken by the prophet:
> 'Behold, a virgin shall conceive and bear a son,
> and his name shall be called Emman'u-el'.

This was substantially how the older English versions (AV and RV)
translated Isaiah 7:14, in spite of the fact that the Hebrew word rendered

as 'virgin' at Isaiah 7:14 meant 'young woman'. Critical commentators on Isaiah 7:14 argued that what mattered in translating the passage was not how it was understood in the New Testament but what it must have meant in the time of Isaiah, i.e. 'young woman'; and this is what is found today in the RSV, NRSV, NJB, REB and GNB. In the 19th century, commentators who said that the reference in Isaiah was to a young woman who was alive at the time when the prophet was speaking, were accused of denying the virgin birth of Jesus and of undermining the inspiration and unity of Scripture. The same charges can still be heard today. The NIV, while not necessarily endorsing these charges, none the less renders Isaiah 7:14 in accordance with its usage in the New Testament: 'The virgin will be with child and will give birth to a son, and will call him Immanuel.'

Another passage, which while not directly quoted in the New Testament was traditionally seen as a prophecy of Christ's crucifixion, was Psalm 22:16b, translated following the ancient Greek translation (the Septuagint) as 'they pierced my hands and my feet', although the Hebrew literally means 'my hands and my feet were like a lion's'. Most modern versions attempt to render the Hebrew rather than the Greek. The NRSV has 'my hands and my feet have shriveled', which is probably the exact opposite of what the Hebrew is trying to convey which is that, in the Psalmist's emaciated state, his hands and feet look grotesquely large and claw-like. The REB has 'they have bound me hand and foot'. Even GNB's 'they tear at my hands and feet' removes the allusion to the Passion narrative. The NIV retains the connection with the Passion in its rendering, 'they have pierced my hands and my feet'.

Our inquirer now has another option. Does she buy a Bible whose translators have deliberately tried to preserve a harmony between the Old and New Testaments and to remove discrepancies where possible; or does she buy a Bible that translates the Old Testament without regard to the New Testament and that is not worried that there may be discrepancies as, for example, between the two opening chapters of Genesis? The question must remain unanswered; but it leads to a further complication that our inquirer must negotiate. Should she buy simply a translation, or should she buy a study Bible, or a study edition of a Bible?

STUDY BIBLES

Most people today are familiar with Bibles that contain simply the biblical text, rather than with study Bibles, although the matter is not quite as simple as this, as will be explained shortly. It comes as a surprise, therefore, to discover that English Bibles without any accompanying commentary are a comparatively new phenomenon, and although what now follows will not directly help our inquirer to decide between the versions and editions available, it may help her to put into historical perspective the question of study Bibles versus Bibles supposedly without comment.

From the beginning of the Reformation, Bibles that were translated into the vernacular such as German or English were accompanied by introductions and explanatory notes. Luther's New Testament of September 1522 contained lengthy introductions to the New Testament and to the letter to the Romans as well as brief introductions to the other books. In doing this Luther was following a tradition that went back to hand-copied and early printed editions of the Latin Vulgate which contained introductions written by Jerome (died 420 CE). Luther also provided notes in the side margins which picked out important names or words, or briefly amplified the text.[13]

Luther's practice was followed by Tyndale. Indeed, if the prefaces to Tyndale's New Testament of 1534 are compared with Luther's it becomes apparent that Tyndale mostly simply translated Luther's prefaces into English.[14] Again, Tyndale published notes in the side margins, although these were not a translation of Luther. When Coverdale was commissioned in 1537 by Thomas Cromwell to produce the first authorized English Bible he was told to avoid marginal comments. This official reluctance to gloss the biblical text was not followed, however, by what became one of the most popular English versions, the Geneva Bible of 1560. This translation, produced by exiles from England during the reign of Mary Tudor (1553–8), contained headings and other notes expressing Reformed doctrine. It was because of its handy format, its notes and its forceful renderings that it remained popular for a century, until the monarchy was restored in England in 1660 following the Civil War and the governing of England as a Commonwealth. Indeed, the Geneva Bible was especially popular with the Puritan leaders of the Commonwealth, and the Authorized Version of 1611 was not able to compete with it in popularity until the 18th century.

The AV itself from the outset contained introductory headings to chapters as well as notes in the side margins and was thus closer to being a study Bible than simply a translation. The mid-18th to mid-19th century, however, was the Golden Age of the study Bible, as editions of the AV were produced accompanied by engravings as well as extensive commentaries. Thus, the Ostervald Bible contained the 'annotations and observations' that had first appeared in French with an edition of the Geneva Bible in 1724. J. F. Ostervald (1666–1747) was a member of the Reformed (i.e. Calvinist) Church at Neuchâtel, Switzerland. One such edition of the AV, in three volumes including Apocrypha with Ostervald's comments, was published by John Harrison of London in 1785. Another popular edition of the AV was John Brown's self-interpreting Bible of 1778. Brown was a Scottish weaver who became a Presbyterian minister. No doubt because of the cost of such editions, Thomas Scott (1747–1821) began to publish his edition of the AV in weekly numbers in 1788. Its popularity was such that, between 1788 and 1812, 12,000 complete copies were printed while in the United States over 25,000 copies were printed between 1809 and 1819. In its 5th edition of 1822 in six volumes, it was printed by being stereotyped.[15] This selection of study Bibles must not give the impression that they were first invented in the 18th century. Matthew Poole's Bible of 1685 (completed by others after his death) was a forerunner, and a famous 19th-century Bible was that by G. D'Oyley and R. Mant (1817; New York 1818–20) whose notes were taken 'from the most eminent writers of the United Church of England and Ireland'.

One of the causes of the decline of the study Bibles was the policy of the British and Foreign Bible Society, founded in 1804, to print Bibles without comment. There is no doubt that the Bible Society did much to make the Bible available at affordable prices. Its policy of no comments was a way of reconciling its Anglican and non-conformist members, each fearful that the other might gain a doctrinal advantage through comments. The policy, however, slowly and subtly changed the habits of readers of the Bible. Previously, the Bible was read, by those who could afford it, as interpreted by Ostervald or Brown or Scott or Poole, or, to add another important name, John Wesley, whose notes dated from 1764. As Bibles without accompanying notes became more common, published not only by the Bible Society but by the Oxford and Cambridge University presses and other authorized printers, the need arose for separate commentaries on biblical books, or series of commentaries, or one-volume commentaries, of which that edited by A. S. Peake (1919) became justly famous.[16]

The marginal comments in Bibles from the Reformation continued the pre-Reformation practice of interpreting the Old Testament as a series of prophecies or anticipations of Jesus Christ. Luther commented on Genesis 3:15 'he will bruise your head':

This is the first Gospel and promise of Christ given [*geschehen*] on earth. That he will overcome sin, death and hell or deliver us from the power of the serpent.

Ostervald comments on the same verse:

By the head of the serpent is meant his power and authority over men, the strength whereof consists in death, which Christ, the blessed seed of the woman, overthroweth, by taking away *the sting of death which is sin, 1 Corinthians 15.55, 56.*

In his introduction to the Psalms Luther summarizes part of his main argument in a marginal note: 'The Psalter speaks clearly of Christ's death and resurrection, of his kingdom and of the nature and being of Christianity.' Ostervald ends a comment on Psalm 22 with the words:

this psalm sets before us the glory to which God has exalted [Christ] after the sufferings, and which he now enjoys at the right hand of his father, and his kingdom is established throughout all the earth.

It is now time to consider modern study Bibles, of which the NJB Study Edition and the NIV Study Bible will be taken as examples. Their respective comments on Genesis 3:15 are instructive. The NIV comment follows the traditional Christian understanding of the passage, going back to the early Church and found, for example, in Luther: 'The offspring of the woman would eventually crush the serpent's head, a promise fulfilled in Christ's victory over Satan – a victory which all believers will share (see Ro[mans] 16:20).' The NJB is more scholarly and distanced.

The Hebrew text, by proclaiming that the offspring of the snake is henceforth at enmity with the women's descendants, opposed the human race to the devil and his 'seed', his posterity, and hints at ultimate victory; it is the first glimmer of salvation, the *proto-evangelium*. The Gk. Version has a masculine pronoun ('he' not 'it' will bruise . . .), thus ascribing the victory not to the woman's descendants in general but to one of her sons in particular, and thus providing the basis for the messianic interpretation given by many of the Fathers.

If the NIV and NJB reflect the ancient Christian understanding of Genesis 3:15, they are sharply divided in their attitude to the results of critical scholarship. In its 'Introduction to the Pentateuch' the NJB accepts that it contains three main traditions, Yahwistic (because it uses the divine name Yahweh), Elohistic (so called after the Hebrew *elohim* meaning 'God') and Priestly (so called because of its concern with priestly and ritual matters), and affirms: 'In the book of Genesis, it is not difficult to recognize and follow the threads of the three traditions: Yahwistic, Elohistic and Priestly.' The NIV firmly rejects such an approach. After outlining the source theory and claiming that the 'Pentateuch is thus depicted as a patchwork of stories, poems and laws' it claims that 'this view is not supported by conclusive evidence, and intensive archaeological and literary research has tended to undermine many of the arguments used to challenge Mosaic authorship.' The two study Bibles under consideration thus have quite different aims. The NJB accepts the main findings of critical biblical scholarship and seeks to help readers to understand the text within that context. The NIV rejects many findings of critical scholarship, and defends traditional views of the authorship and origin of biblical books. At the same time the NIV Study Bible contains many helpful charts, summaries, maps and a concordance.

Perhaps our inquirer will decide against buying a study Bible, preferring to get the plain text and to look at commentaries when she needs help. Will she succeed in getting a 'plain text'? Not exactly. Even Bibles that contain no explanatory comments contain chapter or section headings, and these can predispose readers to see the text in a particular way. An instructive example is a Bible published by the British and Foreign Bible Society in 1956 to commemorate its third jubilee, 1804–1954. While, in accordance with the Bible Society's then charter, there are no comments, and even the section headings are minimal such as, for example, 'Jacob and Laban', 'Jacob and Esau', 'Jacob's children', a feature of this Bible is that some parts of the Old Testament are in much smaller print than the rest of the work. Particularly targeted are lists of descendants, such as the descendants of Esau in Genesis 36 or those in the first nine chapters of 1 Chronicles, along with sections detailing laws (e.g. the so-called Book of the Covenant in Exodus 20:22–23:33) or instructions for offering sacrifices (e.g. the whole of Leviticus and Numbers 1–9). The claim in the preface that the different print sizes do not imply 'any difference in the value of such material' is undermined by the later statement that 'everything essential to the understanding of the message of the Bible has been set in larger type'. It is difficult to see the different print sizes as anything other than an attempt to tell readers what is important and what is not.

This is an extreme example of how a Bible without comment can none the less attempt to predispose readers. What of the versions that our inquirer will find in her bookshop? Of the main modern possibilities, the GNB, NIV, NRSV, NJB, REB, the NIV and REB are generally the most sparing in their headings. If Psalm 110 is considered, the REB and NIV simply print the traditional heading from the standard Hebrew text. The other translations add interpretative headings. Most neutral is probably the GNB with its heading, 'The Lord and His Chosen King'. NJB has 'The Priest Messiah' while NRSV prefers 'Assurance of Victory for God's Priest-King'. While these interpretative headings are not necessarily contradictory or mutually exclusive, they certainly slant matters, and the NJB's use of the word 'Messiah' suggests a covert Christian sense. A psalm where the editors' headings signally diverge is Psalm 84. The GNB heading is 'Longing for God's house' while the NRSV has 'The Joy of Worship in the Temple' and the NJB has 'Pilgrimage Song'.

A book in which headings show up the greatest divergences between modern translations is the Song of Solomon, or the Song of Songs (to give it its Hebrew title). Readers who do not know Hebrew certainly need help with this book. Hebrew has separate words for 'you', depending on whether a man or a woman is being addressed. English has only one word for both genders. Thus, while it is clear from the Hebrew when a woman is addressing a man and vice versa, English cannot make this distinction. Most modern translations try to help readers to know who is speaking in the Song of Songs; only the NRSV does not do this explicitly, although its headings that refer to 'bride' and 'bridegroom' help out at the more difficult points.

The other translations insert the names of the speakers either in the text or margin, and this is where they differ, both in their designation of the speakers, and sometimes in the allocation of the material. The REB divides the participants into the bride, bridegroom and companions, thus immediately suggesting the context of a wedding. The NIV and NJB prefer beloved and lover (respectively, female and male) with the bystanders being the chorus for the NJB and the friends for the NIV. The GNB is more neutral, dividing the material among the woman, the man and the women. When it comes to the allocation of material, the NIV, GNB and REB ascribe 1:8 to the man:

> If you do not know, most beautiful of women,
> follow the tracks of the sheep
> and graze your young goats
> by the tents of the shepherds (NIV).

The NJB ascribes these words to the chorus. Again, the GNB, REB and NIV believe that 1:12–14 are spoken by the woman, whereas the NJB ascribes them to the pair as a duo. However, it is not always NJB that is out of step. The NJB, NIV and GNB all allocate 2:7 to the woman; the REB believes it to be spoken by the bridegroom.

Our inquirer can be forgiven for feeling thoroughly confused by now. She began by going into a bookshop to perform the apparently straightforward task of buying a copy of the Bible. She has now discovered that there are Protestant Bibles and Catholic Bibles, study Bibles and Bibles allegedly without comment but otherwise pre-emptive. She has noted the different content of Bibles and theories about translation and language. All these puzzling variations are symptoms of the complicated process of the origin of the Bible, and the way that it has been used and continues to be used. The remainder of the book will seek to shed some light on these matters.

CHAPTER 2

How Biblical Writers Wrote

The first chapter has indicated that there is no such thing as *the* Bible, if by the Bible is meant a collection of material whose content is identical for each and every copy. It has been noted that there are Bibles with and without the Apocrypha, and that even where the Apocrypha is present it can have several variations. It may be integrated among the books of the Old Testament, or gathered together as a separate section between the Old and New Testaments, and in the latter case may contain extra books such as Psalm 151 and 3 and 4 Maccabees.

It is now necessary to introduce a further complication. In chapter 1 it was noted that the NRSV with its enlarged Apocrypha claimed to represent the Bible as accepted by the Eastern Orthodox churches as well as western Catholics and Protestants. This claim is not quite accurate. The official Bible of the Eastern Orthodox Church is the Septuagint, the Greek version of the Old Testament that began to be produced in the 3rd century BCE. The Septuagint not only contains books not found in the Hebrew Bible; in some cases, its version of books found in the Hebrew text differs significantly from the Hebrew version.

The most conspicuous example of this is found in Jeremiah. First, the order of the chapters differs as between the Hebrew and the Septuagint:

Septuagint	*Hebrew*
25:1–3	25:1–13
25:14–19	49:34a, 35–9
25:20	49:34b
26	46
27	50
28	51

29	47
30:1 – 16	49:7 – 22
30:17-22	49:1 – 6
30:23 – 8	49:28 – 33
30:29 – 33	49:23 – 7
31	48
32	25:13, 15 – 38
33 – 50	26 – 43
51:1 – 30	44:1 – 30
51:31 – 5	45:1 – 5
52	52

The most notable difference that this makes is that the oracles against the foreign nations, chapters 46 – 51 in the Hebrew, occur after chapter 25 in the Septuagint.

However, it is not simply that the material comes in a different order; the Hebrew version of Jeremiah is usually longer than the Greek, and the differences are sometimes significant. The following extract from Jeremiah 27:16 – 22 (Septuagint 34:16 – 22) prints in normal type the material common to the Hebrew and the Septuagint (LXX*). Material in italics is found in the Hebrew only.

16. Then I spoke to the priests and to all this people [LXX: to all the people and the priests], saying, 'Thus says the LORD: Do not listen to the words of your prophets who are prophesying to you, saying, "Behold the vessels of the LORD's house will *now shortly* be brought back from Babylon" for it is a lie which they are prophesying to you.

17. Do not listen to them [LXX: I have not sent them]; *serve the king of Babylon and live, Why should this city become a desolation?*

18. If they are prophets, and if the word of the LORD is with them, then let them intercede with the LORD of hosts [LXX: with me], *that the vessels which are left in the house of the LORD, in the house of the king of Judah, and in Jerusalem may not go to Babylon.*

19. For thus says the LORD *of hosts concerning the pillars, the sea, the stands,* and the rest of the vessels that are left in this city,

20. which *Nebuchadnezzar* king of Babylon did not take away, when he took into exile from Jerusalem *to Babylon* Jeconiah *the son of Jehoiakim, king of Judah, and all the nobles of Judah and Jerusalem —*

21. *thus says the LORD of hosts, the God of Israel, concerning the vessels which are left in the house of the LORD, in the house of the king of Judah, and in Jerusalem*:

22. They shall be carried to Babylon *and remain there until the day when I give attention to them,* says the LORD. *Then I will bring them back and restore them to this place.'*[1]

It is clear that we have two different versions of Jeremiah's words, one of which (the Hebrew) envisages the ultimate return of the vessels of the temple and the king's house to Jerusalem, the other of which (the Septuagint) foresees only their removal. One of the implications of these differences is that the version of the Bible accepted as sacred by the Eastern Orthodox Church is not the same as that received by the Western churches, although even this point is complicated by the fact that agencies such as the Bible Societies have produced translations into the languages of Eastern Christians based on the Hebrew and not the Septuagint. However, these theological matters are not of concern at this point. The reason for introducing the issue of the difference between the Hebrew and the Septuagint at the level of content is that it is a way in to the topic of this chapter, how the biblical writers wrote. This, in turn, will open the way for consideration of the origin and growth of the material of which the Bible (or, Bibles) consists.

The traditional view of the origin of the Bible is that it was written by identifiable individuals. Early Jewish and Christian tradition identified Moses as the author (i.e. writer) of the Pentateuch (Genesis to Deuteronomy), Joshua as the author of Joshua, Samuel as the author of Judges and Ruth, David as the author of many of the psalms, Solomon as the author of most of the Book of Proverbs, as well as of Ecclesiastes and the Song of Solomon, and the prophets as the authors of the books named after them. For the New Testament, the traditional view attributed the Gospels to Matthew (Levi) the tax collector and disciple of Jesus (Matthew 9:9), John Mark the erstwhile companion of Paul (Acts 15:37), Luke the physician (Colossians 4:14) and the apostle John. Paul was responsible for the majority of the letters, the others being attributed to James, Peter and Jude, while Luke was responsible for Acts and the apostle John for the letters of John and the Book of Revelation.

The view that identifiable individuals had written the biblical books fitted well with theories about the inspiration of the Bible that developed in Judaism and Christianity. In post-Reformation Protestantism, for example, the view was held that the Bible was verbally inspired, that is, that God through the Holy Spirit had guided the thoughts and writing of the biblical authors to the point where God could be said to be the author of every word of the Bible. This theory began to break down in the 18th century as biblical criticism began to be established as an academic profession, and as the composition of biblical books started to be examined critically. Today it is found in this extreme form only among fundamentalist groups (see chapter 7). However, many ordinary people who have no religious axe to grind are resistant to the theories of the composition of biblical books that have been proposed by modern scholarship. Readers are most familiar with works that have been written by one author. The idea, proposed by modern biblical scholarship, that the Bible was composed by various processes of amalgamation of originally separate sources, or by the supplementation of original sources, and that all this was done by several if not many hands, perhaps over a long period, is alien to the experience of modern readers, and needs to be explained and justified.

A good starting-point is the example given above from Jeremiah 27. From a comparison of the two versions, the Hebrew and the Septuagint, it could be argued that the Septuagint is simply a shortened version of the Hebrew. This possibility can, however, be ruled out. Hebrew manuscripts from among the Dead Sea Scrolls discovered in 1947 onwards show that there was a Hebrew version of Jeremiah shorter than the Hebrew version that is translated in our English Bibles. In some, but not all, points this shorter Hebrew version supports the Septuagint. It is therefore clear that the Septuagint is a translation of a Hebrew version of Jeremiah that is shorter than the traditional Hebrew text. This means that the traditional Hebrew text translated in our English Bibles is an expansion of an originally shorter version, and this gives us a clue as to how this traditional text reached its final form.

The expansions in the longer Hebrew text are of two kinds. First, they make the statements more explicit. The shorter version merely refers to 'the rest of the vessels that are left in this city, which the king of Babylon did not take away when he took into exile from Jerusalem, Jeconiah' (Jeremiah 27:19–20). The longer version identifies Jeconiah as the son of Jehoiakim and adds that the nobles of Judah and Jerusalem were also exiled at the same time (in 597 BCE). It also reminds readers that Jeconiah was exiled to Babylon. Further, whereas the material common to both versions notes that 'the vessels of the LORD's house' had been taken away (verse 16) the longer version defines the remaining vessels as those 'left in the house of the LORD, in the house of the king of Judah, and in Jerusalem'.

The second expansion, at the end of the passage, alters the content of the prophet's message so as to make him say that the vessels will not only be removed but returned. No doubt this addition was made in the light of the return of some of the descendants of the exiles after 540, and the rebuilding of the temple. It has several implications. First, the Septuagint version is probably closer to what Jeremiah may actually have said than the Hebrew version. Second, the words of prophets as well as written versions of their words were not regarded as sacrosanct by the editors who worked upon the Hebrew text. Third, the biblical writers did not hesitate to adapt traditions from the point of view of hindsight, or later events. A similar thing has probably occurred in the Book of Micah. At the end of chapter 3 the prophet forecasts that Jerusalem will be destroyed and never rebuilt:

> Zion shall be ploughed as a field;
> Jerusalem shall become a heap of ruins,
> and the mountain of the house a wooded height (3:12).

However, immediately following this utterance is a passage that is also found in almost identical form in Isaiah (Micah 4:1 – 5, Isaiah 2:2 – 4) that looks forward to the day when Jerusalem and its temple become the centre of pilgrimage for all nations. It looks as though the later editors of Micah have been influenced by the fact that Micah was wrong about Jerusalem not being rebuilt, even if he was right about it being destroyed.

What has emerged from these examples is that biblical tradition grew by various forms of addition and supplementation. Another clear instance of this is the account of the battle between David and Goliath in 1 Samuel 17 and 18 where the Septuagint again translates what was once a much shorter account than that in the traditional Hebrew version, which has added verses 12–31 and 55–8 to chapter 17 and verses 10–11 and 17–19 to chapter 18.[2]

The process of addition is responsible in some cases for the existence of books in the Apocrypha. The most conspicuous example is the Prayer of Manasseh. In 2 Chronicles 33:18, the reign of Manasseh is summarized in words beginning: 'Now the rest of the acts of Manasseh, and his prayer to his God . . .', with this prayer being a reference back to the information in 33:12–13 that Manasseh prayed to God when he had been taken captive to Babylon and that God received the prayer and restored him to Jerusalem. The prayer is said in 2 Chronicles 33:18 to be recorded in the Chronicles of the Seers, though critical scholars are doubtful about the existence of such a source.

Because tradition abhors a vacuum, the Prayer of Manasseh was composed probably sometime during the 2nd to 1st century BCE to fill the gap; and it is a sublime expression of the awesomeness of God, leading to confession of sins and the plea for forgiveness. Unfortunately, little is known about its origin, and even the language in which it was originally composed is disputed.

Another instance of enlargement that has led to Apocryphal books as well as differences between Bibles in English concerns the Book of Esther. The traditional Hebrew text contains roughly 160 verses and, notoriously, no reference to God. However, the Septuagint contains eight additional passages amounting to around 100 verses. These additions add somewhat to the action but, most importantly, they introduce a specifically religious element lacking in the Hebrew. An addition which follows Esther 4:17 in the numbering found in English Bibles of the Old Testament Book of Esther, contains two prayers prayed respectively by Mordechai and Esther when they discover Haman's plot to destroy the Jews. That of Esther is especially sublime, beginning: 'my Lord, you only are our King; help me, who am alone and have no helper but you, for my danger is in my hand' (NRSV). The treatment of these additions sheds some light on the difference between Bibles.

In the Septuagint the additions are part of the text of Esther. This was also the case with Latin versions until Jerome, in his championing of the Hebrew text at the end of the 4th century, removed them to the end of Esther. When chapter and verse numbers were added to the Latin Vulgate by Stephen Langton (died 1229) the additions were numbered as 10:4–13 (the Hebrew of Esther ends at 10:3) and chapters 11–16. At the Reformation, these additions were separated from Esther and placed with the rest of the Apocrypha between the Old and New Testaments. This arrangement lasted until the Revised Standard Version Apocrypha of 1957. However, more recent translations, including the NEB, REB, GNB and NRSV, have translated the whole of the Septuagint version of Esther in their Apocryphas, thus setting the additions in context. The NJB has also restored the additions to their original contexts, but as part of the Old Testament. In the NJB the material found only in the Septuagint is printed in italics while roman type is used for the material in Hebrew. A note in the NJB Study Edition says that 'The Church [i.e. the Roman Catholic Church] has accepted those passages in the Gk. Version not contained in the Hebr. Text'.

The Greek additions to Esther were made probably towards the end of the 2nd century BCE (see chapter 4). They illustrate, as do the additions to the longer Hebrew text of Jeremiah, that, until 'canonization' (a process to be discussed later in the book and provisionally defined for the moment as an official freezing of the number of books counted as Scripture) editors and translators felt free to expand texts in smaller or larger ways.

So far, the examples given have concerned instances in which, by comparing Hebrew and Greek versions of texts, the expansion process can be observed. Can anything be said about composition processes where such controls are lacking? Obviously, without controls scholars can only make informed guesses; but if these informed guesses can be shown to conform to practice otherwise observable in the ancient world, they can claim plausibility if not probability.

The suggestion that parts of the Old Testament were composed by combining together originally separate accounts of the same incident, has long been accepted in academic circles. The classic example is the Flood narrative in Genesis 6:5–9:19, where, it is held, two sources have been skilfully woven together. These two sources are usually called J and

P: J because this source typically uses the name Yhwh* (English versions: 'the LORD') for God, and because the theory was taken over from Germany, German J being the equivalent of English Y; P because of this source's interest in priestly matters. P also avoids the name Yhwh prior to Exodus 6:3 where this source relates the revelation to Moses of this special name. Other characteristics of the two sources are that J's style is simple and direct, while that of P is repetitious, and has a particular interest in chronology. A typical division of part of the Flood narrative into J and P is as follows.[3]

J	P
The LORD saw that the wickedness of man was great in the earth, and that every imagination of the thoughts of his heart was only evil continually. And the LORD was sorry that he had made man on the earth, and it grieved him to his heart. So the LORD said, 'I will blot out man whom I have created from the face of the ground, man and beast and creeping things and birds of the air, for I am sorry that I have made them' (Genesis 6:5–7).	Now the earth was corrupt in God's sight, and the earth was filled with violence. And God saw the earth, and behold, it was corrupt; for all flesh had corrupted their way upon the earth. And God said to Noah, 'I have determined to make an end of all flesh; for the earth is filled with violence through them; behold, I will destroy them with the earth' (Genesis 6:11–13).

This is a straightforward case of doublets which substantially duplicate the material found in each. The divine name is consistently different. Later on in the Flood narrative the originally separate accounts are neatly dovetailed.

J

P

Noah was six hundred years old
when the flood of waters came upon
the earth.

Noah and his sons and his wife and
his sons' wives with him went into
the ark, to escape the waters of the
flood. Of clean animals, and of
animals that are not clean, and of
birds and everything that creeps on
the ground, two and two, male and
female, went into the ark with Noah,
as God had commanded Noah. And
after seven days the waters of the
flood came upon the earth.

In the six hundredth year of Noah's
life, in the second month, on the
seventeenth day of the month, on
that day all the fountains of the great
deep burst forth, and the windows of
the heavens were opened.

And rain fell upon the earth forty
days and forty nights.

On the very same day Noah and his
sons, Shem and Ham and Japheth,
and Noah's wife and the three wives
of his sons with them entered the
ark, they and every beast according
to its kind, and all the cattle
according to their kinds, and every
creeping thing that creeps on the
earth according to its kind, every bird
of every sort. They went into the ark
with Noah, two and two of all flesh
in which there was the breath of life.

> And they that entered, male and
> female of all flesh, went in as God
> had commanded him;

and the LORD shut him in.

Again we have duplication of material as well as characteristic features of the two sources that are found in the whole of the Flood narrative (Genesis 6–9). These include the precise chronology of P and its much more elaborate style compared with J.

Before the implications of this type of composition process are discussed, it is necessary to consider an objection to the theory that two sources have been combined. It has been argued that there is no evidence from the ancient world that writers combined sources in this way, and that the duplications can be explained as typical of ancient Near Eastern literature. Also, the different, but valid, objection has been made that whatever may have been the process of composition, the interpretation of the Bible should be concerned with the text as we have it in its final form.[4] This latter point is not, however, pertinent to the present chapter, whose aim is to inform readers about the composition processes of the books of the Bible so that the books lose some of their strangeness and become more comprehensible.

The objection that there is no evidence that ancient writers combined separate sources can be answered in two ways. First, research into the growth of the Mesopotamian *Epic of Gilgamesh** from separate stories to its familiar form in Akkadian shows that ancient writers did use sources which they adapted, rewrote or used as a basis for selection.[5] Second, there exists from the early Christian era a text which shows exactly how it was possible to produce a reasonably coherent text by combining separate sources using a 'scissors-and-paste' method. The text is Tatian's *Diatessaron*. The *Diatessaron* which is known from citations and commentaries was composed either in Syriac or Greek in the latter third of the 2nd century. It is a harmony of the four Gospels which enables them to be read as one account. It was so successful that, in some parts of the early Church, it supplanted the four Gospels themselves. The following account of the baptism of Jesus is a mosaic based on Matthew

3:13–16, Luke 3:21–3 and John 1:29–31. In the following extract Matthew is in roman type, Luke in italics and John in bold.[6]

Then Jesus came from Galilee to the Jordan to John, to be baptized by him (Matthew 3:13). *Jesus, when he began his ministry, was about thirty years of age being the son (as was supposed) of Joseph* (Luke 3:23). **[John] saw Jesus coming towards him, and said, 'Behold the Lamb of God, who takes away the sin of the world! This is he of whom I said "After me comes a man who ranks before me, for he was before me". I myself did not know him; but for this I came baptizing with water, that he might be revealed to Israel'** (John 1:29–31). John would have prevented him, saying, 'I need to be baptized by you, and do you come to me?' But Jesus answered him, 'Let it be so now: for thus it is fitting for us to fulfil all righteousness.' Then he consented (Matthew 3:14–15). *Now when all the people were baptized, Jesus also was baptized* (Luke 3:21a). He went up immediately from the water, and behold, the heavens were opened (Matthew 3:16a) *and the Holy Spirit descended upon him in bodily form, as a dove, and a voice came from heaven, 'Thou art my beloved Son; with thee I am well pleased'* (Luke 3:22).

If it is accepted that one of the composition techniques of biblical writers was the combination of originally separate sources, what is gained? First, it helps us to appreciate that the distinction between author, editor and copyist was much smaller in the ancient world than in the modern world, and that in some instances these functions could overlap. Thus, while it is not being suggested that there were no ancient authors in the sense that we would understand authors, it is being pointed out that the ancient world could regard as an author both an editor who combined existing narratives, and a scribe who expanded a narrative in the way that the longer text of Jeremiah was produced from the shorter text.

Second, if some biblical narratives were produced by the combining of separate narratives, this accounts for parts of the Bible whose narratives may sometimes be chaotic and repetitious. A case in point is 1 Samuel 8–26. There appear to be three accounts in these chapters of how Saul became king: (a) 8:4–22 and 10:20–27, (b) 9:1–10:13 and (c) 11:1–15. The saying 'Is Saul also among the prophets?' occurs at 10:12 and 19:24, Saul is twice rejected from the kingship by Samuel (13:8–14, 15:1–35),

David twice deserts to the Philistine Achish King of Gath (21:10–15, 27:1–4) and twice spares Saul when he could have killed him (24:1–22, 26:1–12). Furthermore, the narrative does not read connectedly. It was most likely composed, therefore, from several sources, which the author preferred to combine rather than replace by a completely new version based on the sources.

If the problem of the narrative being less than connected occurs in a book that is primarily narrative, it becomes acute in a prophetic book such as the opening chapters of Jeremiah. Anyone who tries to read through chapters 1–6 will soon be in the difficulty that, following the account of the call of Jeremiah (Jeremiah 1:1–10), the remainder of chapters 1–6 consists of prophetic oracles with no narrative clue as to their setting or context. The same is true of smaller prophetic books such as Hosea. This is because the editors of these books have put together originally separate sayings in ways that are far from obvious to modern readers, while later editors have added further material, perhaps from long after the time of a prophet. They have also rewritten some of the material as in the case of the longer version of Jeremiah.

The different view of authorship in the ancient world compared with today leads next to the important problem of pseudonymity, a problem that is felt acutely by users of the Bible from conservative backgrounds.[7] Pseudonymity is claiming as the author of a book someone who is not the author. (It does not correspond to the modern phenomenon of writers using a pen-name.) It is to be distinguished from mistaken claims about authorship by tradition, such as that the letter to the Hebrews is by Paul, whereas the book itself makes no such claim. Pseudonymity is a claim in a work, implicitly or explicitly, that the author is a well-known or otherwise identifiable figure, as against the conviction of critical scholarship that the well-known person cannot have been the author.

An example of a claim implicit from the text would be the Book of Isaiah where 1:1 reads: 'The vision of Isaiah the son of Amoz, which he saw concerning Judah and Jerusalem in the days of Uzziah, Jotham, Ahaz, and Hezekiah, kings of Judah.' Slightly less elaborate formulae are found at 2:1 and 13:1, while chapters 6 and 8 are in the first person singular (cp. 8:1: 'Then the LORD said to me'). However, nowhere is there an explicit claim by Isaiah in the book to be the author. The formulae at 1:1, 2:1 and 13:1 could be, and most probably are, the work of editors, and the most that could be claimed is that the Book of Isaiah *contains* words or writings of Isaiah and not that Isaiah actually wrote the book. Even this is sufficient to create a problem. It has long been asserted by critical scholarship that chapters 40–55 record the words of a prophet who lived among the exiles in Babylon in the mid-6th century, and that chapters 56–66 date from the late 6th to early 5th centuries, and are set in Jerusalem. 'Isaiah of Jerusalem' lived in 8th-century Jerusalem. Further, certain parts of chapters 13–39 have been attributed to periods later than that of 'Isaiah of Jerusalem'.

The problem of the 'authenticity' of the Book of Isaiah, i.e. the question whether it contains the words of one prophet ('Isaiah of Jerusalem') or of several prophets from different centuries, was a fiercely contested battleground in the 19th century between traditionalists and critical scholars, and is still a live issue in conservative circles. Thus the NIV Study Bible defends the unity of Isaiah and claims that the prophet may well have written chapters 40–66 in his later years. The prevailing view of modern scholarship is that the Book of Isaiah is the product of an Isaiah school (the disciples mentioned in 8:16) that existed for at least two centuries, which recorded the words of several different prophets, but which tried to make the book a literary unity in its final form, for example, by beginning and ending it with the fate of Jerusalem.

Explicit instances of pseudonymity include the attribution to Paul of the letters to Timothy and Titus (the so-called Pastoral Epistles*). It can be added that some modern scholars also doubt whether Paul wrote Ephesians or Colossians.[8] Concentrating for the moment on the Pastoral Epistles, it can be summarized that their Pauline authorship has been questioned since the early 19th century on the grounds of their different vocabulary, doctrinal outlook and presumed circumstances of writing, compared with the undoubtedly genuine Pauline epistles such as Galatians, Romans and 1 and 2 Corinthians. This raises an acute question not only for theologically conservative readers, but for readers with a modern view of authorship. 1 Timothy begins with the words: 'Paul, an apostle of Christ Jesus by command of God our Saviour and of Christ Jesus our hope, To Timothy, my true child in the faith.' There follow personal details such as 'I urged you when I was going to Macedonia . . .'

(1:3) and 'certain persons have made shipwreck of their faith, among them Hymenaeus and Alexander' (1:19–20). If modern scholars are convinced that 1 Timothy was not written by Paul, what are we to make of this material? Words such as 'forgery' and 'fiction' with all their negative implications spring readily to mind, and it is no surprise that the NIV Study Bible states that 'evidence is still convincingly supportive of Paul's authorship'. The matter needs to be approached from several angles.

First, it was generally accepted in the classical world that historians would freely compose speeches and letters and attribute them to the main characters about whom they were writing.[9] Books such as 1 Maccabees and the Acts of the Apostles contain respectively speeches delivered by Judas Maccabeus and by Peter and Paul, and it is likely that they are free compositions of the authors of the books, in accordance with this custom. Second, in the rhetorical schools a common method of teaching was to make pupils imitate the style of great philosophers or orators. This did not, however, permit students to pass off their own work as that of Plato or Cicero, to take two examples, and a literary criticism designed to identify and discredit forged works was certainly practised in the classical world. Third, there were situations in which pseudonymity was a form of necessary anonymity. The Book of Daniel, for example, which was probably written to encourage the Jews during their persecution by Antiochus IV in 167–164 BCE, shielded the identity of the author through the explicit claim that the book was the work of Daniel (Daniel 8:1) who had lived in the 6th century (1:1–7). If the view is correct that the book of Jonah was written in opposition to the policies of Ezra and Nehemiah in the 5th century BCE, in order to plead for a more tolerant attitude to non-Jews than that enforced by Ezra and Nehemiah, we have another example of pseudonymity as anonymity. The 5th-century author, who was perhaps not fully Jewish, concealed his identity by implicitly attributing the book to a prophet who had lived in the 8th century (cp. 2 Kings 14:25).

Fourth, pseudonymity was a device which placed a writing within an established tradition. Thus, given the strong traditions that David was the psalmist *par excellence* (2 Samuel 23:1) and that Solomon was the great speaker of proverbs (1 Kings 4:29–34), many psalms were ascribed to

David and books such as Ecclesiastes, the Song of Solomon and the Wisdom of Solomon were attributed to Solomon. That it was possible to attribute something to a figure of the past and to be perfectly aware that it was an innovation, albeit in the spirit of the great figure of the past, is indicated by the notion of the 'Halakah* of Moses given at Sinai' in the Judaism of the early common era.

On an occasion when it was necessary to reinterpret the written and oral laws of Judaism to apply them to new situations, the Rabbis both made new rulings and described them as laws given to Moses at Sinai. The story is told of R. Akiba (died *c.* 135 CE) that Moses in heaven was shown Akiba expounding the law to his disciples. Moses did not understand what was being said but was reassured when Akiba replied to a student who asked 'how do you know this?' that it was a Halakah of Moses given at Sinai.[10]

Returning to the Bible and the problems of the Pastoral Epistles, the most likely solution is that these letters were written by someone who was a member of a Pauline church and who believed that he had apostolic authority, directly or indirectly from Paul, to write in the apostle's name. A. T. Lincoln's definition of pseudonymity as 'a device for passing on authoritative tradition in a creative way' is helpful here.[11] The same would apply to Ephesians and Colossians, if those scholars are correct who believe them not to be the work of Paul. It can be assumed that the original recipients of these letters were aware that they were not by Paul. As time passed, this was forgotten, and the letters were presumed to be Pauline until critical scholarship began to question this fact from the early 19th century onwards.

This last point sheds some light on why the churches did not agree about the exact contents of the Old Testament. In a situation where there were pseudonymous books, such as the Wisdom of Solomon or Tobit, there could be different opinions about the extent to which their pseudonymity should be taken seriously. Alongside the fact that writers could believe that they had apostolic or other authority to write in someone else's name was an early form of literary criticism that examined claims to authorship and pronounced against books that were deemed not to be authentic. One simple test of authenticity was whether or not an Old Testament book had been written in Hebrew, and this was sufficient to decide the issue in broad terms. But the matter of which books should be included in the Hebrew and Greek collections ultimately depended on factors such as the popularity or appeal of books, and whether or not they had influential backers. Ironically, in the case of the pseudonymous Pauline letters, once it had been forgotten that they were not actually by Paul, it was the claim in their contents to be Pauline that ensured their inclusion in the New Testament canon.

To the discussions of composition methods and pseudonymity there now needs to be added a third factor, that of 'book' production. When a writer finishes a book today and it is printed and bound, it is complete and it is circulated as such. It can only be altered if a new edition or a pirate edition is brought out. It was otherwise in the ancient world. Books, in the sense of sheets of paper or parchment bound at one edge so that the pages can be turned back and forth, did not make their appearance until the 2nd century CE. The biblical books were written on scrolls prepared from the skins of animals, or on sheets of papyrus. They could only be reproduced by being copied by hand, and the copying process could easily be an opportunity for new material to be introduced. This was illustrated at the beginning of this chapter with an example from Jeremiah 27. A further complication is this. If 'books' are written on separate scrolls or sheets of papyrus, how do they become collections?

Libraries, in the sense of catalogued collections of archives and other texts, date back to *c.* 2,600 BCE in the ancient Near East,[12] and although initially they existed for administrative purposes, as time went on they included letters and literary texts. In ancient Greece from the 5th century BCE there were libraries collected by the philosophical schools as well as in private possession. The same was true later in Rome.[13] This tradition was taken over into the early Church. Leading apologists such as Irenaeus (*c.* 130–*c.* 202), Hippolytus (*c.* 170–*c.* 236) and Tertullian (*c.* 160–*c.* 225) evidently possessed or had access to libraries as did the Catechetical Schools of Alexandria (*c.* 200). In Caesarea, Origen established a famous library around 231. It can be assumed, therefore, that the main early Christian centres in places such as Alexandria, Jerusalem, Antioch, Corinth and Rome began to collect 'books', which would include books which later formed the Old and New Testaments.

An instance of a Jewish 'library' is furnished by the caves near Qumran at the north-west end of the Dead Sea. The older view, that the caves contained the library of the covenanters* who lived at Qumran, is now being modified to allow for the heterogeneous nature of the material; i.e. the 'library' may also contain material deposited in the caves by groups other than the covenanters. However, what is important is that the caves provide evidence that biblical texts (Old Testament, Apocryphal and pseudepigraphical*) and texts relating to the beliefs and practices of the covenanters were being collected by at least one group during the 1st century BCE to 1st century CE.

One of the Dead Sea Scrolls, the Psalms Scroll from Cave 11 (11Q^{psa}), has an order of the psalms from Psalm 100 onwards that is highly unusual. It contains a number of items that are not part of the canonical Book of Psalms, such as Psalms 151–155 (the canonical version stops at Psalm 150), as well as an irregular order. Thus, Psalms 106–8 are omitted, and the order after 103 is 109, 118, 104, 147, 105, 146, 148. At this point a more normal sequence from 120–32 resumes, but 119 follows 132.[14] This may be evidence that the order of what are now called Books 4 and 5 of the Psalms (90–106 and 107–50) was not fixed when the scroll was compiled (early in the 1st century CE); but it certainly illustrates that 'book' production in the form of handwritten manuscripts can lead to interesting variations.

Some examples can also be considered from the New Testament. Among the earliest collections of New Testament 'books' are the Chester* Beatty papyri. P^{46}, dated around 200 CE, originally contained ten letters of Paul, but apparently not the Pastoral Epistles plus Hebrews placed between Romans and 1 Corinthians. It is, however, evidence for an early collection of letters of Paul. Codex Sinaiticus, the famous 4th-century codex first discovered by C. Tischendorf in the Monastery of St Catherine in Sinai in 1844, is the only uncial (i.e. manuscript written in capital letters) that contains the entire New Testament. But it also contains the Epistle of Barnabas* and the Shepherd of Hermas*, two popular 2nd-century CE texts that were not included in the canonical New Testament. Codex Alexandrinus, a 5th-century uncial, contains, in addition to parts of every New Testament book, the First and Second Letters of Clement* of Rome, again, early texts (end of 1st century CE) that were not included in the New Testament. Codex Bezae, a 5th-century uncial, is bilingual (Greek and Latin), and has the four Gospels in the order Matthew, John, Luke, Mark.[15] These codices raise fascinating and unanswerable questions, such as did the churches that produced Sinaiticus and Alexandrinus regard Barnabas, Hermas and 1 and 2 Clement as part of the New Testament? The matter belongs properly to the subject of canon, to be discussed in chapter 6. But the evidence of these sources is a reminder that when we think of 'authors' and 'books' in regard to the Bible, we must cast aside our modern notions of what these words mean. A joke is sometimes told about someone who said that if the Authorized Version (i.e. the King James translation of 1611) of the Bible was good enough for Paul (the 1st-century apostle), it was good enough for him. This polemic against modern translations is not only absurd because Paul pre-dates the AV by more than 1,500 years and because much of the New Testament had not been written by the time of Paul's death. It overlooks the fact that Paul had no experience of books as we know them, and that for him the Bible (probably in Greek) existed only as a collection of *separate* scrolls.

Selected Old Testament Chronology

13th–12th centuries BCE

Israelites settle in hill country of Ephraim, Galilee and parts of northern Trans-jordan. Philistines settle in coastal plain.

11th century

Growing conflict between Philistines and Israelites leads to emergence of Israelite 'kingship' under Saul (c. 1020).

10th century

David defeats Philistines, makes Jerusalem his capital and unites Israel and Judah (c. 1000–960). Solomon succeeds David and builds temple in Jerusalem (c. 961–931). Israel secedes from Judah after death of Solomon.

9th century

Under Omri (c. 885–874) Israel becomes a dominating small nation in its area, controlling Judah, Moab and southern Syria.
Jehu (841–813) overthrows the dynasty of Omri but becomes subject to Shalmaneser III of Assyria, and suffers at the hand of Hazael of Damascus.

8th century

The Assyrians crush Damascus and leave Judah and Israel to enjoy peace under Jeroboam II of Israel (c. 782–747) and Uzziah (Azariah) of Judah (*c.* 767–739). The prophets Hosea and Amos criticize social injustice and religious syncretism in Israel (*c.* 740). Tiglath-pileser III of Assyria (745–727) campaigns against Israel, and the northern kingdom, Israel, is destroyed in 722/1. Under Hezekiah (*c.* 728–699) Judah assumes the role of Israel and Judah. Judah is invaded by Sennacherib of Assyria in 701 and Hezekiah is forced to pay tribute.

7th century

During the reign of Manasseh (699–643) Judah is a vassal of Assyria. The decline of Assyria and the rise of Babylon from *c.* 630 encourages Judah to assert its independence under Josiah (640–609). Josiah carries out a reform of the nation's religion.

6th century

Babylon under Nebuchadnezzar (605–562) dominates the region and captures Jerusalem in 597, exiling its king and nobles. A revolt in 588 leads to the destruction of Jerusalem a year later. In 540 Cyrus king of Persia defeats the Babylonians. Some exiles return from Babylon and the temple is rebuilt (*c.* 515).

5th century

Judah is the Persian province of Yehud. Nehemiah (445–?430), governor of Jerusalem, rebuilds the walls of the city.

4th century

Alexander the Great's defeat of Persia and his conquest of Syria, Palestine and Egypt (333–323) begin an era of Greek influence in Judah.

3rd century

Judah is ruled by the Ptolemies, the Greek rulers of Egypt descended from Alexander's general Ptolemy. The establishment of Jewish colonies in Egypt, especially Alexandria, causes parts of the Old Testament to be translated into Greek.

2nd century

Judah comes under the control of the Seleucids, the Greek rulers of Syria (*c.* 198). The Hellenization of Judaism and interference by the Seleucid king Antiochus IV in Jewish affairs including the desecration of the temple (168–164) leads to the Maccabean revolt led by Judas Maccabaeus (166–160). The temple is rededicated in 164. Simon the brother of Judas Maccabaeus is appointed high priest (143). Aristobulus I assumes the title of king as well as high priest (104).

1st century

Disputes between the brothers Hyrcanus II and Aristobulus II (67–63) lead to the intervention of Rome under the general Pompey. Judah becomes a Roman province. Herod the Great is appointed king (37).

CHAPTER 3

The Making of the Old Testament

Writing in the ancient world was an activity mainly confined to a professional class of scribes who were employed by temples or rulers. In other words, writing was controlled by powerful interests. If it is asked why the Old Testament was written, the answer has to be sought in terms of groups and occasions that could, or needed to, produce writings. Given that the content of the Old Testament is diverse, including narratives, psalms, laws, proverbs, regulations about sacrifices and priesthood, prophetic literature and 'wisdom'* writings (e.g. Job and Ecclesiastes) it will be necessary to investigate the origin and occasion of each type of literature. This exercise has to be tempered, however, by the fact that little is known about the extent or function of literacy in ancient Israel. Just as the previous chapter has warned against assuming that biblical writers were similar to modern writers, so here it must not be assumed that the intended readers of biblical writings were similar to modern readers, even if it is not easy to be more precise. It must also be remembered, as pointed out in the previous chapter, that Old Testament 'books' were not a single creation, but that they evolved through various processes of redaction and editing.

The aim of the chapter will be to outline the enormous diversity of the material found in the Old Testament, and to indicate the varied origins of the material. A tentative attempt will then be made to sketch how these disparate writings were brought together to form something like the collection that is called the Old Testament. This is not the same as asking how these writings became Scripture. That question, that of the formation of the canon, will be dealt with in chapter 6, although there is inevitably some overlap between what is attempted here and the matter of the emergence of the canon. The chapter will be broken down into the following headings: Historical writings, Laws, Prophetic literature, Psalms, 'Wisdom' literature, Other writings (apocalyptic, love poetry, novelistic writings, laments).

HISTORICAL WRITINGS

More than half of the books of the Old Testament are 'historical' books in the sense that they tell the story of ancient Israel from the time of Abraham to the time of Ezra and Nehemiah (5th century BCE). These books are parts of Genesis, Exodus and Numbers, and the whole of Joshua, Judges, 1 and 2 Samuel, 1 and 2 Kings, 1 and 2 Chronicles, Ezra and Nehemiah. Traditionally in biblical scholarship these books have been grouped under three main headings: the Tetrateuch (Genesis, Exodus and Numbers), the Deuteronomistic History (Joshua, Judges, Samuel and Kings), and the Chronicler's History (Chronicles, Ezra and Nehemiah). While it is possible to question details within these broad divisions, they can serve as convenient sub-headings for the present discussion.

The Tetrateuch

Strictly speaking, the Tetrateuch includes Leviticus as well as Genesis, Exodus and Numbers, but because Leviticus is entirely a collection of laws, it will not be considered here. Also the first eleven chapters of Genesis (the so-called primeval history) and the legal sections of Exodus and Numbers will be discussed later.

The narrative parts of Genesis, Exodus and Numbers tell a connected story, beginning with Abraham who is said to have migrated to ancient Canaan from Haran in northern Mesopotamia (Genesis 11:31–2). Abraham and his descendants (Isaac and Jacob) settle in Canaan until famine forces Jacob and his family to move to Egypt, where one of his sons, Joseph, has risen to power after being sold by his brothers to traders travelling to Egypt. The growth in numbers of the Hebrews leads to their enslavement and the official killing of newly born boys by the Egyptians, until Moses, who had escaped death and had been brought up in the Egyptian court, leads his people from Egypt to the Sinai wilderness. The Exodus* from Egypt is accompanied by divine miracles on behalf of the Hebrews, and the departure is marked and commemorated by the passover*. The remainder of the narrative of the Tetrateuch concerns the Hebrews' wanderings in the wilderness back to Canaan, and closes with the people having conquered parts of Trans-jordan, but not having crossed the river Jordan into Canaan.

It is unlikely that the story ended here in its original conception; indeed, it is continued in the Deuteronomistic History with the Book of Joshua's account of the conquest of Canaan. For reasons that will be given later, however, it will be convenient to deal with the 'story so far'.

Why and how was the story composed? The traditional view, that Moses wrote it (at least as far as Numbers), offered no reason other than the implied one, that God told him to do so. With the rise of critical scholarship, this view was replaced by the theory that it was in the reign of Solomon (c. 961–931 BCE) that the traditions about Israel's origins were collected and put into something approaching the form in which we have them. Solomon's reign, it was argued, provided the necessary conditions for such writing: a period of peace and stability, and the establishment of a scribal bureaucracy that administered the small Davidic/Solomonic empire. The reason for writing the story was to show how God's promises to Abraham that his descendants would inherit the land of Canaan had been fulfilled in the Davidic/Solomonic monarchy. The scribe or author responsible for collecting the traditions and fashioning the narrative was usually called the Yahwist.

This critical scholarly consensus is currently disintegrating under pressure from two directions. First, archaeological investigations are increasingly questioning whether there was much of an Israelite state in the time of David and Solomon let alone a small Israelite empire. Secondly, some literary experts are dating the Yahwist's work to the exilic* period (6th century BCE) rather than the time of Solomon. An intermediate view, and one provisionally accepted here, is that the most likely time for the composition of the Tetrateuchal narratives is the reign of Hezekiah (c. 727–698).[1]

Early in Hezekiah's reign, in 722/1, the Assyrians captured Samaria, the capital of the northern kingdom, Israel. (The united kingdom of

David and Solomon had split into Judah and Israel *c.* 931.) This ended the political independence of the northern kingdom, and brought refugees from there to Jerusalem, the capital of the southern kingdom, Judah. Among the latter were groups possessing written or oral traditions such as those about Elijah and the religious practices of associated prophetic groups. From now on, Judah and in particular Jerusalem took over the role of 'all Israel', and this provided the impetus for collecting past traditions and for fashioning them into a comprehensive story about Israel's origins. The traditions about Abraham and Jacob, containing stories centred mainly in Hebron and Bethel respectively, were probably traditions about ancestors of groups located in southern Judah (Hebron) and central Canaan (Bethel). That the Judahite Abraham should be the grandfather of the Israelite Jacob reflects the fact that it was in Judah that the overall story was shaped. Precedence was given to the Judahite ancestor in spite of the fact that Jacob was celebrated in the tradition as the immediate ancestor of the tribes of Israel (cp. Genesis 29:31–30:13). Isaac, probably another southern Judahite ancestor (cp. Genesis 26), became the link in the story between Abraham and Jacob. How far the Abraham and Jacob traditions contained historical memories, for example, of their origins in northern Mesopotamia, is hard to say.

The story of the sojourn in Egypt, the Exodus and the journeyings to the land of Canaan was possibly contributed by descendants of a group of Semites* who had made the journey from Egypt to Trans-jordan, and whose faith in a divine deliverance had become the common possession of larger groups which they had joined. In their present form, the Exodus and wilderness wandering traditions have been shaped by liturgical celebration and theological meditation. Whether, in the first phase of the collection and shaping of the Tetrateuchal narratives, the story of Joseph was present is uncertain. Readers who compare the Abraham (Genesis 12–25) and Jacob (27–35) cycles with the story of Joseph (37–48) will immediately notice the contrast between the episodic nature of the first two narratives and the carefully crafted and dramatic nature of the story of Joseph. That the latter is superbly composed does not necessarily make it later than the other material; but similarities in theme between the story of Joseph and the undoubtedly later stories of

Daniel and Esther (they all centre on Jews in exile who gained high office) suggest that Genesis 37–48 may be later than the Abraham and Jacob cycles.

The Deuteronomistic History

It has long been noted that the Books of Joshua, Judges, Samuel and Kings contain, to a greater or lesser degree, heavy traces of the distinctive theology of the Book of Deuteronomy. According to this theology, Israel's obedience to the covenant laws* revealed by God will bring blessing, while disobedience will bring disaster. It is because this theology is not present in the narratives in the Tetrateuch that the latter have been discussed separately in the present chapter, even though the Deuteronomistic History continues the story begun in the Tetrateuch.

The Deuteronomistic History relates how the Israelites occupied Canaan under the leadership of Joshua, experienced a period of transitional leadership under the judges*, and then saw the emergence of institutionalized and dynastic leadership beginning with Saul and passing to David and Solomon and their successors in the divided kingdoms of Judah and Israel. The narrative ends with the destruction of the temple by the Babylonians in 587 BCE. The last event recorded, in 2 Kings 25:27–30, is the release from prison in Babylon of king Jehoiachin, who had been taken into exile in 597. The date of his release, 560, gives the date after which the Books of Kings and therefore the Deuteronomistic History must have reached their present form. It does not follow, however, that all the material in the Deuteronomistic History was composed after 560.

A widely held view is that a substantial first draft was composed during the reign of Josiah (640–609 BCE; see 2 Kings 22:1–23:5). The king initiated a sweeping reform of Judah's religious and political life after 622, as a way of asserting his country's independence from the rapidly decaying Assyrian empire. The reform was also inspired by the ideals of the 8th-century BCE prophets as embodied in the Book of Deuteronomy, which book is believed by many experts to have been substantially written during the 7th century. On this scenario, a school of writers who shared the ideals expressed in Deuteronomy set down

Israel's history from the time of Joshua to the reign of Josiah, borrowing and adapting in the process some parts of the story that already existed as a continuation of the narrative of the Tetrateuch.

It has been argued in addition that the Book of Deuteronomy and the Deuteronomistic History were influenced by Assyrian vassal treaties*. The latter required vassal kings to swear allegiance to the Assyrian king on pain of severe punishment in case of rebellion; and Judah had been an Assyrian vassal prior to Josiah's reform. Josiah, it is suggested, used the treaty form to require his people to pledge allegiance to the God of Israel, on pain of incurring divine punishment if they turned to other gods. The retelling of Israel's past history was then cast in such a way as to illustrate how Israel had been blessed when obedient to God, and punished when it had turned from God. The whole theory certainly gives a plausible rationale for why the first draft of the Deuteronomistic History was composed in Josiah's reign, and what it aimed to do.

Unfortunately, the hopes excited in Josiah's reign were disappointed. He was killed in battle in 609 BCE by the Egyptian king Necho II, and twelve years later (in 597) the Babylonians captured Jerusalem and took Josiah's grandson, Jehoiachin, into exile together with the nobles and leaders of the people. The temple was destroyed ten years later. It was in the aftermath of this tragedy that the Deuteronomistic History reached its final form, sometime after 560. The account of Jehoiachin's release from prison was probably meant to arouse hope in those who read or heard the Deuteronomistic History. The final editors are also believed to have inserted passages such as 1 Kings 8:27–53. This part of Solomon's prayers at the dedication of the temple strongly implies that the Israelites are in exile (8:46), and it asks God to restore them to the land if they repent and pray fervently towards their land (8:48).

What has been written so far has sought to suggest a plausible occasion and purpose for the writing of the Deuteronomistic History. It has said nothing about the sources used. These included extracts from temple accounts* (cp. 2 Kings 18:13–14), the annalistic chronicles* of the kings of Judah and Israel (cp. 2 Kings 15:26, 36), and traditions about Elijah and Elisha and popular stories about figures such as Joshua, Deborah and Jael (Judges 4–5), Gideon (chapter 8), Abimelech (9), Jephthah (12), Samson (13–16), Samuel (1 Samuel 1–5), Saul (chapters 9–15) and

David and Jonathan (16–26). The historical framework that was thus created has been considerably modified if not entirely rewritten in some cases by modern research.[2]

The Chronicler's History

Whether or not the Books of Chronicles, Ezra and Nehemiah were composed by the same author or school they are intended to be read consecutively, in that Ezra 1:1 begins explicitly where 2 Chronicles 36:22–3 ends. The Books of Chronicles take the history of Israel back to Adam by way of genealogies that occupy the first nine chapters. The narrative as such begins at 1 Chronicles 10 with Saul and then concentrates upon David and Solomon before recounting mainly the history of the southern kingdom, Judah, until the destruction of the temple in 587 BCE. The Book of Ezra then takes up the story and, with the Book of Nehemiah, relates the return from exile in the reign of the Persian king, Cyrus, the rebuilding of the temple in 515 and the reforms of Ezra and Nehemiah in the reign of Artaxerxes I (465–423).

Chronicles is usually dated to 400–350 BCE, and seen as the production of a temple-based community in Jerusalem, one of whose main aims was to stress continuity between the first temple and the second temple. In some particulars, Chronicles has material that is almost identical with material in the Books of Samuel and Kings (e.g. 2 Samuel 5:6–9 = 1 Chronicles 11:4–8; 2 Kings 14:2–6 = 2 Chronicles 25:1–4), so much so that it has been generally accepted that Chronicles used Samuel and Kings as a source.[3] However, Chronicles almost goes out of its way to give an alternative view of events as compared with the Deuteronomistic History. This is especially apparent in the treatment of individual kings. Rulers declared good in the Deuteronomistic History are found to be with faults in Chronicles (e.g. Josiah at 2 Chronicles 35:20–24 compared with 2 Kings 23:25) while redeeming features are attributed to bad kings (e.g. Manasseh at 2 Chronicles 33:18–20 compared with 2 Kings 21:10–15).

Ezra and Nehemiah deal with the question of the boundaries that demarcated the Jewish community, and tell how the citizens of Judah who had married non-Jews were excluded. Their occasion of writing (as a first draft in the late 5th century BCE) could well have been a move by the Persian authorities, who had defeated the Babylonians in 539 and of whose empire Judah was now part, to regulate the community in Judah by recognizing and authorizing the enforcement of Jewish law as though it was the Persian king's law.

It is noteworthy that, in the Hebrew Bible, the books that comprise the Deuteronomistic History belong to the second part of the canon and are labelled 'Former Prophets' whereas Chronicles, Ezra and Nehemiah belong to the third part of the canon, the Writings and, indeed, conclude the Hebrew Bible in the order Ezra, Nehemiah, Chronicles. (The first part of the canon is the Pentateuch, i.e. Genesis to Deuteronomy.)

LAWS

The legal sections of the Old Testament are in Exodus, Leviticus, Numbers and Deuteronomy. They often combine together what we today would separate out as civil laws and cultic or ceremonial laws (i.e. regulations for ritual in worship and daily life), and while ancient Israelites may well have been unaware of such a distinction, it will be convenient here to treat the two classes separately.

Civil laws

The first point that needs to be made under this heading is that the civil laws of the Old Testament are only a selection of the laws that must have existed in order to regulate society in ancient Israel. Thus, there are no laws dealing with marriage or divorce, or adoption, or rights of prisoners-of-war, or redress against a physician or a builder. That such laws were known in the ancient world is evident, for example, from the laws of Hammurabi of Babylon (1792–1750). It may well be, then, that the civil laws of the Old Testament are to be regarded as evidence for ancient Israel's ethics rather than its legal practice.[4]

The earliest collection of civil laws (of course, it also contains cultic regulations) is the Book of the Covenant in Exodus 21:1–23:19, and so called on the basis of the ceremony described in Exodus 24:3–8 where

Moses reads 'the book of the covenant' and the people promise to observe it. It presupposes an agricultural, slave-owning society in which damages to persons and property have to be regulated. It also covers cases in which property or cattle are put in the temporary care of a neighbour and then damaged or stolen, the seduction of a virgin who is not betrothed, and the conditions under which loans can be made.

Some of this material is practical and straightforward, such as that dealing with compensation when an ox has gored a man or another ox (Exodus 21:28–32). However, there is a strongly compassionate tone throughout, and a deliberate bias towards slaves, the poor, and even domesticated animals. The protection of the latter, for example, is cited as a main reason why no work should be done on the Sabbath (Exodus 23:12). A passage which sums up God's solidarity with the poor in the Book of the Covenant is Exodus 22:25–7:

If you lend money to any of my people with you who is poor, you shall not be to him as a creditor, and you shall not exact interest from him . . . If he cries to me, I will hear, for I am compassionate.

It is impossible to be sure about the origin of the Book of the Covenant, assuming it to be a unity. Some of its laws reflect the settling of disputes by the parties involved rather than by recourse to a court of law, e.g. Exodus 21:22 where the husband of a woman accidentally injured in a fight between men determines the damages. (The immediately following reference to judges is a later expansion.) However, the collection in its present form implies the existence of courts of law and, presumably, was promulgated under royal authority. The best guess is that it was sponsored by either a king of Judah or of Israel who was in sympathy with the ideals of the prophetic movements*. More cannot be said.

We are on surer ground in dealing with the civil laws in the Book of Deuteronomy, noting again that this book also contains cultic material. While Deuteronomy clearly reached its final form during or after the Babylonian exile (cp. Deuteronomy 30:1–8), it is still widely agreed that a substantial first draft was composed during the 7th century BCE, and was the basis or justification for Josiah's reform of 622, which centralized worship in Jerusalem and closed down provincial shrines.

Some of the material in Deuteronomy, such as that which advocates the execution of all males in a city conquered by the Israelites (Deuteronomy 20:10–18), is highly distasteful to modern readers, even though it probably belongs more to the rhetoric of warfare in the ancient world than to actual practice.[5] This apart, however, the laws of Deuteronomy stress compassion (cp. Deuteronomy 24:10–22), give women slaves the same right of release as male slaves (15:12; Exodus 21:7–11 exhibits no such equality) and command support to the poor (Deuteronomy 15:7–11). Deuteronomy has often been regarded as an attempt to legislate the social justice demanded by the 8th-century prophets.

The best-known collection of civil laws is contained in the Ten Commandments (Exodus 20:1–17 and, in a slightly different form, Deuteronomy 5:6–21), the second group of which, from Exodus 20:13 onwards, prohibits murder, adultery, theft, false evidence and coveting. Yet it has to be asked whether these really are civil laws. No penalties are prescribed, neither are legal procedures enjoined for dealing with offenders, although some of these deficiencies are remedied elsewhere (e.g. murder is dealt with at Exodus 21:12–14). The Old Testament itself presents the Ten Commandments as part of Covenant Law, the law enjoined upon Israel as its part of an agreement between God and the nation. This is probably the most likely origin for the Ten Commandments, even though it is difficult to be precise as to date and place.

Ceremonial laws

The bulk of these laws is to be found in the latter part of Exodus, the whole of Leviticus and Numbers 1–20. According to the Old Testament these laws were given by God to Moses at Mount Sinai (cp. Leviticus 26:46), but the opinion of critical scholarship is that these laws reached their final form as late as the 5th century BCE. One reason for this is that there appears to be no trace of the Levitical* system of priesthood and sacrifice in the narratives of books such as Judges, where Gideon, not a priest, offers a burnt offering (Judges 6:25–7) and 1 Samuel (where Samuel, also not a priest, offers various sacrifices, cp. 1 Samuel 7:9–10).

However, cultic laws are very robust in that the specifics of various types of ritual, such as consecrating priests and offering particular sacrifices, are passed on from generation to generation, with little modification. Given this, the likelihood is that what we have in the Old Testament represents the possibly quite ancient cultic practices of various religious centres such as Bethel, Shiloh and Jerusalem. These were probably brought together and consolidated when Josiah made Jerusalem the sole legitimate sanctuary in Judah in 622 BCE, and they were written down after the destruction of the temple in 587. Whether they were ever put into practice in their amalgamated form is an interesting point. The sacrifices specified for the various feasts in Jerusalem in Leviticus and Numbers would require several hundred oxen and over 1,000 sheep and goats to be killed annually, and we do not know whether the post-exilic community possessed the economic base to provide animals for sacrifice on such a scale. As with the civil laws, the sacrificial laws of the Old Testament may be a witness to Israel's theology rather than to practice.

PROPHETIC LITERATURE

Following the historic-like narratives, the next main category of Old Testament writing in terms of quantity is the prophetic literature. Jewish tradition reckons that there are four prophetic books: Isaiah, Jeremiah, Ezekiel and the Book of the Twelve Minor Prophets, and they appear in this order in the Hebrew Bible. English non-Catholic Bibles insert Lamentations after Jeremiah and Daniel after Ezekiel, while Catholic Bibles further add Baruch after Lamentations. In the present section only the four books recognized by the Hebrew Bible will be discussed.

The earliest prophet after whom a book is named was probably Hosea who operated in the northern kingdom of Israel from around 750 BCE. However, it is clear from the Books of Samuel and Kings that Hosea was not the first prophet in Israel, and the biblical tradition even claims Abraham (Genesis 20:7) and Moses (Deuteronomy 18:15) as prophets. Prophecy was probably not a uniform phenomenon in Israel, a fact perhaps recognized in 1 Samuel 9:9 where it is said that 'he who is now called a prophet was formerly called a seer'.[6] Samuel (1 Samuel 19:20), Elijah (2 Kings 2:3) and Elisha (2 Kings 4:38) are represented as heads of groups of ecstatic* prophets. Amos claimed that he was not a prophet

(Amos 7:14), and Isaiah had ready access to the royal court whereas Micah seems to have been an elder in the provincial town of Moresheth-gath and highly critical of Jerusalem. Ezekiel was a priest. Recent research suggests that some, at least, of the prophets after whom books are named were supported by groups of disciples who collected and preserved their masters' sayings.

Much of the material in the named prophetic books began as oracles spoken by the prophets in specific situations, such as at gatherings of the people in the temple area (e.g. Jeremiah 7:1). The prophets employed a variety of spoken forms, and in particular the form used by ambassadors who conveyed orally the messages of kings to one another (for an example of the ambassadorial form see Judges 11:12–27). They also used funeral dirges (cp. Amos 5:1–3) and love songs (cp. Isaiah 5:1–7) and acted out events that they foresaw (Ezekiel 4:1–12). Some prophets were employed by kings to predict the future and to influence it for good (1 Kings 22:5–6), and prophets after whom books were named were certainly consulted by kings even if they were not on the royal pay roll (e.g. Isaiah at Isaiah 37:2, Jeremiah at Jeremiah 38:14). However, the 'true' prophets ('false' prophecy was an acute problem – see Jeremiah 28) were mostly highly critical of the leaders of the nation, and demanded social justice and fair dealing in the name of God.

In the first instance the prophets' words were recorded by disciples, and Jeremiah 36 states that he dictated to a scribe, Baruch, the prophecies that he had previously uttered. The main impetus for the production of the prophetic books, however, was the fall of Jerusalem in 587 BCE. This major disaster was seen as a fulfilment of the threats of coming divine judgement that had been articulated for many years by the prophets. Now that disaster had struck, the prophets began to be taken very seriously, and their words were studied to see what lessons could be learned. Possibly the first books to reach something like their present form were Jeremiah and Ezekiel. Both prophets had explicitly warned of the imminent destruction of the temple in the years shortly before this happened. Jeremiah was also aligned with the group in Judah's administration that had been involved in Josiah's reform according to the ideals of Deuteronomy, and his book was therefore finally edited by members of that school.

Isaiah probably reached its final form later than Jeremiah or Ezekiel, being the product of a school of disciples that existed for some 200 years. It included the words not only of Isaiah of 8th-century BCE Jerusalem, but of Deutero-Isaiah of 6th-century Babylon (chapters 40– 55), and of one or more prophets of late 6th-century Judah (chapters 56–66). Last to be put into its final form was the Book of the Twelve. An original collection of sayings of six pre-exilic prophets (Hosea, Amos and Micah from the 8th century BCE, and Zephaniah, Nahum and Habakkuk from the late 7th century) was gradually expanded into a collection of twelve. This involved not only adding later prophets, but also inserting new material into the earlier collection, such as the hopeful ending of Amos (Amos 9:11–15) and the vision of a restored Jerusalem in Micah 4:1–4. The latest material in the Book of the Twelve, Zechariah 9–14, probably dates from after 330 BCE; thus, the Book of the Twelve had a long literary history, and almost certainly contains a different prophetic activity from that of words spoken by a prophet; that is to say that, as time went on, prophecy became a matter of scribal interpretation and elaboration of words of prophets rather than a spoken activity.

PSALMS

The Book of Psalms is the only book in the Old Testament where an attempt was made in ancient times to indicate to readers who it was who had composed a particular psalm, and in what circumstances. The first such piece of information comes in Psalm 3 and reads: 'A Psalm of David, when he fled from Absalom his son', referring the psalm to the incident of Absalom's rebellion against David in 2 Samuel 15–18. Another such heading, relating to Psalm 51, connects the psalm to Nathan's rebuke to David following his adultery with Bath-sheba (2 Samuel 12:1–14).

It is difficult to know how old these headings are. They are substantially reproduced in the Greek Septuagint, the main difference being the tendency of the latter to attribute to David psalms such as 93–9, which have no title in the Hebrew. This means that the titles may go back to the 2nd century BCE. On the other hand, they all presuppose the existence of the Books of Samuel in substantially their present form, which indicates that they cannot be earlier than the 6th–5th centuries BCE. Modern critical scholarship regards the titles as evidence for later, personal use of the psalms, rather than as evidence for their origin (see below). It is interesting to note how the psalm titles have fared in recent translations. The NEB omitted them, but the REB restored them, printing them in italics. The GNB relegates them to footnotes.

Probably the best way in to the difficult task of accounting for the Psalms is to classify them according to their content. The largest category is that of laments. There are roughly thirty-two national and twenty-six individual laments. Other categories include hymns of praise (roughly thirty), 'songs of ascents' (fifteen) and royal psalms (roughly eleven). The 'songs of ascents' (Psalms 120–34) have been thought to have been composed by or for the use of pilgrims visiting Jerusalem at times of festivals (Psalm 84 would also be appropriate for this occasion). Although their content is varied (Psalm 130 has often been used in Christian services at funerals) they generally centre on Jerusalem (called Sion) and the security that comes from that place as the city of God.

Much attention has been devoted to the royal psalms (2, 45, 47–8, 72, 93, 95–9, 110) and attempts have been made to connect them with an annual or periodic celebration in Jerusalem of the kingship of God, in which the king played an important role. A plausible reconstruction has linked the ceremony to God's covenant with the descendants of David (cp. 2 Samuel 7:11–16 and Psalm 132 – a 'song of ascents'!), and the ritual has been fleshed out to include a symbolic search for the Ark* of the Covenant (Psalm 132:6–7), a circumambulation of Jerusalem (48:12–14), an entry to the city accompanied by challenges from the gate-keepers (24) and a solemn re-placing of the ark in the temple to the accompaniment of fanfares and the shout 'the LORD is king' (cp. 132:8–10, 47:5–7, 93:1, 97:1, 99:1). If this is correct (and it remains no more than an illuminating piece of guesswork), then some psalms originated in the royal ceremonies of the first temple, when there was still a king. There was no king of Jerusalem after 587 BCE until Simon the Maccabee united the high priesthood with unofficial kingship in 141. Attempts to date some royal psalms to this very late period were once popular, but do not enjoy widespread support today.

The national laments and hymns most likely originated in the context of public mourning and celebration, although it is difficult to know whether the setting was the first or second temple, or some other assembly. Individual laments may have been texts provided for worshippers who came to the Jerusalem temple or a local sanctuary, needing a form of words to express their grief, or their prayer for recovery from illness or some other disaster. Again, we can only guess from the content of the psalm. The so-called 'wisdom' psalms form a small category of psalms not so far mentioned, which contemplate the problem of evil and suffering. Psalms 73 and 94 are good examples.

Although the psalms had different origins according to their content, they began to be collected together into separate collections. The earliest was probably Psalms 3–41, most of which are connected in their titles with David. Traditionally, this was taken to mean that David had actually composed them. The modern scholarly view is that the Hebrew article ?, meaning 'of' or 'to' David, does not necessarily denote authorship: the matter will be reconsidered below. A second collection was a group of psalms (42–9) attributed in their titles to the sons of Korah, while Psalms 73–83 are attributed to Asaph. These were probably musicians in the time of the second temple (at 1 Chronicles 25:1 Asaph is placed in the time of David). The 'songs of ascents' seem to have comprised a separate collection as did the group of 'David' psalms (135–45).

Gradually, these collections were brought together in the form in which we know them and, perhaps on the analogy of the five books of the Pentateuch, were divided into five books (1–41, 42–72, 73–89, 90–106, 107–50) each of which ended with a doxology*. In the process, an important change in their perspective occurred. Psalm 1, the preface to the collection, is not about worship at all, but about meditation on God's law. Similarly, Psalm 119, an elaborate composition in which each eight verses begin with a successive letter of the Hebrew alphabet, and which may at one point have concluded the Psalter, is entirely concerned with personal meditation on the law. This indicates that, while the psalms were never divorced from public worship, the Book of Psalms as a whole was conceived as a vehicle for personal prayer and meditation. It was at this point that the psalm titles were added, linking many of them to incidents in the life of David and pseudonymously ascribing them to David.

In 1 Chronicles 16:8–36 a psalm that was sung by Asaph when David brought the Ark of the Covenant to Jerusalem is recorded. In fact, it is a composition made up of Psalms 105:1–15, 96:1b–13 and 106:1, 47–8. At 2 Chronicles 6:41–2, Psalm 132:8–10 is quoted in the context of Solomon's prayer at the dedication of the temple. The refrain 'For he is good, for his steadfast love endures for ever' (Psalm 136) is found at 2 Chronicles 5:13, 7:3 and Ezra 3:11. These are the only glimpses that the Bible allows us to have of how the psalms might have been used in worship.

'WISDOM' LITERATURE

The Books of Proverbs, Job and Ecclesiastes are usually classified under the heading of 'wisdom', and this is convenient so long as it does not obscure the very great differences between them, or indeed, within the Book of Proverbs itself.

Proverbs

Proverbs, in the sense of short, pithy sayings embodying sound advice based on experience of life, are apparently to be found universally in all cultures. Expressing as they do human observation, they are secular rather than religious. In the ancient Near East they were also used to train scribes in the art of writing, thus providing them with a reason and occasion for being written down. Old Testament tradition (1 Kings 4:29–34) credits Solomon with many proverbs and songs, and a heading at Proverbs 25:1 mentions 'proverbs of Solomon which the men of Hezekiah king of Judah copied'. There is thus good reason to connect the existence of the Book of Proverbs with the scribal and administrative class in Judah, at least from the time of Hezekiah (727–698 BCE).

This does not invariably imply that the scribal class composed the Proverbs or that the proverbs reflect the interests of the scribal elite. On the contrary, the proverbs are firmly rooted in the life of families, and partly consist of advice of a father to his son. Further, the families seem to be moderately prosperous land-owning units who practise hard work and thrift, and who defend the integrity of the family unit by warning of the perils of prostitution and adultery. Kings and the affairs of court are not excluded (cp. chapter 25), but certainly do not predominate.

The biblical Book of Proverbs is divided into several sections. The verses 1:2–9:18 contain a series of poems which, in addition to good advice about thrift and the avoidance of misbehaviour, introduce wisdom personified as a woman. In 8:22–36, Wisdom, speaking in the first person, claims that she was present when God created the world. This not only establishes her credentials to give good advice about how life should be lived if it is to be in harmony with creation; it adds a theological tone to the opening nine chapters of the book. It is likely that chapters 1–9 was the last section to be added to the book, with the purpose of putting its largely secular material within a religious framework.

The central collection is chapters 10:1–22:16, and consists mostly of two-line proverbs employing devices such as antithesis:

> A man who is kind benefits himself,
>> but a cruel man hurts himself (11:17),

comparison:

> It is better to be of a lowly spirit with the poor
>> than to divide the spoil with the proud (16:19),

and observation:

> The sluggard does not plough in the autumn;
>> he will seek at harvest and have nothing (20:4).

Although the subject matter is largely secular, there are groups of proverbs such as 16:1–11 that set behaviour in the context of God's control of the world. The section 22:17–24:22 is in part strikingly similar in content, but not order, to the Egyptian text, the Instruction of Amen-em-Opet, which is usually dated to around 1300 BCE.[7] While the likelihood is that the Egyptian and Israelite texts are dependent on not necessarily identical but common sources, the similarity demonstrates the international character of the wisdom tradition.

The final chapters of Proverbs include sections headed enigmatically 'The words of Agur son of Jakeh of Massa' and 'The words of Lemuel, king of Massa, which his mother taught him' (30:1, 31:1). The collection in chapter 30 in particular is unique with its numerical proverbs:

> Three things are too wonderful for me;
>> four I do not understand (30:18),

and its riddle-like quality:

> Who has ascended to heaven and come down?
>> Who has gathered the wind in his fists?
> Who has wrapped up the waters in a garment?
>> Who has established all the ends of the earth?
> What is his name, and what is his son's name?
>> Surely you know! (30:4).

The whole book ends with an acrostic poem (a poem in which each verse begins with a successive letter of the Hebrew alphabet) praising the perfect wife (31:10–31).

The Book of Proverbs probably emerged in several stages. The core was the collection in 10:1–22:16, most likely begun in court circles in the pre-exilic period. To this was added, after the exile, the smaller collections from 22:17 onwards, and the whole was prefaced with the first nine chapters with their picture of wisdom as God's companion at the creation.

The Book of Job

The Book of Job is one of the high points of the Old Testament and has inspired poetry, art and music, most famously William Blake's *Illustration of the Book of Job* (1825).[8] Basically, it is the story of a man who loses all his possessions and his children as a result of a wager between God and the Satan* (who is not the devil of later Christian theology).

The Satan argues that Job is pious only because he is prosperous, and that he will curse God if misfortune strikes him. The opening prologue of two chapters is then followed by thirty-five chapters of poetic dialogue in which Job argues about his fate with three (later, four) comforters. These maintain that Job must have sinned grievously for such misfortunes to have befallen him, while he insists that he has done nothing to merit his abject situation. The dialogues explore a number of themes, such as the justice of God, God's transcendence, and the problem of innocent suffering. In chapters 38:1–41:34 God intervenes and speaks out of a storm. He makes no attempt to answer the questions raised in the dialogues, but poses a series of rhetorical questions that concern both the awesomeness and, to human interest, the triviality of the created order (cp. 39:13 and its treatment of the ostrich). Job responds to the divine revelation by repenting (42:5–6), after which Job is restored to his former position of wealth and prosperity.

The Book of Job probably reached its present form in at least two stages. The first was the composition of the cycles of speeches framed by the prologue (chapters 1–2) and the epilogue (chapters 42:7–17) without which the speeches lack context. The second stage was the insertion of the Elihu speeches (chapters 32–7). These differ from the other speeches of the comforters in that they are a monologue without any reply of Job. By the time the Elihu speeches were added, some material from chapter 24 onwards had possibly been lost, because the third cycle of speeches is incomplete.[9] The two authors (it is also possible that there was only one author, who later expanded the work) were clearly men of deep sensitivity and poetic genius, and it is usually supposed, although direct evidence is lacking, that they lived in Judah in the 5th–4th centuries and were wealthy Jews suffering from the hardships of post-exilic Judah. The book is also regarded as an attack on the world-view of wisdom with its assumption of a moral universe in which virtue is rewarded and vice is punished; although the Book of Proverbs is not as naïve as this (cp. Proverbs 28:6, 11–12). It is possible that underlying Job is the actual experience of an educated sufferer who had to endure counselling from self-opinionated champions of a religious orthodoxy who were more interested in the vindication of their beliefs than the good of the sufferer. In this case, Job was the product of a remarkable individual in the post-exilic community, whose outpourings were able to find a place in the growing collection of writings that later came to be regarded as Scripture.

Ecclesiastes

Ecclesiastes, or, to give it its Hebrew name Qohelet, meaning something like 'preacher', 'teacher' or 'philosopher', is another remarkable composition on account of its general pessimism. Although the implicit claim of the book is that it was composed by Solomon (Ecclesiastes 1:1), modern scholars date it to the 3rd century BCE, when Judah was ruled by the Greek rulers of Egypt descended from Alexander the Great's general, Ptolemy. Opinions differ as to Qohelet's status and world. One view is that he was an upper-class person enjoying comparative prosperity. Another view is that he belonged to the middle classes at a time when the economic policies of the Ptolemies were bringing about great economic and social changes in Judah. Whatever his circumstances, Qohelet regarded his society as corrupt and unjust, and felt that little could be done to improve matters. Further, God seemed to be remote, with death the great leveller provided by God to remind people of their transience. Humans lived lives over which they had little control (Ecclesiastes 3:1–9) and the world provided no clues about any deeper purpose to life (3:11). However great a person's achievements, that person shared the same fate (death) as everyone else, while the achievements of one generation could quickly be undone by the next generation.

Insofar as Qohelet has a religious content, this is couched in conventional formulae such as the concluding verses, including, 'Fear God and keep his commandments; for this is the whole duty of man' (12:13). Not surprisingly, sentiments such as these have been suspected of being later additions designed to make the book more acceptable to a religious establishment. Yet, arguably, the religious value of Qohelet lies precisely in its transparent honesty. Along with Job, some of the psalms, and parts of Jeremiah it displays a 'courage to doubt' that enhances rather than diminishes the Old Testament as a collection of religious texts.

OTHER WRITINGS

Apocalyptic

In Jewish and Christian writings of the period 200 BCE–200 CE a distinctive genre called 'Apocalyptic' (from a Greek word meaning 'to unveil or uncover') can be found. These writings take the form of visions about the future that are interpreted by heavenly intermediaries; they employ symbolism drawn from official and popular mythology which features monstrous creatures; they are dualistic, often interpreting events in the world in terms of a cosmic struggle between God and his angels and Satan and demons. Apocalyptic has been seen as developing out of prophecy or, in more recent scholarship, as connected with mantic wisdom.[10] The latter, which derived from Babylon and spread throughout the Graeco-Roman world, combined divination, that is discovering the future by interpreting signs such as the stars or the entrails of animals, with a knowledge of mythological texts and traditions. This accounts for the concern for the future and the use of mythological imagery in apocalyptic literature. It is also possible that the dualistic eschatology* of Jewish apocalyptic was influenced by Zoroastrianism* when Judah was part of the Persian empire in the 6th–4th centuries BCE.

The Old Testament contains only one instance of the genre, the Book of Daniel, and in the strict sense only Daniel chapters 7–12 is apocalyptic in the sense of visions couched in imagery drawn from mythology. However, the first six chapters concern an encounter between Babylonian divination and God's revelation to Israel in which the central characters, Daniel and his companions, constantly demonstrate the superiority of the young Jews* who have been taken captive to Babylon.

Most scholars connect Daniel with the persecution of the Jews by Antiochus Epiphanes around 169 BCE, the reason being that the visions in chapters 8–11 are veiled references after the events to the defeat of the Persians by Alexander the Great in 333 BCE, to the break-up of Alexander's empire after his death, and to the struggle between Alexander's successor in Egypt (the Ptolemies) and Syria (the Selucids) for control of Palestine at the close of the 3rd century BCE. The 'little horn' of Daniel 7:8 has been identified with Antiochus Epiphanes. However, it is also generally agreed that the stories which comprise chapters 1–6 of Daniel were popular stories perhaps going back to the 6th century; and some additional popular stories about Daniel can be found in the Apocrypha (the Story of Susanna, Bel and the Dragon). Thus popular stories about the superiority of God's wisdom over foreign wisdom, and about the deliverance of God's servants when threatened by foreign powers, were combined with visions which set Judah's tribulations of the Seleucid persecution of 169 in a cosmic perspective, and promised vindication for all who suffered.

Love poetry

The joys and vicissitudes of love between men and women is such a universal human phenomenon that it is no surprise that love poems as a genre can be found in Egypt going back to the 14th–12th centuries BCE. Neither is it surprising that such love poems contain the universal themes of praise for the beauty of the beloved, the obstacles to the realizing of a longed-for liaison, the pain of separation and the joy of meeting. The Song of Songs (also called the Song of Solomon in some Bibles) is the only instance of the genre in the Old Testament, but it is a truly beautiful composition made up of a number of separate poems and possibly composed in the 4th century BCE. Its traditional ascription to Solomon derives from 1:1: 'The Song of Songs, which is Solomon's', and the apparent witnessing of a procession of Solomon being carried on a litter (3:6–11). According to some interpreters it originated from a marriage ceremony, and some translations present it in this manner (see chapter 1). It is easier, however, to regard it for what it is – genuine love poetry whose popularity was based upon its appeal to human emotions.

That it should appear in the Old Testament (it does not mention God) results from the fact that in Jewish interpretation, it came to be regarded as an allegory of God's love for Israel. Christian interpretation similarly allegorizes it in terms of Christ's love for the Church, or the intimate relationship between Christ and the individual believer. Modern interpretation lets the poems speak in their freshness, exuberance and frustration as expressions of deepest human feelings.

Novelistic writings

Just as love songs have a universal appeal, so do popular short stories about heroes and heroines. There are two such works in the Old Testament, Ruth and Esther. Ruth is a young Moabite woman who leaves her own country and people to return with her widowed mother-in-law, Naomi, to Bethlehem. Naomi had earlier left Bethlehem for Moab with her husband and two sons because of a famine. After the deaths of all the males in her family, Naomi decides to return home, and Ruth, now a widow, decides to accompany her. The story relates how Ruth marries Boaz, a wealthy kinsman of Naomi, and how the family of Naomi is thus continued when Ruth has a son by Boaz. A concluding genealogy identifies Boaz as the great-grandfather of king David.

The story of Esther is set in the court of the Persian king Xerxes (486–465), who is called Ahasuerus in the biblical book. Esther is a Jewish orphan brought up and adopted by her uncle Mordechai, who, because of her beauty, is recruited to the royal harem where she is made queen. The story relates how, with the help of Mordechai, Esther played a key role in preventing a courtier named Haman from organizing and carrying out a mass destruction of Jews in the Persian empire. The book connects the story with the Jewish festival of Purim (at which the story of Esther is still today read publicly) because Haman cast a lot known as Pur to determine the month in which he hoped to destroy the Jews (Esther 3:7, 9:24–8). The popular nature of the two stories is indicated by the fact that God is not mentioned at all in Esther (see also chapter 2 above) and not frequently in Ruth. Esther is usually dated to the 2nd century BCE while Ruth is harder to pinpoint. A popular theory is that Ruth, with its positive picture of a foreign Moabite woman, was written to counteract the policies of Nehemiah, who required Jews who had married non-Jews to divorce them. Taken together, Ruth and Esther are two poles of Jewish popular story-telling, the one exhibiting openness to non-Jews, the other showing the necessity for the closing of Jewish ranks in the face of a determined persecutor.

Laments

A third type of literature with a universal presence, if not appeal, is the lament. Since death and disaster are as ubiquitous as love, it is not surprising that laments should be part of the communal rituals used by peoples to help them to come to terms with grief. In the Old Testament there are hints of popular laments in some of the dirges of the prophets (see above). In the Book of Lamentations there is a series of poems lamenting the destruction of Jerusalem. Laments at the destruction of cities are known from other parts of the ancient Near East, and such laments share common themes with the biblical Book of Lamentations, such as references to the destruction, comments on the fate of survivors, denunciations of enemies.

Lamentations was traditionally ascribed to Jeremiah, and follows Jeremiah in English Bibles, but is placed among the Writings in the Hebrew Bible. In their present form the poems are highly sophisticated compositions. The first four are acrostic poems, poems in which each verse, or in the case of chapter 3 each three verses, begin with a successive letter of the Hebrew alphabet. Chapter 5 is not an acrostic, but its number of verses (22) corresponds to the number of letters of the Hebrew alphabet. The poems also contain many instances of *qinah* or lament rhythms, in which three stressed syllables are followed by two stressed syllables. A plausible origin for Lamentations can be found in communal gatherings at which the destruction of Jerusalem in 587 BCE was remembered. It is more difficult to say how what was expressed at these gatherings relates to the poems that we now have, with their sophisticated acrostic structure and allusions to many images and symbols found elsewhere in Old Testament poetry.

THE MAKING OF THE OLD TESTAMENT AS A WHOLE

It was suggested above that the first material to be collected and put into a coherent narrative was the story of Israel's origins. It was also suggested that the time of Hezekiah (727–698) was a plausible occasion for this activity. The destruction of the northern kingdom in 722/1 and the migration to Jerusalem of scribal and prophetic groups that preserved traditions about the northern ancestor Jacob, as well as about the prophets Elijah and Elisha and, perhaps, a group that had escaped from slavery in Egypt, was the catalyst for undertaking the task of constructing a grand narrative. Because this was undertaken in Judah, traditions about the Judahite ancestor Abraham preceded those about the Israelite ancestor Jacob.

The narrative beginning with Abraham could well have been taken to the time of Hezekiah himself. An important second stage was the emergence and work of the Deuteronomists in the 7th century BCE before and into the reign of Josiah. Here, laws probably deriving from the northern traditions formed the bulk of the legal sections of Deuteronomy. The narrative from the account of Joshua onwards was heavily re-edited to show that the tragedies that had overwhelmed the people, including the loss of the northern kingdom, had come about because of the sins of the people, and especially their rulers particularly in the northern kingdom. At this point the narrative was probably brought down to the time of Josiah (640–609).

The next stage was the destruction of Jerusalem in 587. This necessitated further reflection on the overall narrative and also turned attention to two other areas, law and prophecy. Because the prophets had consistently warned of an impending disaster if rulers and people did not observe the law, the collection and editing of the oracles of the prophets became a priority, as did the collection and study of laws. As a result of this the first two sections of the later Hebrew canon, the law – Genesis to Deuteronomy – and the prophets – Joshua, Judges, Samuel, Kings, Isaiah, Jeremiah, Ezekiel and the Twelve – began to approach their present form. However, a major stage of editing, that from priestly circles, was still to come, and this was probably undertaken in Jerusalem in the 5th–4th centuries. This revision affected particularly the Tetrateuch (Genesis to Numbers), and saw not only the inclusion of the ritual, priestly and sacrificial laws of Exodus, Leviticus and Numbers, but also the use of the so-called priestly history as the basic structure of the whole narrative. The narrative now began with the creation of the world (Genesis 1), and also incorporated non-priestly traditions such as the story of the Garden of Eden (chapters 2–3) and Cain and Abel (4).

The work was carried out in priestly circles in the Jerusalem temple, and to these circles can also plausibly be reckoned the collection and editing of the Psalms, the Book of Proverbs especially with its linking of Wisdom to the creation (Proverbs 8:22–31), and Lamentations. A later generation of priestly writers composed the Books of Chronicles, with their stress on the continuity of their temple with the worship of the time of David and Solomon. They also probably adapted the material now known as Ezra and Nehemiah.

Jerusalem of the 4th–3rd centuries saw the emergence of a more diversified, urban society than previously, and it was in these circles that works such as Job, Ecclesiastes and the Song of Songs were produced. It is also necessary to suppose that a library, or libraries, was established if we are to account for the preservation and availability of these texts for later inclusion in the Old Testament. The final crisis that precipitated literary activity was the persecution under Antiochus Epiphanes in 169 BCE, which produced Daniel and possibly Esther.

However, it must be remembered that the production of 'books' was not a matter of an author completing something that was then finished. The composition process was open-ended, with the work of authors shading into that of copyists via editors. Thus, although this section has looked for major crises or contexts which especially stimulated literary activity, the ongoing process via editing and copying must not be overlooked. The Old Testament, as the evidence from the Greek Septuagint and from the Qumran findings shows, was in some parts still being edited/composed up to the time when Jewish and Christian canonizing called a halt to the process.

Conjectural Chronology of the Composition of Books of the Old Testament and Apocrypha

10th–9th centuries BCE

Records of administration of temple and court compiled in Jerusalem and Samaria.

8th century

Beginnings of collections of written material that will become or be part of the Old Testament: oracles of the prophets Hosea, Amos, Micah and Isaiah (c. 740–700); first drafts of story of Israel and Judah from Abraham to time of Hezekiah; collections of laws, proverbs and psalms.

7th century

Collection of words of prophets Jeremiah, Nahum, Zephaniah; first drafts of Deuteronomy; overall story of Israel and Judah extended to time of Josiah (640–609).

6th century

Collection of words of prophets Jeremiah, Ezekiel, Deutero-Isaiah (Isaiah 40–55), Habakkuk, Haggai, Zechariah (1–8), Trito-Isaiah (Isaiah 56–66); further editorial work on story of Israel and Judah from Abraham to the destruction of Jerusalem (587) and on Deuteronomy. Further psalms, and Lamentations composed.

5th century

The Pentateuch (Genesis to Deuteronomy) begins to assume something like its final form, as do Joshua to 2 Kings, the prophetic books and Proverbs. New compositions include many psalms, Ezra and Nehemiah, and possibly Jonah and Ruth.

4th century

New compositions include the Books of Chronicles, possibly Malachi and the later chapters of Zechariah, Song of Songs, Job and Ecclesiastes, Esther.

3rd century

New compositions include Isaiah 24–9 and parts of Enoch (1–36, 72–92).

2nd century

New compositions include Daniel, 1 and 2 Maccabees, the Wisdom of Jesus ben Sirach (Ecclesiasticus), other parts of Enoch, Wisdom of Solomon.

1st century

Composition of 3 and 4 Maccabees, Tobit, Judith, Baruch, Prayer of Manasseh.

CHAPTER 4

The Making of the Apocrypha

In chapter 1 it was pointed out that the term 'Apocrypha' is used in different ways by the main branches of the Church. For Protestants the Apocrypha consists of books that appear in a separate section between the Old and New Testaments, while for Roman Catholics these same books are integrated into the Old Testament and regarded as deutero-canonical. The term Apocrypha is used by Roman Catholics to refer to 3 and 4 Esdras, the Prayer of Manasseh and Psalm 151.[1] No major Catholic translation in English includes these books.

The definition of the term 'Apocrypha' has been complicated by the fact that, in 1977, the committee responsible for the RSV issued translations of 3 and 4 Maccabees and Psalm 151, thus producing an expanded Apocrypha.[2] The aim was to produce a Bible that contained books recognized by the Orthodox churches. This policy was continued in the NRSV Apocrypha. Ironically, these extra books, as well as those designated as Apocrypha by Protestants and as deuterocanonical and Apocrypha by Catholics, are all regarded as deuterocanonical by the Orthodox. The following table seeks to make the position clearer, using Roman typeface to indicate 'Apocrypha', and italics to indicate 'deuterocanonical' books.[3]

'Protestant' (as in NRSV)	Catholic	Orthodox
Tobit	*Tobit*	*Tobit*
Judith	*Judith*	*Judith*
Additions to Esther	*Additions to Esther*	*Additions to Esther*
Wisdom of Solomon	*Wisdom of Solomon*	*Wisdom of Solomon*
Ecclesiasticus (Sirach)	*Ecclesiasticus (Sirach)*	*Ecclesiasticus (Sirach)*

Baruch	*Baruch*	*Baruch*
Letter of Jeremiah	*Letter of Jeremiah*	*Letter of Jeremiah*
Song of the Three	*Song of the Three*	*Song of the Three*
Daniel and Susanna	*Daniel and Susanna*	*Daniel and Susanna*
Bel and the Dragon	*Bel and the Dragon*	*Bel and the Dragon*
1 & 2 Maccabees	*1 & 2 Maccabees*	*1 & 2 Maccabees*
1 Esdras	1 & 2 Esdras	*1 Esdras*
Prayer of Manasseh	Prayer of Manasseh	*Prayer of Manasseh*
Psalm 151		*Psalm 151*
3 Maccabees		*3 Maccabees*
2 Esdras		*2 Esdras*
4 Maccabees		*4 Maccabees*

The present chapter will deal with the enlarged Apocrypha as found in the NRSV. Because these may be the books of the Bible least familiar to readers, they will be listed here, grouped under the headings according to which they will be considered. The present chapter will follow the broad divisions used in the previous chapter.

Historical writings: 1, 2 and 3 Maccabees, 1 Esdras.

Psalms: Prayer of Manasseh, Psalm 151.

'Wisdom' literature: Baruch (of which chapter 6 is sometimes separately designated as The Letter of Jeremiah), 4 Maccabees, Wisdom of Solomon, Wisdom of Jesus ben Sirach (Ecclesiasticus).

Apocalyptic: 2 Esdras.

Novelistic writings: Tobit, Judith, additions to Esther, additions to Daniel (Prayer of Azariah, Daniel 3:24–50; the Song of the Three Young Men, Daniel 3:51–91; the Story of Susanna, Daniel 13; Bel and the Dragon, Daniel 14).[4]

Compared with the content of the Old Testament it is noticeable that there are no prophetic books and practically no psalms. The whole collection is evidence of the growth of educated literary individuals among the Jewish communities of the Hellenistic world. None of the books are accepted as Scripture by the Jewish community, although the Wisdom of Jesus ben Sirach (Ecclesiasticus) was often quoted and referred to in Jewish literature of the early Common Era.

HISTORICAL WRITINGS

1 Maccabees

This work of sixteen chapters describes events in Judah from 175 BCE, the year of accession of the Seleucid king Antiochus IV Epiphanes of whose empire Judah was part, to 135 BCE, the year of the death of the high priest and ruler of Judah, Simon, and the accession of his son, John Hyrcanus. The introductory verses of 1 Maccabees describe the victories of Alexander the Great over the Persians (333–331) and tell that Antiochus IV was descended from Alexander's generals who divided up and became kings in what had been Alexander's empire. The first four chapters then recount the banning of Judaism by Antiochus in 167, the revolt inspired by the priest Mattathias of Modein, and the defeat of the Syrians and the cleansing of the temple in 164 by Mattathias's third son, Judas Maccabeus.

What began as a revolt to re-establish freedom to practise Judaism became, after 164, a fight for Jewish independence. This brought Judas into the world of the internal and external politics of the Seleucid empire, including its problems of accession to the kingship and its relationships with Rome. Judas was killed in battle in 160 to be succeeded by his youngest brother Jonathan. In 152, Jonathan, profiting from a struggle for the Seleucid throne between Demetrius I and Alexander Balas, was appointed high priest in Jerusalem by Alexander. Jonathan was killed by Typho, a powerful governor of Antioch and self-appointed king-maker, in 143, whereupon he was succeeded by the eldest son of Mattathias, Simon, with whose death, in 135, 1 Maccabees ends.

As this summary indicates, 1 Maccabees is concerned solely with the dynasty of Mattathias, how it restored the temple and how it won independence for Judah. Its author is generally thought to have been a resident in Jerusalem who composed the work in Hebrew, although it now exists only in Greek and Latin, and translations dependent upon the Greek. According to one view, the author lived during the reign of John Hyrcanus (134–104), while other experts suggest a later period, such as the reign of Alexander Jannaeus (103–76). Among the sources used were possibly an official Seleucid chronicle for the complicated events of the Seleucid empire, a life of Judas, and archive copies of official letters such as that at 10:18–20 appointing Jonathan as high priest.

The aim of the work is clear. It is an official attempt to justify the Hasmonean dynasty (the dynasty of Mattathias), especially because it had assumed the high priesthood (beginning with Jonathan in 152), for which it was not strictly speaking qualified. This action is justified by the loyalty of Mattathias and his sons to the observance of the Jewish law and the upholding of the ancestral religion. It should be pointed out that modern historians, although grateful for 1 Maccabees as an historical source, do not necessarily accept its account of the causes of the revolt at face value.[5]

2 Maccabees

This book is of similar length to 1 Maccabees and overlaps with it to some extent. It claims to be an abridgement of a five-volume work by Jason of Cyrene (2 Maccabees 2:23–31), an otherwise unknown writer who, as a Jew living in North Africa (Cyrene was the capital of the Roman province of Cyrenaica (now Libya) in North Africa), possibly reflected the outlook of the Jewish community in Alexandria. The book concentrates on two sets of events: those beginning in 187 BCE and leading up to the banning of Judaism by Antiochus in 167 and the Maccabean revolt to the cleansing of the temple in 164 (3:1–10:9), and the campaigns of Judas after 164, culminating in the defeat of the Syrian general Nicanor in 161 (10:10–15:36). Its first part, on the origins of the banning of Judaism, has often been largely, if uncritically, followed by modern historians.

The date of 2 Maccabees, which was written in Greek, is usually placed in the first half of the 1st century BCE (i.e. between 100 and 50), its place of composition being North Africa or Egypt. In its second chapter (2:13–14) it claims that Nehemiah founded a library and collected books about the kings and prophets, and the writings of David, and that also Judas (Maccabeus) had collected all the books that had been lost in the war. This passage will be useful later when the matter of canonizing is discussed (see chapter 6).

The purpose of the book is not to glorify the Maccabees but rather to account for the two festivals of Hanukkah (commemorating the rededication of the temple in 164) and Nicanor's Day, the latter being a festival that was observed until 70 CE. It has a much more supernatural flavour than 1 Maccabees with the intervention of angels (2 Maccabees 3:26) and other heavenly agents (10:29–31). Also, it glorifies martyrdom, as in the story of the martyrdom of the seven brothers and their mother (chapter 7).

3 Maccabees

It is arguable that this book should be included in the section on novelistic writings rather than here, for it is primarily a story about how the Jews in Alexandria were threatened with destruction by the Ptolemaic king Ptolemy IV Philopator (221–204 BCE) and how they were miraculously preserved. However, unlike similar books such as Esther and Judith, there is no central hero or heroine responsible for the deliverance. Rather, deliverance results from the combined resistance and prayers of the people as a whole, although the Jerusalem high priest Simon and an Alexandrian priest Eleazar are prominent at crucial moments.

The book begins with an account of Ptolemy IV's attempt to enter the Jerusalem temple. Being prevented by a paralysis inflicted by God, Ptolemy returns to Egypt where he plans to destroy the Jews in Alexandria by having 500 drugged elephants trample them to death. Further divine intervention on three occasions persuades the king to deal generously with the Jews.

The author is generally regarded as an Alexandrian Jew who composed the book in Greek in the 1st century BCE. Its purpose may have been to justify a Jewish festival in Alexandria commemorating a deliverance from persecution.

1 Esdras

This book is a history of the Jerusalem temple from Josiah's passover (sometime after 622 BCE) up to the reorganization of religious life by Ezra (458–428). It is based upon, and is a translation into Greek of,

2 Chronicles 35–6, Ezra 1:1–10:44 and Nehemiah 7:72–8:13a. However, the Hebrew text used was not identical with the later, traditional Hebrew text. There are two sections (1 Esdras 1:23–4 and 3:1–5:6) which have no parallel in the Old Testament, and of which the second records a contest between three bodyguards. Each defends respectively before the Persian king Darius the view that wine, the king or women is the strongest thing, with the third adding that truth wins the victory over all things. The victor, the third bodyguard, is Zerubbabel, who is consequently given authority and material support to return to Jerusalem in order to rebuild the temple. One other difference between 1 Esdras and its biblical source is that the correspondence between Zerubbabel's opponents and king Artaxerxes in Ezra 4:7–24 (1 Esdras 2:15–26) is put *before* the mission of Zerubbabel (in the biblical Ezra this correspondence is placed *after* Zerubbabel's mission). The result of this transposition is to make the story more logical, since the correspondence relates to the temporary official prohibition of building work in Jerusalem.

The overall effect of 1 Esdras is to provide a more integrated and interesting version of material most of which is in the Old Testament. It is usually dated to the lower end of 150–100 BCE. Whatever its purpose might have been, it indicates that the text of (later) biblical works such as Chronicles, Ezra and Nehemiah was not regarded, in some circles at any rate, as sacrosanct or beyond improvement, and was subjected to revision and supplementation.

PSALMS

The Prayer of Manasseh

This composition of fifteen verses was occasioned by the brief reference in 2 Chronicles 33:18 to Manasseh's prayer to God, and to the notice at 33:13 that he prayed to God and was restored, after he had been taken captive in fetters to Babylon. It falls into two main parts: verses 1–7 recount God's greatness in creation and in justice and mercy, verses 8–15 are a confession of sins and a plea for mercy. It was composed, probably in Greek, at the end of the pre-Christian era, and probably by a Jew, although there are few indications about these matters.

Psalm 151

This is not so much a psalm as a poetic composition about David's anointing as king and his defeat of the Philistine Goliath, all in the first person singular. In its form in the Septuagint it has seven verses, and it is this that is translated in the NRSV. However, a Hebrew version found at Qumran among the Dead Sea Scrolls, which comprises two psalms, is somewhat longer, and has evidently been abbreviated in the Greek version (similarly in a version in Syriac) producing in the process a verse 3 that makes little sense:

> And who will tell my Lord?
> The Lord himself; it is he who hears.

With regard to the origin of the psalm, a distinction must be made between its presumed Hebrew original found in Cave 11 at Qumran and its Greek version. The former *may* come from Essene circles if the Qumran covenanters were Essenes and the Psalms scroll from Cave 11 was their work, but this is not certain. Whatever its origin, it is again evidence that the biblical tradition was not regarded as complete or sacrosanct at the end of the pre-Christian era, and that an individual and no doubt pious Jew was ready to compose a psalm as though it had been spoken by David himself.

'WISDOM' LITERATURE

Baruch

This has been put here under the heading of wisdom on account of the long poem in praise of wisdom in Baruch 3:9–4:4. The book's content, however, does not belong to one type of literature only, and it is likely that it is the work of several writers. It begins by claiming to be the words of Baruch, Jeremiah's secretary (cp. Jeremiah 36:4) who is in captivity in Babylon after the fall of Jerusalem. Following the introduction, there is a prayer of confession and penitence (1:15 – 3:8) of which part (1:15 – 2:19) is dependent upon Daniel 9:5 – 19. The latter section (4:5 – 5:9) consists of several poems, each introduced by the phrase 'take courage', which speak consolation to Israel and Jerusalem in language reminiscent of Isaiah 40 – 55. The last such poem, Baruch 5:5 – 9, which almost quotes Isaiah 40:4, occurs in almost identical form in Psalms of Solomon 11:2 – 7. The Psalms of Solomon are eighteen psalms that are held to be a response to the Roman occupation of Judah in 63 BCE and subsequent events.

Chapter 6 of Baruch is, in the Septuagint, a separate book entitled the Letter of Jeremiah. Seventy-three verses long, it purports to be a letter sent by Jeremiah to captives taken to Babylon in 597 (cp. Jeremiah 29 for such a letter in the Old Testament). It is almost entirely a denunciation of the Babylonian worship of idols, and draws heavily upon Jeremiah 10:3 – 9, 14 and Psalm 115:4 – 8, as well as being reminiscent of Isaiah 40:18 – 20 and 41:6 – 7. A refrain, repeated nine times with slight variations, is 'that they [the idols] are not gods'.

A date for the varied contents of Baruch is difficult to give. A fragment of the Letter of Jeremiah in Greek has been found at Qumran and has been dated to 100 BCE, while 1:15 – 2:35 is thought to have been composed originally in Hebrew. On the other hand the dependence of 5:5 – 9 on the Psalm of Solomon 11:2 – 7 (assuming the dependence to be this way round) suggests a date after 63 BCE for the final form of the poems of 4:5 – 5:9. Because there are other works in existence attributed to Baruch (e.g. the Apocalypse of Baruch – not discussed in the present book), it is clear that the figure of Baruch was a convenient one both for the pseudonymous attribution of works, and the cataloguing/collecting of various other items.

4 Maccabees

This work of eighteen chapters is included here under 'wisdom' rather than historical writings because of its aim, which is to show that reason is superior to the emotions, and that truly to be both human and Jewish is to be ruled by reason. Its classification as 4 Maccabees results from the fact that the writer illustrates this thesis by dwelling in some detail on the story of the martyrdom of Eleazar and of the seven brothers and their mother, taken from 2 Maccabees 6:18–7:42, and expanded into chapters 15–18. In the earlier chapters the examples of Moses, Jacob and David are cited, and the figure of Isaac as the prototype martyr is alluded to several times. The writer believes in immortality (14:5) and the necessity of the Jewish law; but he has also been trained philosophically and uses the Stoic term for reason (*logismos*) and cites the Stoic virtues of rational judgement (*phronesis*), justice (*dikaiosune*), courage (*andreia*) and self-control (*sophrosune*). Thus 4 Maccabees exhibits a fusion of Judaism and Greek philosophy as well as furnishing some interesting examples of biblical interpretation. It was most likely written in Alexandria, although Antioch has also been proposed, sometime between 50 BCE and 30 CE.

The Wisdom of Solomon

A prayer in chapter 9 of this book contains the words:

you have chosen me to be the king of your people . . .
you have given command to build a temple on your holy mountain (9:7–8),

and thus constitutes an implicit claim to Solomonic authorship. However, it is generally agreed that the author wrote in Greek and was a Jew probably living in Alexandria in the period 100–50 BCE.

The book divides into three parts. The first, 1:1–5:23, deals with two themes: the incompatibility of wisdom and wickedness, and the respective fates of the righteous and the wicked, of whom only the former will enjoy immortality. Part two has a central section (6:12–8:21) which describes and praises wisdom. This central section is preceded by an exhortation to receive wisdom (6:1–11) and followed by a prayer to God, implicitly by Solomon (9:1–18). The third part (10:1–19:22) is an interpretation of the history of Israel from the time of Adam to the Exodus from Egypt in the light of wisdom. Interpolated into it is a section (13:1–15:19) that is a polemic against idolatry. It is noteworthy, however, that the word 'wisdom' that is so prominent in the first ten chapters, appears only twice in the concluding nine chapters. This has led some experts to suggest that the work had at least two authors.

The polemic against idols is in parts reminiscent of the Letter of Jeremiah (see above), while at 8:17, the Stoic virtues of self-control, prudence, justice and courage are mentioned (cp. 4 Maccabees 1:6). The book is thus another example of the combination of Judaism and Greek philosophy prevalent in the Jewish diaspora of the end of the pre-Christian era.

The Wisdom of Jesus ben Sirach (Ecclesiasticus)

This book presents a series of fascinating problems generated by recent discoveries and by the fact that this is the one book about whose authorship there is some reliable information! Until the end of the 19th century, Sirach was known only in Greek, Latin and Syriac. In this form it begins with a prologue written by the grandson of Jesus ben Sirach. He relates how he came to Egypt in the thirty-eighth year of Euergetes II, king of Cyrenaica 170–163 BCE and of Egypt 145–116. This would put the grandson's arrival at 132 BCE. He relates further that he translated his grandfather's work from Hebrew to Greek, naming his grandfather as Jesus (the Greek form of Joshua). His full name, Jesus ben Sirach, occurs at 50:27. It is deduced from these details and from the mention of a school at 51:23, that Jesus probably headed an academy in Jerusalem and that he composed the book around 190–180 BCE.

The translation of Sirach offered in the Authorized or King James version utilized Greek and Latin versions which today are regarded as inferior, and are held to contain interpolations. The standard Greek text published today is a shorter version, which means that modern translations such as the NEB, REB, RSV, NRSV, GNB and NJB frequently omit verses and indicate in footnotes the additional matter that has been left out. Further, there is more than one numbering system. The Parallel Apocrypha is most instructive here, printing as it does the Douay and AV translations alongside four modern versions. This enables readers to note different numbers (in Douay), and longer (AV) and shorter (GNB, NRSV, NJB) versions.

But there is a fourth modern version in The Parallel Apocrypha, the

(Catholic) New American Bible, which differs from the other modern translations in being based primarily on the Hebrew manuscripts of Sirach that have been discovered since 1896 in Cairo and since 1947 at Qumran and Massada. Five (or possibly six) manuscripts derive from Cairo, two (from Caves 2 and 11) derive from Qumran and one from Massada. These Hebrew discoveries give access to two-thirds of Sirach in Hebrew.

The textual history of Sirach is too complicated to be summarized, but raises this question: should modern translations be based on the best Greek version with readings adopted from the Hebrew where necessary, or should they be based on the Hebrew where it is extant? That this is not simply a purely academic question is indicated by the introduction to Sirach in the NJB Study Bible where it is stated that 'the Greek text is the only one recognized by the Church as canonical, and it is from this that the present translation has been made . . .' (p. 1076). The issue of the canonicity of Sirach presents no problems to Protestants (for them it is not canonical) and it is therefore surprising that translations such as the REB and NRSV should be based primarily on the Greek text, while a Catholic translation, the New American Bible, gives preference to the extant Hebrew.

From the point of view of its content, Sirach is a series of collections of sayings on many topics, beginning with a poem in praise of wisdom and ending with an acrostic poem on the search for wisdom (Ecclesiasticus 51:13–30). A well-known passage is 44:1–50:21, beginning with the words 'Let us now praise famous men'. Starting with Enoch* it epitomizes the work of selected heroes, ending with the high priest Simon II, son of Onias III, *c.* 220–195 BCE. Sirach was a popular composition among Jews and Christians. Although the former did not admit it to their canon, they quoted from it freely, while Christians nick-named the book Ecclesiasticus and valued it on account of its advice on matters not otherwise dealt with in the Old Testament.

APOCALYPTIC

There is only one apocalyptic work in the Apocrypha, namely, 2 Esdras. In the appendix to the Latin Vulgate this is numbered as 4 Ezra. A further complication is that the work as originally written seems to have comprised only chapters 3 – 14. These were written in Hebrew or Aramaic around 100 CE as a response to the destruction of the second Jerusalem temple by the Romans in 70 CE. The Semitic original is lost and these chapters are known only in translations into Latin, Syriac, Ethiopic, Arabic, Coptic, Armenian and Georgian. However, the Latin version contains additional material in the form of chapters 1 – 2 and 15 – 16, which are both independent compositions and are often referred to as 5 Ezra and 6 Ezra respectively. These are almost certainly Christian compositions that were added later to the Jewish work, as can be seen from the similarity between 2 Esdras 2:42 – 8 and parts of the Book of Revelation in the New Testament. Thus, in the 2 Esdras passage, Ezra sees a great multitude praising God on mount Sion, in whose midst is a young man taller than the rest who is placing crowns on the heads of the others. Ezra is told that the young man is the Son of God, and that those being crowned have confessed him to the world and have died (cp. Revelation 7:9 – 14). In available English translations, the AV lacks 2 Esdras 8:36 – 105, because this material was missing from the manuscripts of the Vulgate used by the AV translators. The passage was possibly omitted deliberately from the Latin because it explicitly rules out prayers for the dead – a missed opportunity for the Protestant translators! English versions, from the RV onwards, restore the passage, thus once again creating the situation in which, depending on what version of the Bible one uses, there will be differences in content.

The main part of the book (chapters 3 – 14) consists of seven visions: (a) 2 Esdras 3:1 – 5:20, (b) 5:21 – 6:34, (c) 6:35 – 9:25, (d) 9:26 – 10:59, (e) 11:1 – 12:51, (f) 13:1 – 58, (g) 14:1 – 48. The earlier visions, drawing heavily on the story of Israel from the Old Testament, reflect on why the temple has been destroyed by the Babylonians (by which they mean the second temple's destruction by the Romans), given that Ezra has found Babylon to be just as sinful as Israel had been. The answer is that humankind cannot understand God's ways. This material contains many analogies drawn from everyday life, as well as explanations about the origin of sin because of Adam, and reflections about the creation and about the hereafter. This extensive and explanatory material about origins and destinies, not found elsewhere in the Bible, undoubtedly accounts for the book's enormous popularity in the early Church as indicated, for example, by the number of languages into which it was translated.

Two visions call for special comment. The fifth, the eagle vision (11:1–12:51), is reminiscent of Daniel 7, and just as the latter alludes to the recent history of the Seleucid empire, so the fifth vision in 2 Esdras alludes to recent events in the Roman empire – either to events culminating in the reign of Nero, or events at the close of the 1st century CE. The seventh vision (chapter 14) contains the legend of Ezra and the composition of the books of the Old Testament. According to this, Ezra dictates ninety-four books to five men over the space of forty days. Of these, twenty-four, which clearly refer to the books of what is now called the Hebrew Bible, are to be read by the worthy and the unworthy. The remaining seventy are to be reserved for the wise only. The idea of secret and hidden wisdom is a stock-in-trade of apocalyptic.

The content of 2 Esdras is too rich and complex to summarize. Its purpose of composition is clear: a response to the destruction of the Jewish temple and the heart-searching that followed within certain Jewish circles. Yet it was taken over and preserved only by the Christian community. This was made possible by the fact that, on the surface, the book deals with the destruction of the first temple in 587 BCE, and by the fact that it is explicit about human origins and destiny, matters on which the Old and New Testaments are silent.

NOVELISTIC WRITINGS

Tobit

This is a charming story which recounts how two pious Jews were delivered by God from their afflictions in response to prayer. The first, Tobit, resides in Nineveh having been taken there as a captive from

Israel in the late 8th century. Under Shalmaneser (V) he prospers, but under Sennacherib his property is confiscated because he reverently buries any Jew executed by the king. Restored to favour in the reign of Esarhaddon through the intercession of Ahikar, Tobit's nephew and the king's chief administrator, Tobit loses his sight when sparrow droppings fall in his eyes as he sleeps in the open. He prays to God that he may die.

The second person to pray is Sarah, daughter of Raguel, who lives in distant Ecbatana, Raguel being Tobit's cousin (Tobit 7:2). She is plagued by a demon who has, on their wedding nights, killed seven men who were betrothed to her. She, too, prays that she might die. The story tells how God delivers Tobit and Sarah by sending an angel, Raphael, to accompany Tobias the son of Tobit from Nineveh to Ecbatana where he seeks Sarah's hand in marriage. On the journey, the capture of a large fish provides a heart, liver and a gall. By burning the first two with incense Tobias repels the demon; with the gall he restores his father's sight on returning to Nineveh with his bride Sarah. The story ends with the death of Tobit, aged 158, who has told his son and daughter-in-law to return to Ecbatana, believing that Nineveh will be destroyed in accordance with the words of the prophet Jonah or Nahum (there are two textual traditions). Tobias does so, and before he dies in Ecbatana he hears the news that Nineveh has fallen.

The story is a combination of biblical, extra-biblical and folkloristic elements, punctuated with prayers and hymns of praise. Thus, Tobias's journey to Ecbatana to seek Sarah has overtones of Abraham sending a servant to seek Rebekah for Isaac (Genesis 24). The references to Ahikar (Tobit 1:21, 11:18, 14:10) indicate knowledge of the popular story of Ahikar, according to which this chancellor under kings Sennacherib and Esarhaddon was deposed by his nephew, but survived eventually to resume his office. Various wisdom collections are attributed to Ahikar, of which one version was found in Aramaic at the 5th-century BCE Jewish colony of Elephantine on the Upper Nile.[6]

Tobit was written in Hebrew or Aramaic, probably around 200 BCE and presumably in Mesopotamia, where the story is set. Cave 4 at Qumran has provided two Hebrew fragments and one Aramaic fragment of Tobit, although the standard translations in the Bible depend on

Greek versions of which there is a longer and a shorter version. The shorter Greek version is translated by the AV, RV and RSV, while the longer is used by the NRSV, NJB, GNB and NAB. Their differences can be easily noted in The Parallel Apocrypha.

Jerome's Latin version, based apparently on an Aramaic text which a local Jew translated into Hebrew for him, shows some divergences from the Greek. This can be best seen by comparing the Douay and Knox* versions, which translate the Latin in The Parallel Apocrypha, with the other versions there. Differences include the fact that Tobit's blindness is caused by swallows, not sparrows (Tobit 2:10 or 11 – the numbering varies) while the three nights of chastity of Tobias and Sarah in the Latin of 8:4 are not in the Greek. Also, the summary of the story of Ahikar, found at 14:10 in the Greek editions, is missing from the Latin, and thus from Douay and Knox. An interesting point at which to observe the divergences of the Greek versions and of the Latin from both is Tobit 14. The Latin makes no mention of the prophetic forecast of Nineveh's destruction, nor that Tobit hears of its fall. Tobias's departure from Nineveh is because his father knows that its iniquity will bring destruction. In the shorter Greek version it is Jonah's prophecy of Nineveh's destruction that evokes Tobit's advice to his son to leave the city. In the longer Greek version the prophet is Nahum.

Tobit is thus full of interest – as a story in its own right, as an indication of popular Jewish piety containing allusions to biblical stories, other literature and folklore, and as showing how books could circulate in several different versions, of which three are represented in Bibles in English.

Judith

Like Tobit, this book does not exist in one version, although its textual history is not as complicated as that of Tobit. However, the Latin version of Jerome, again claimed by the translator to be based on an Aramaic original, differs considerably from the Greek version. This can be seen in The Parallel Apocrypha by comparing Douay and Knox (based on the Latin) with the other versions represented there. This indicates that chapter 2, for example, is much shorter in the Latin version, comprising eighteen verses as against twenty-eight in the Greek edition. Thus, again, we have a book which appears in two different versions in Bibles in English.

The story itself, which takes considerable liberties with Israelite and ancient Near Eastern history and geography, is set in the reign of Nebuchadnezzar, king of Assyria(!). Following this king's defeat of an otherwise unknown king Arphaxad of Media, and his rebuttal by countries to the west including Judah and the inhabitants of Samaria, he sends his general Holofernes westwards, the latter eventually camping in the Valley of Jezreel in Galilee. This alarms the Jews, many of whom are said to have returned recently from captivity (another historical liberty). They pray fervently to God for deliverance.

An ally presents himself in the form of Achior, an Ammonite, who summarizes Israelite history, and who urges caution upon Holofernes. Achior is shouted down, however, and deported and taken to the Israelite town of Bethulia (evidently a fictitious name) where he is welcomed. Holofernes then advances and surrounds Bethulia, seizing the springs upon which it depends for water. The story then recounts how Judith, a pious widow, persuades the elders of Bethulia to let her go to the Assyrian camp on the pretext of giving information to Holofernes. Finding her beauty and charm irresistible, Holofernes allows her to stay in the camp and gives a banquet at which he becomes drunk. Left alone with Holofernes, Judith cuts off his head, puts it into a bag and escapes with her maid back to Bethulia. The next day the Israelites attack and defeat the Assyrians. The Ammonite Achior accepts circumcision and thus becomes an Israelite.

Whether the book was originally written in Hebrew or Greek is disputed; but its date is generally agreed to be around the middle of the 2nd century BCE. It evokes the atmosphere of the time after the Maccabean revolt when Judah experienced a number of invasions from the north as the Hasmonean dynasty strove for the independence of the nation.

Additions to Esther

It was pointed out above that there exist in the Greek version of Esther a number of additions to the Hebrew version, the Hebrew being the basis for English translations of Esther in the Old Testament. The additions expand the story at crucial points, and, above all, introduce prayers which thus give the Greek Esther a religious flavour that is lacking from the Hebrew edition, which notoriously does not mention God. If the view is dismissed, as most likely it should be, that the Hebrew is a *shortened* version of the longer Greek edition, we have further evidence of the way in which the biblical tradition developed, i.e. a popular story of a Jewish heroine was expanded by additions designed to make the writing more overtly religious.

Esther and its additions are also valuable for considering how Bibles have come into being. When Jerome translated Esther into Latin he did the work in two stages. First, he translated the Hebrew text. Second, he translated the additions from the Greek, placing them as an appendix to Esther. In due course, these were numbered as Esther 10:4–16:24. At the Reformation these additions were removed from after Esther 10:3 to the Apocrypha as a separate section between the Old and New Testaments in Protestant Bibles. English tradition, illustrated by the AV, kept to Jerome's order of the additions. Luther, however, rearranged the additions, and omitted 12:1–6 because of the similarity with Esther 2:21–3, 6:3 and 3:1–6. Luther's order was 13:1–7, 13:8–14:19, 15:1–16, 11:1, 16:1–25, 11:2–12 and 10:6–13. Catholic Bibles in English continued to have the additions at the end of the Old Testament Book of Esther.

An interesting situation exists in recent translations. Some, including the NEB, REB and GNB, have translated the whole of the Greek version of Esther in the Apocrypha, so that the additions can be read *in situ*. Catholic versions, such as the NAB and NJB, have put the Greek additions back into the body of the Old Testament text of Esther (which is translated from Hebrew), the NJB distinguishing the additions by printing them in italics. These modern translations have, in this way, produced two different versions of the longer form of Esther, because, the additions apart, there are differences between the Hebrew and Greek versions of Esther. This can be seen easily in The Parallel Apocrypha by comparing the NRSV (which translates the Greek Esther) with NJB (which translates the Hebrew). Differences include the name of the Persian king (Artaxerxes in the Greek, Ahasuerus in the Hebrew), the name of his rejected wife (Astin in the Greek, Vashti in the Hebrew), and also other names of officials. There are many other slight variations.

The Greek version of Esther, with its additions, was produced sometime before either 114 or 78 BCE, depending on the accuracy and interpretation of a scribal note at 11:1.

Additions to Daniel

There are four additions to Daniel: the Prayer of Azariah, the Song of the Three Young Men, the Story of Susanna, and Bel and the Dragon. Slight variations of these titles can be found in English translations. In Catholic Bibles, the first two additions are numbered as Daniel 3:24–50 and 3:51–91.[7] Susanna is Daniel 13 and Bel and the Dragon is Daniel 14 in Catholic Bibles.

These additions have had a complicated textual history, but since this is not reflected in English versions (in contrast to Tobit and Esther) the matter will be touched upon only lightly. The Septuagint version of the Old Testament Book of Daniel, which includes the additions, differs significantly from the Hebrew and Aramaic book that is found in the Old Testament. The early Church found this divergence so intolerable that it adopted for Greek Bibles the Greek translation of Daniel made by Theodotion of Ephesus in the middle of the 2nd century CE. This translation was much closer to the Hebrew and Aramaic Daniel; but its version of the additions also differed in some respects from the Septuagint. Several of the differences will be noted below where appropriate. All English translations of the additions are based upon Theodotion and not the Septuagint.

The Prayer of Azariah and the Song of the Three Young Men occur at the point in Daniel when Hananiah, Mishael and Azariah (cp. Daniel 1:6–7) are put into the fiery furnace for refusing to bow down to the golden statue that Nebuchadnezzar had made. Azariah's prayer is a noble confession of the unworthiness of the people of Israel and a prayer for deliverance without, however, alluding to the specific circumstances of the fiery furnace. It makes allusions to many parts of the Old Testament. The Song of the Three Young Men consists mainly of a call to all the forces and parts of nature to praise God. Verses 35–66a (57–88a in Catholic Bibles) have, since the late 4th century CE, been used as the canticle known as the 'Benedicite', and beginning: 'O all ye Works of the Lord, bless ye the Lord: praise him, and magnify him for ever' (Book of Common Prayer). In the first English Prayer Book of 1549 it was appointed as an alternative to the 'Te Deum' at Mattins during Lent, and although the restriction to use only in Lent was removed in the 1551 Prayer Book, the tradition of singing the 'Benedicite' during Lent has survived to today in some parts of the Church of England.

The Story of Susanna relates how two elderly Jews in Babylon were seized with passion for the beautiful Susanna, wife of Joakim, and how they tried to take advantage of her while she was bathing in a private garden. Refusing their advances by shouting for help, Susanna finds herself accused by the two men, who are also judges, of having been seen by them having intercourse with a young man. She is condemned to death by the people meeting in her husband's house. However, Daniel, described as a young boy, refuses to agree with the sentence, and by cross-examining the judges proves that they are lying. In accordance with the Old Testament laws of false evidence (Deuteronomy 19:18–19), they receive the sentence that had been passed on Susanna.

The Septuagint version differs in that there is no bathing scene, the examination of Susanna takes place in the synagogue and not her husband's house, and Daniel is a young man rather than a young boy. The two versions stress different themes. Theodotion focuses on the wronged young woman, while the Septuagint contrasts the young judge who is filled with divine wisdom with the corrupt and deceitful elder judges.

Bel and the Dragon describes a contest between Daniel and Cyrus, king of Persia, regarding an idol named Bel. By spreading ashes on the floor of the temple Daniel proves, from the footprints left by the priests, that the idol does not consume the food left for it, but that the priests do so, using a secret entrance to the temple. Next, Daniel destroys a dragon by feeding it with pitch, fat and hair. Its priests are so angry that

Daniel has to be handed over to them by the king. They put him in a lion pit, where he stays for six days. While in the pit he is fed by the prophet Habakkuk, who is transported from Judah to Babylon by an angel holding him by his hair. Daniel survives the ordeal in the lion pit to the king's great joy.

The Septuagint has a title at the beginning of the story which reads: 'From the prophecy of Ambakum [Habakkuk], son of Jesus [Joshua] of the tribe of Levi'. Generally, the Septuagint version gives Daniel a much more prominent role in the action, and after he has destroyed the dragon all the people cry out: 'The king has become a Jew. He has destroyed Bel and killed the dragon.' This pressure causes the king to put Daniel into the lion pit.

The date of the additions is not easy to determine, nor the language in which they were originally written. Given that popular stories about Daniel circulated probably from the 6th to 5th centuries, they may have a long oral history. In their present form they are not older than the middle of the 2nd century BCE.

THE MAKING OF THE APOCRYPHA AS A WHOLE

It will be clear from the foregoing that the above heading is at best misleading and at worst nonsense. There is no such thing as the Apocrypha. This is indicated by the different contents of the Apocrypha as outlined in chapter 1. The present chapter has also shown that even where churches agree that certain books are Apocryphal or deuterocanonical and collect them together in some way, these books often exist in quite different versions in the extant manuscripts, and these different versions are represented in English translations. This is especially true in the cases of the Wisdom of Jesus ben Sirach (Ecclesiasticus), Tobit, Judith and Esther. These differences show that the growth of the biblical tradition was open ended, and that it was not until the invention of printed books that anything like standardization began to be achieved. Even so, as the cases of Tobit, Judith and Esther have shown, complete standardization was never achieved.

EXCURSUS: THE DEAD SEA SCROLLS

Allusions have been made in this chapter and the preceding one to the 'library' at Qumran and to the presence there of fragments of Apocryphal books such as Tobit and the Wisdom of Jesus ben Sirach (Ecclesiasticus). The aim of this excursus is to place these remarks in the wider context of the so-called Dead Sea Scrolls, especially because the Scrolls and their origins continue to be subjects of scholarly controversy that impinge upon the general public by way of popular books and television programmes.

The story of the first, and accidental, discovery of manuscripts in a cave at the northern end of the western side of the Dead Sea by Bedouin in 1947 or late 1946 has been told many times.[8] The publication of most of the important biblical and non-biblical manuscripts from eleven caves followed in the late 1940s and the 1950s, as did the excavation of the remains of ancient buildings at Khirbet Qumran (Khirbet being the Arabic for 'ruin'). By the end of the 1950s a scholarly consensus had emerged which ran roughly as follows. The scrolls were produced by a community that lived at Qumran, and which was to be identified with a group known from Jewish and classical sources as Essenes. This was a pacifist, celibate group within Judaism which practised commonality of possessions, engaged in corporate worship and study of the law, and had several stages of admission to the community from novitiate to full membership. The community regarded itself as the true Israel which, in the final days at the end of the world, would play a key role in a cosmic battle between good and evil. The community was believed by scholars to be descended from Hasideans, devout followers of the Jewish law who initially supported the Maccabees in their struggle against Antiochus Epiphanes when he banned Judaism in 167–164 BCE, but who later withdrew their support and sought the seclusion of the wilderness. There was also evidence from material discovered in the caves near Qumran, as well as material discovered at the end of the 19th century in a synagogue in Cairo, that the community also existed in 'camps' that were dispersed throughout Judea.

The community's founder, or a key figure in its history, was the

'Teacher of Righteousness' mentioned in several non-biblical texts. A passage from the Commentary on Habakkuk aroused particular interest:

Woe to him who causes his neighbours to drink; who pours out his venom to make them drunk that he may gaze on their feasts (Habakkuk ii, 15).

Interpreted, this concerns the Wicked Priest who pursued the Teacher of Righteousness to the house of his exile that he might confuse him with his venomous fury. And at the time appointed for rest, for the Day of Atonement, he appeared before them to confuse them, and to cause them to stumble on the Day of Fasting, their Sabbath of repose.[9]

From this text it was surmised that the Teacher was the leader of a community that observed a different calendar from that of 'official' Judaism, and that he was possibly a legitimate high priest who had been ousted by the Wicked Priest. The latter had come to Qumran ('the house of his exile') when the community, but not 'official' Judaism, was observing the Day of Atonement, in order to 'confuse him'. Some interpreters suggested that this meant that the Teacher was killed by the Wicked Priest. Various attempts were made to identify the Teacher and the Wicked Priest from personages known in the 2nd–1st centuries BCE. The history of the community came to an abrupt end in 68 CE when the Romans destroyed Qumran during the Jewish Revolt of 67–73 CE. Before the destruction the manuscripts were deposited for safety in caves nearby, where they remained undisturbed until their discovery in 1946/47. This consensus view is what is presented to visitors to Qumran today, and buildings such as the scriptorium (where the scrolls were written or copied) and the hall where the members of the community held their assemblies are identified in accordance with the consensus view. The consensus view has also remained largely intact, and is defended by Vanderkam and Vermes in their recent books.

If the scrolls have come to public attention in recent years it is because the fragments found in Cave 4, reckoned to amount to 575 titles,[10] were far too many for the small original team of scholars and their successors to handle. Publication of the material came almost to a standstill, a situation exacerbated by the refusal of the scholars concerned to grant general scholarly access to the fragments. This situation inevitably gave rise to speculation, now known to be groundless, that the unpublished material was being suppressed because it would prove highly embarrassing to the churches in its implications for Christian origins. It is only since 1991 that all the scrolls and fragments have become generally available to scholars, and that is why Geza Vermes's *The Complete Dead Sea Scrolls in English* appeared only in 1997, fifty years after the first discoveries!

It is beyond the scope of the present work to engage with the consensus view in detail.[11] However, several points will be made that are pertinent to the present chapter. On the consensus view, the manuscripts from near Qumran represent the library of a Jewish group that was outside the main stream of Judaism, in the sense that it regarded the Jerusalem temple, its priesthood and worship, and its calendar as illegitimate. It also included among its library, books such as Tobit, the Wisdom of Jesus ben Sirach, Jubilees* and parts of Enoch, which were not later accepted as Scripture by Judaism. Further, in its Scroll of Psalms from Cave 11, it included a number of compositions that are not in the traditional Hebrew collection of the Psalms. It could therefore be said to be unrepresentative of the Judaism of the closing centuries before the Common Era. The challenges to the consensus view result in positions that imply that, far from being unrepresentative of the Judaism of the period, the works found near Qumran are evidence for a considerable diversity so that it becomes difficult to speak of a main stream in Judaism before the fall of Jerusalem in 70 CE.

For present purposes, recent challenges to the consensus have questioned whether all the manuscripts found in the caves originate from the Qumran community. Even back in the 1950s it was conceded by some that the Copper Scroll from Cave 3, an inventory of places where treasure was buried inscribed on copper sheets, was not the work of the community.[12] With the passage of time, the opinion has grown that the material found in the eleven caves cannot have been the product of a single community. One reason for this is the number of different types of handwriting found in the fragments, amounting to at least 150 identified. Philip Davies believes that the final number of hands will be much greater and observes that

The problem is not merely the number of hands (this is embarrassingly high), but specifically the ratio of hands to texts: a smallish community with a scribal school should produce for the same number of different texts a much higher proportion in the same hand. It is now being conceded that a large number of manuscripts – the majority, perhaps – do not emanate from a single scribal school or from a single religious community.[13]

The present work is not the place to enter in to these controversies. That there was no connection between the buildings at Qumran and the manuscripts found in caves in the region seems to be ruled out by the fact that Cave 4 is part of the promontory on which the buildings stood. It does not follow from this, however, that all the caves were connected with Qumran. Cave 1 is about a mile north of Qumran and Cave 3 is nearly two miles away. These facts do not, of course, prove anything; but they leave open the possibility that groups other than those at Qumran could have used caves in the area to deposit writings, either to keep them safe or because they were no longer fit for use.

If Davies is correct to say that a large number of the manuscripts do not come from a single scribal school or a single religious community, then we have evidence for the diversity that there was in the Judaism of the 2nd–1st centuries BCE. Summarizing the content of the Scrolls and assuming them, uncritically, to represent differing interests, it can be said that there were groups that rejected the temple, its priesthood and its worship, groups that were organized in 'camps' within general society, groups that had an expectation that they would be involved in the final battle in the last days against evil, and groups that regarded highly books such as Tobit, Jubilees and parts of Enoch. It was as part of this complexity, including the contribution made by Jews living in Alexandria, that the books of the Apocrypha were written, and early Christianity emerged. Paradoxically, after the fall of Jerusalem in 70 CE, it was the early Church rather than Judaism that retained, in what Protestants call the Apocrypha, the Jewish compositions that bear witness to this complexity.

Chronology of the New Testament Period

1st century BCE

Birth of Jesus of Nazareth (7 or 6 BCE). Death of Herod the Great (4 BCE). Herod Antipas ruler of Galilee and Peraea, southern Trans-jordan (4 BCE–39 CE).

1st century CE

Pontius Pilate Roman procurator of Judea (26–36 CE).
Beginning of public ministry of John the Baptist (27).
Baptism and beginning of public ministry of Jesus (27–8).
Beheading of John the Baptist by Herod Antipas (29).
Crucifixion of Jesus (c. 30).
Conversion of Paul of Tarsus (c. 33–5).
Paul's first missionary journey (c. 46–8).
Paul's first visit to Jerusalem and second missionary journey (c. 49–52).
First Pauline letter (1 Thessalonians, c. 50).
Bulk of main Pauline letters written (Romans, 1 and 2 Corinthians, Galatians, Philippians, c. 51–7).
Paul's third missionary journey (c. 53–6).
Paul's journey to Rome as a prisoner (c. 58–62).
Death of Paul (? 63/4).
Destruction of Jerusalem by Titus and removal of the Jerusalem Church to Pella (70).
Gospel of Mark (70–80).

Gospels of Matthew and Luke, Acts, Deutero-Pauline letters (Ephesians, Colossians, 1 and 2 Timothy, Titus), 1 Peter, James, Hebrews (80–90).
Gospel of John, Johannine letters, Revelation (90–100).

2nd century

Jude, 2 Peter (100–110).

CHAPTER 5

The Making of the New Testament

The New Testament differs from the Old Testament and Apocrypha in several respects. First, the works of which it is made up were written in a comparatively short space of time – about seventy years if 1 Thessalonians is dated to around 50 CE and 2 Peter to *c.* 120 CE. Second, these works were written because of a fundamental difference of opinion in the early Church between Paul and his followers, and those who wanted to keep Christianity within, or at least close to, 1st-century Judaism. In turn, this dispute about Christian identity affected relationships between the Church and the Synagogue, and fed back in to the writing of the Gospels, where a key issue became the attitude of the Founder of Christianity to Judaism, the law, the temple and non-Jews.

That such a dispute should have arisen is not surprising. On the principle that there is no smoke without fire, the catalyst for dissension was the life and teaching of Jesus of Nazareth. The Gospels must be used with caution as historical documents; but their picture of Jesus as befriending the outcast, challenging the strict interpretation and observance of the Jewish law and challenging the notion of the indispensability of the Jerusalem temple probably reflects the facts. This being so, the question was bound to arise whether the movement initiated by Jesus would become part of the rich spectrum of Judaism before the fall of Jerusalem in 70 CE, or whether it would move outside the limits of Judaism.

Because the present chapter is about the making of the New Testament and not the history of Christian origins, these matters will not be pursued in detail. But they will remain the backcloth to the chapter, given, as stated above, that the New Testament writings took the form that they did because of a fundamental dispute about the significance of Jesus in relation to the Judaism of his day. The main protagonist of what, in one sense, became the winning side, was Paul, and because his writings are both the earliest and most numerous in the New Testament, this chapter will begin with them. This may well surprise readers who might expect such a chapter to begin with the four Gospels, but these belong to the later stages of the growth of the New Testament, and can be understood better if seen in the light of the controversies mirrored in the Pauline letters. The chapter will be organized as follows.

The Pauline letters: 1 Thessalonians, Galatians, 1 and 2 Corinthians, Romans, Philippians, Philemon.

The Deutero-Pauline letters: Ephesians, Colossians, 2 Thessalonians.

The pastoral letters: 1 and 2 Timothy, Titus.

The Church in Syria (?): Mark, 1 Peter.

The Church in Antioch (?): Matthew.

'The Lukan history': Luke, Acts of the Apostles.

The Church in Ephesus: John, 1, 2 and 3 John, Revelation.

Miscellaneous books: Jude, 2 Peter, James, Hebrews.

It must be explained that, while some of the above suggestions represent majority viewpoints in New Testament scholarship, for example, assigning Matthew's Gospel to Antioch and John's Gospel to Ephesus, other suggestions, such as assigning Mark's Gospel to Syria, are more contentious.[1]

THE PAULINE LETTERS

1 Thessalonians

It is generally accepted that this is Paul's earliest extant letter. Placing it in the context of Paul's ministry raises the question of whether that ministry should be reconstructed by combining the information in Acts about Paul's missionary journeys with information in the letters, or whether we should be satisfied with a somewhat more fragmentary reconstruction based on the letters alone. The view taken here is that it is safer to depend on the letters alone. While autobiography is not necessarily infallible, Paul's letters were written in a situation where, being in dispute with people who wished to discredit him, he had everything to lose if he falsified the details of what he had done in the churches to which he wrote. The author of the Acts of the Apostles, writing some forty years later, could only at best have relied upon the memories of members of the churches which Paul had founded. Paul's letters are immediate, if not detailed, evidence for his movements.

A good reason why the information in Acts must be treated with caution arises in connection with Paul's stay in Thessalonica. According to Acts 17:1–10, Paul stayed in Thessalonica for only three successive sabbaths until opposition from local Jews necessitated his hasty evacuation under cover of darkness. 1 Thessalonians 2:7–12 suggests a much longer stay, with Paul practising his trade as a tent-maker in order not to be a financial burden on the Church. Philippians 4:16 mentions two occasions on which the Church at Philippi sent some sort of aid to Paul while he was in Thessalonica. Finally, there is the point that if Paul really only stayed for no more than a month in Thessalonica (Acts 17:1–10) his achievement in founding a church which then proceeded to witness so effectively to the whole of Macedonia and Achaia was quite breathtaking. It will be assumed, then, that Paul had spent some time, presumably at least some months, in Thessalonica (modern Thessalonike/Salonike in northern Greece), the capital of Macedonia.

According to the letter, there were two reasons why Paul had written. First, he was concerned that those whom he describes as 'hindering us from speaking to the Gentiles' (1 Thessalonians 2:16) may have gone to Thessalonica and tried to subvert his teaching. So concerned was he at this that he had sent Timothy from Athens to Thessalonica to see how the Church was faring. Having received a reassuring report, Paul was now writing possibly from Athens, or more likely from Corinth (where we know from the Corinthian letters that he stayed for some time).

The second reason was to answer a question that was troubling some members of the Thessalonican Church. There was, in that church, and perhaps in other churches also, a firm belief that the world would soon end and that Jesus would be seen to return in glory. However, some believers had died before this had happened. What would be their fate?

Would they miss witnessing their Lord's return? In reply, Paul reassures
these members that, when Jesus returns in glory, Christian believers will
be resurrected and, together with the living believers, will be taken up
to meet the Lord in the air (1 Thessalonians 4:17). However, Paul warns
the Thessalonians to be less concerned with when this will happen and
to be more concerned with being ready for that day. They should put
on faith and love as a breastplate and hope of salvation as a helmet, and
should live accordingly (5:8).

The earliest written witness to Christianity from inside the Church,
1 Thessalonians, indicates one of the lines along which this new faith
had developed less than twenty-five years after the death of its founder. It
indicates a community living in the firm conviction that divine judgement
upon the world is imminent, but that believers will be saved from
condemnation, not on their own account, but because the message about
the death and resurrection of Jesus has enabled them to turn in faith
and hope to the God and Father of Jesus (1:4–10). This message does
not depend upon human persuasion, but is the power of God (2:13),
and it calls for a life style of unassuming service (2:7–12), upright living
(4:1–8) and mutual support of believers in the local church and beyond
(4:9–12). It brings with it the possibility of misunderstanding and persecution (2:14–16).

Galatians

If 1 Thessalonians was written because Paul had been reassured by
Timothy's visit and report back that the Church there was holding fast
to the Gospel as Paul understood it, Galatians was written when Paul
heard that the Church there had repudiated his teaching and gone over
to the Judaizers. Scholars are not agreed as to where to place the letter
in the Pauline series, although the view taken here is that it comes after
1 Thessalonians. However, the exact placing is unimportant for present
purposes. What matters is that Galatians is full of autobiographical
material that is valuable for understanding the fundamental dispute in
the early Church that caused Paul to write his letters.

At the heart of this dispute was whether the Gospel message should
be preached to non-Jews and, if it was so preached and accepted by

non-Jews, what obligation the latter should have to the Jewish law. It was common ground between Paul and his opponents that the life and teaching of Jesus had been a fulfilment of what the Jewish community accepted as 'the Scriptures'. The point at issue was whether the Jewish law, based upon the laws of the Old Testament, was binding on non-Jews who became Christian believers.

In Galatians, Paul justified his position that non-Jewish Christians were not obliged to observe the Jewish law in several ways. First, he outlined his conversion from zealous observance of the Jewish law to Christianity, mentioning a special revelation from God which included a commission to preach to non-Jews (Galatians 1:13–16). Second, he described a conference held in Jerusalem fourteen years after his conversion at which it was agreed with Peter, James, John and other leaders of the Church, that Paul's mission should be to non-Jews (2:1–10). Third, Paul argued theologically that the Jewish law was a provisional ordinance in force only until the coming of Jesus Christ (3:1–4:31). Fourth, he maintained that, with the coming of Christ and the giving of the Spirit of God, or Holy Spirit (4:5–6), Christians were guided by the Spirit whose fruits included love, joy and peace (5:16–26).

Reading between the lines, it is clear that the agreement at the Jerusalem conference about the spheres of operation of Paul and the other leaders had not necessarily clarified the issue of the obligation of non-Jewish Christians to the law. Paul relates in Galatians 2:11–14 a bitter encounter between himself and Peter at Antioch where the latter, under pressure from people sent by James to Antioch from Jerusalem, refused to eat with non-Jewish Christians, although he had done so before James's emissaries arrived.

1 and 2 Corinthians

That Paul wrote more than two letters to the Church in Corinth is evident from the passages in the extant letters. Thus, at 1 Corinthians 5:9 Paul writes: 'I wrote to you in my letter . . .' while 2 Corinthians 2:3 reads: 'I wrote as I did . . .', with verse 9 adding: 'this is why I wrote'. Another reference to correspondence is at 2 Corinthians 7:8: 'For even if I made you sorry with my letter . . .' A minimalist interpretation of these references would be that 1 Corinthians 5:9 refers to a first letter to Corinth, now lost, that 1 Corinthians was Paul's second letter and that 2 Corinthians was his third, with 2 Corinthians 2:3, 9 and 7:8 referring back to 1 Corinthians. Another possibility would be that 2 Corinthians 2:3, 9 refers to a letter, now lost, that was written in between 1 and 2 Corinthians. If the same was also true of 2 Corinthians 7:8, this would give us five letters.

But scholars have long doubted the unity of 2 Corinthians, and, noticing the change of mood and subject-matter of chapters 10–13, have suggested that these chapters are part or whole of a separate letter. Another suggestion has been that fragments of the lost letters can be found both in 1 and 2 Corinthians. These matters are far too complicated to be discussed here, and there is, in any case, little scholarly agreement about how many Corinthian letters were written and how they relate to the extant letters. For present purposes, the attempt will be made to pick up some of the clues in the Corinthian letters about why Paul wrote however many letters he did.

Going chronologically through the letters in their present form, the first clue is at 1 Corinthians 1:11. Paul has heard from Chloe's people (about whom nothing is otherwise known) that the Corinthian Church is divided into factions. He writes to point out that, fundamental to Christianity, are service and weakness rather than domination and human power. Thus, there is no place for vying for power or for factionalism, and that the Corinthians' descent into these things is a sign of immaturity (1:10–4:21). Second, although Paul had warned in an earlier letter (5:9) against immorality, he has had reports of immoral behaviour, which he now condemns. Third, it is stated at 7:1 that the Corinthians have written to Paul asking for advice on marriage (chapter 7), and on whether Christians should eat food offered to idols (chapter 8). It is not easy to comment in the same way about the remainder of 1 Corinthians. Chapters 12 and 16 begin, as do 7 (verse 25) and 8, with the words: 'Now concerning . . .', and it is not impossible that Paul is referring back to matters raised in the Corinthians' letter. If this is the case, Paul deals, in reply, with spiritual gifts and the regulation of worship (12:1–14:40) and with a collection to support the Church in Galatia (16:1–3). More difficult to place are 11:2–34 and 15:1–58. The former passage, about the observance of the Lord's Supper, may have been provoked by an adverse report to Paul (11:18), while the latter, about the resurrection of the dead, may be a reply to a query in the letter.

From 2 Corinthians, there are the following clues. In 1:15–2:4 it is clear that Paul had visited Corinth and that the visit had been painful (2:1). Instead of a planned further visit, Paul instead wrote a letter that was painful both to him and the recipients (2:3–4 and 7:8, 12 – if these refer to the same letter). At 12:14 and 13:1 there is reference to a third visit, ahead of which Paul is writing, to assure the Corinthians that he will not be a burden upon them. He also defends his right to admonish and advise the Corinthians on two grounds: the sufferings that the service of the Gospel have brought upon him in terms of beatings, imprisonments and shipwrecks (11:24–33), and a mystical experience of being caught up into the third heaven (12:1–10) which has left Paul content with his weakness as a human being. Thus, the Corinthian correspondence came into being as a result of a turbulent relationship between Paul and the Church, in which he admonished them on the basis of reports, answered their queries raised in a letter or letters, wrote after a very painful visit, and wrote in preparation for a third visit, whose purpose included defending his right to admonish and teach them.

Romans

Paul's reason for writing Romans is given in Romans 15:22–9. He intends to travel from his present place of residence (Corinth or Ephesus?) to Jerusalem taking with him the financial aid for the Jerusalem Church that he has been collecting (cp. 1 Corinthians 16:1–3). From Jerusalem he will go on to Rome and thence to Spain. His letter is thus meant to introduce him to Rome, and, hopefully, to give him opportunity for missionary work there (Romans 1:15). It has been argued, however, that Paul was as much addressing the Church in Jerusalem as in Rome, and that the contents of his letter would be reported to Jerusalem. Whether or not this is correct, it is certainly the case that Romans is much more conciliatory in its attitude to the Jewish law and to the Jewish people than is Galatians. Indeed, although Romans does not lack a hint of controversy (cp. 14:1–15:13) it is not written out of a situation of anguish, as are Galatians and the Corinthian letters. Given its origins, then, it is not surprising that Romans is both Paul's longest letter and his fullest attempt to explain his understanding of Christianity. For this reason, it has become the letter that has received more scholarly attention than any other Pauline writing. It has also been regarded as one of the two most important theological writings in the New Testament (the other being the Gospel of John).

Scholars are divided in their opinion about chapter 16. It consists of a number of greetings to people well known to Paul. Could these people be in Rome, which Paul had never visited, or was Romans distributed to more than one church, with chapter 16 attached to the copy destined, say, for Ephesus? The matter is important here only by way of reminder that it is not impossible that multiple copies of Romans were circulated, or that a sheet from another letter could have become attached to a copy of Romans, which originally ended at chapter 15.

Philippians

This letter, if it is *one* letter, was written by Paul whilst in prison (Philippians 1:13). Traditionally, this imprisonment was connected with that recorded in Acts 28:16 – a kind of house arrest in Rome. This view is hardly consistent with the content of Philippians, however, which envisages Paul keeping in touch with the Philippians by sending Timothy (Philippians 2:19) and Epaphroditus to them (2:25, 4:18). This would be a very long journey from Rome, and therefore a closer venue for Paul's imprisonment has been sought, either Caesarea (Acts 23:35) or, more likely, Ephesus (1 Corinthians 15:32, 2 Corinthians 11:23).

It has been questioned whether Philippians is a unity. Certainly, 3:1b–4:1 appears to break the continuity of the letter, and can be argued to be a separate composition. Some have also seen 4:10–20 as a separate letter or part of a letter. If 3:1b–4:1 is a separate piece, its sharp polemic against 'Judaizers' would put it earlier in Paul's life at around the same time as Galatians or 1 Thessalonians, and express Paul's concern that the Philippian Church should stand firm to Paul's teaching. The remainder of Philippians, with its more eirenic content, would be an expression of Paul's concern for a community which he was unable to visit personally.

Philemon

This brief letter of twenty-five verses, written by Paul in his own hand (verse 19), in prison (verse 10) and in what he considers to be old age (verse 9), is a note to an otherwise unknown Philemon concerning his slave Onesimus. The traditional view, that Onesimus was a runaway slave who had become a Christian believer, and whom Paul was now sending back to his master with this letter, has been modified by some interpreters as follows: Onesimus had been sent to Paul by Philemon in order to get Paul's advice on a domestic matter. For present purposes, this scholarly dispute is immaterial. What matters is that Paul has a clear purpose in writing – on a personal and pastoral level to a named individual. If the information at Colossians 4:9 can be trusted, then Philemon may have lived in or near Colossae. The place of Paul's imprisonment has traditionally been taken to be Rome, but, as with Philippians, some experts prefer Ephesus.

THE DEUTERO-PAULINE LETTERS

The view taken here, that Paul did not write Ephesians, Colossians and 2 Thessalonians is not universally accepted but, as pointed out in chapter 2 (see note 8), is supported by moderately conservative critics such as Lincoln (Ephesians) and Dunn (Colossians). In the present section, a possible scenario for the production of these letters will be outlined. Detailed justification for regarding the letters as deutero-Pauline will not be given; interested readers can pursue the subject in the commentaries by Lincoln and Dunn.

Ephesians

It is possible that this letter was intended for several churches, not for one. All modern translations note that the words 'at Ephesus' are not in the best manuscripts at Ephesians 1:1, and these words are, in fact, omitted by the RSV and NJB. Even the very conservative NIV Study Bible accepts that the letter may have been intended for a number of churches, including that at Ephesus. The letter is addressed entirely to non-Jews (2:11) and has as main themes the unity of the Church under the cosmic headship of Christ, and the necessity for loyalty to the ministers of the Church, whose ministries are the gift of Christ through the Holy Spirit.

The purpose for writing the letter must be put in the context of a growing sense in the early Church that it is a unity, and that its ministry is more than a merely local phenomenon. It is possible, as has been suggested, that the letter was written after Paul's death to remind the churches of their debt to Paul (3:1–21). Another suggestion is that an attempt was being made to introduce a more formal hierarchy into church leadership, and that Ephesians opposes this by pleading for unity based upon ministries which are the gift of the Holy Spirit. There can be no doubt, however, that the concern with church order and with the regulation of family life (5:21–6:9) indicates a setting in a church situation removed from that in, for example, Galatians and the Corinthian letters. Its date and place of writing are hard to determine, although 80–90 CE is often suggested. It is generally accepted that the writer knew, and drew upon, Colossians.

Colossians

This letter is written to correct 'errors', yet it lacks the sharp polemical tone of Galatians or Philippians 3. While the 'errors' have been traced to Greek cults and philosophies, those commentators seem to be on firmer ground who see the 'errors' as being those of Judaism. Yet the controversy is not that of Galatians. While the Jewish law and circumcision are referred to (Colossians 2:11–15) and it is argued that Christ has made circumcision unnecessary and has cancelled the debt owed to the law; and while those people are criticized who are concerned with food regulations and the observance of festivals (2:16–23), the main thrust of Colossians is to emphasize the cosmic significance of Christ. Through him all things were created (1:16) and his death on the cross has stripped their power from the 'principalities and powers' (2:15).

The letter marks a new phase in the development of the early Church's theology, that of dialogue with other communities that do not necessarily directly threaten the Church's existence. The theology is Pauline, but is developed in new directions. It has been suggested by some authorities that the hymn in praise of the cosmic Christ in 1:15–20 is an adaptation of a pre-Christian hymn to Wisdom.[2] The letter's date and place of writing cannot be determined. Similarities between personal names mentioned in Colossians 4:9 (Onesimus), 4:10 (Aristarchus, Mark) and 4:14 (Luke and Demas) and in Philemon (cp. verses 23–4) have been pointed out, and have led to such suggestions as either that Colossians was written very soon after Philemon by a companion of Paul, or that Philemon was a source used by a later leader of a Pauline church.

2 Thessalonians

This brief work of three shortish chapters elaborates material from 1 Thessalonians, dealing with two problems. There are those who claim that the day of the Lord has already come. The answer of the letter is that it cannot come until a lawless enemy of God arises, who is an agent of Satan, and whose coming will be accompanied by false signs and wonders. Second, there are members of the Christian community who expect to be fed without working. The letter indicates the kind of beliefs and attitudes that could arise in a church, and how they were dealt with by the writing of letters.

THE PASTORAL LETTERS

1 and 2 Timothy, Titus

The situation presupposed by 1 and 2 Timothy and Titus has moved on a stage compared with Colossians and Ephesians. Two noticeable themes are, first, the importance of teaching sound doctrine (1 Timothy 6:3, 2 Timothy 2:1–2, 8–13, 4:1–5), and second, the mention of the offices of bishop and deacon (1 Timothy 3:1–7 and 8–10; Titus 1:7–9), and the qualifications necessary for these offices. Even if 'bishop' (Greek *Episkopos*) is not the office as later understood, it is on the way to becoming this. An important function of a 'bishop' is to 'hold firm to the sure word as taught, so that he may be able to give instruction in sound doctrine and also to confute those who contradict it' (Titus 1:9). In connection with the stress on doctrine, the pastoral letters contain brief, credal or hymn-like summaries of the essentials of the Christian faith, such as 1 Timothy 3:16:

> He was manifested in the flesh,
> vindicated in the Spirit,
>   seen by angels,
> preached among nations,
> believed on in the world,
> taken up in glory.

Another noticeable concern is that Christian communities should earn the respect of the outside world through modest behaviour that is without reproach. A positive view is taken of secular authority, with instructions for prayers and thanksgivings to be offered for kings and those in high authority (1 Timothy 2:1–4, cp. Titus 3:1–2). Advice for proper behaviour is extended to various types of widow (e.g. older or younger widows), rich members of the congregation, older men and younger men. There is no trace of the sense of the imminent end of the world and of the return of Christ in glory, although believers may be living in the latter times (cp. 1 Timothy 4:1).

Notoriously, and especially for modern readers sensitive to women's issues, 1 Timothy 2:11–12 requires the silence and submissiveness of women, and permits 'no woman to teach or to have authority over men'. This clause has been explained in terms of the imposing upon the Church of the model of the household, in which the rights of the male householder were absolute. It contrasts with the genuine Pauline letters which mention women such as Phoebe, Prisca, Mary, Tryphaena, Tryphosa and Julia as among Paul's helpers (Romans 16:1, 3, 6, 12, 15).

The community or communities addressed by these letters are therefore second or third generation Pauline churches, organized hierarchically, and concerned with handing down correct teaching and with maintaining good relationships with the outside world. The problem of their explicit claims to be written by Paul are discussed in chapter 2 above. Ephesus has been suggested as the place of writing and a date at the latter end of 80–100 CE has been proposed; but there is very little to go on in deciding such matters.

THE CHURCH IN SYRIA (?)

Mark

The traditional view of the origin of Mark's Gospel is that it was written in Rome by John Mark, Paul's erstwhile companion (Acts 12:25, 13:13), recording the reminiscences of Peter (1 Peter 5:13). The tradition goes back to Papias of Hierapolis (*c.* 130 CE) as preserved by the 4th-century Church historian Eusebius. According to Eusebius, Papias said: 'Mark, indeed, having been the interpreter of Peter, wrote accurately, howbeit not in order, all that he recalled of what was either said or done by the Lord.'[3] This Mark was connected with the person at whose mother's house the Jerusalem Church met, according to Acts 12:12, and even with the mysterious youth who fled naked from the Garden of Gethsemane on the night of Jesus's arrest (Mark 14:51). The traditional view gave reassurance that Mark's Gospel was a reliable source of information about the life and teaching of Jesus.

If critical scholarship has taken a different view this is not because of any desire to discredit Mark's Gospel as a source for the life of Jesus. The two questions, however, that of the origin of Mark's Gospel, and that of how much can be known about the historical Jesus, are best kept separate. It must also be noted that the study of the origin of the Gospels has generated an enormous amount of technical scholarly literature. While this scholarship has been successful in highlighting some important questions and problems, it has been less successful in proposing solutions that carry anything like universal acceptance. What follows must be read in the light of this lack of general agreement.

Two points that have been made that are relevant to the origins of Mark's Gospel are as follows:

1. On the assumption that Matthew and Luke used Mark as a source, they both omit Mark 4:26–9 (the Parable of the Seed Growing Secretly),

7:32−7 (the healing of the deaf mute), 8:22−6 (the healing of a blind man in Bethsaida), and 13:33−6 (the Parable of the Master's Unexpected Return). Luke, in addition, has a large omission, from Mark 6:43 to 8:27. From these facts it can be surmised that Luke used a version of Mark shorter than the final version and that material was added to Mark after its use as a source by Matthew. The table overleaf illustrates these points.

2. Mark contains doublets, primarily 6:31−44 and 8:1−9 (the Feeding of the 5,000 and the 4,000). Passages such as Mark 3:13−35 seem to disturb the order of the narrative. In 3:7−12 Jesus comes to the lakeside in Galilee and tells his disciples to have a boat ready so that he is not crushed by the crowd. At 4:1 he gets into the boat and teaches from it. The intervening material, 3:13−35, which is set on a mountain, introduces abrupt changes of scene.

On the basis of these and other considerations one view of the origin of Mark's Gospel is that it emerged in two stages. Initially, there was a basic composition that began with John the Baptist, described Jesus's ministry in Galilee and the Greek cities of the Decapolis* and climaxed in his journey to Jerusalem where he taught prior to arrest and crucifixion. This was already a nuanced theological composition which emphasized the reluctance of Jesus to be identified as Messiah, gave to Peter a leading role among the disciples and emphasized the failure of the disciples to understand or be faithful to Jesus. It concentrated particularly on the Passion of Jesus. The second stage was an enlargement of the basic composition, which introduced some of the doublets and unevennesses.

This view leaves open the question of the purpose and the sources of the two compositions, especially those of the basic composition. Some general observations can be made. First, Mark's Gospel is not a biography of Jesus in the sense of a modern biography. It probably had its origins in missionary preaching and in the celebrations of the Lord's supper, at which the Passion story was recounted. It is an account of Jesus's life and teaching from the perspective of a community that believed that God had raised Jesus from the dead and had exalted him to a position of authority. Second, even if there was a strong apologetic tone to the basic composition, this does not mean that it contains no reliable information about Jesus's life and ministry. It is inconceivable that the early Church had no interest in the life and teaching of Jesus.

The table follows the order of the first nine chapters of Mark to show how the order is followed in Matthew and Luke. Three passages that occur only in Mark are in bold type. Luke's 'great omission' is indicated by putting the material from Matthew and Mark that was evidently unknown to Luke in italics. Note how Luke, who has been following Mark's order closely, suddenly jumps from Mark 6:43 to 8:27.

Description	Matthew	Mark	Luke
Ministry of John the Baptist	3:1–12	1:1–8	3:1–20
Baptism of Jesus by John	3:13–17	1:9–11	3:21–2
Temptation of Jesus	4:1–11	1:12–13	4:1–15
Arrest of John the Baptist, first preaching of Jesus	4:12, 17	1:14–15	
Call of the first disciples	4:18–22	1:16–20	5:1–11
Healing of demoniac in Capernaum synagogue		1:23–8	4:33–6
Healing of Peter's mother-in-law	8:14–15	1:29–31	4:38–9
Healing of many sick and diseased	8:16–17	1:32–4	4:40–41
Retirement of Jesus for solitary prayer		1:35–9	4:42–4
Healing of a leper	8:1–4	1:40–45	5:12–16
Healing of a paralytic in Capernaum	9:1–8	2:1–12	5:18–26
Call of Levi (Matthew), discourse at feast	9:9–17	2:13–22	5:27–39
Sabbath controversy with Pharisees	12:1–8	2:23–8	6:1–5
Healing of man with withered arm	12:9–14	3:1–6	6:6–11
Retirement of Jesus with disciples		3:7–12	
Commissioning of the twelve disciples	10:1–4	3:13–19	6:13–16
The blasphemy against the Holy Spirit	12:24–37	3:22–30	
Jesus and his relatives	12:46–50	3:31–5	8:19–21
Parables: the Sower	13:3–23	4:2–20	8:5–15
the Candle	5:15	4:21–3	8:16
the Seed Growing Secretly		**4:26–9**	
the Mustard Seed	13:31–2	4:30–32	13:18–19
Conclusion of parables		4:33–4	
The stilling of the storm	8:24–7	4:35–41	8:23–5
The Gerasene demoniac	8:28–34	5:1–20	8:26–39

Healing of Jairus's daughter and woman with the issue of blood	9:18–26	5:22–43	8:41–56
Jesus's rejection in 'his own country'	13:53–8	6:1–6	
The mission of the twelve	10:5–42	6:7–13	9:1–6
Death of John the Baptist	14:1–12	6:14–29	9:7–9
Feeding of the 5,000	14:13–21	6:31–44	9:10–17
Jesus's walking on the water	*14:24–33*	*6:47–51*	
Healings at Gennesaret	*14:34–6*	*6:53–6*	
Controversy over pollution with scribes and Pharisees	*15:1–20*	*7:1–23*	
Healing of daughter of Syro-Phoenician woman	*15:21–9*	*7:24–30*	
Healing of deaf mute		**7:32–7**	
Feeding of the 4,000	*15:32–9*	*8:1–9*	
The 'leaven' of the Pharisees	*16:5–12*	*8:14–21*	
Healing of the blind man at Bethsaida		**8:22–6**	
Peter's confession that Jesus is the Christ	16:13–21	8:27–30	9:18–20
First prediction of the Passion	16:21–8	8:31–8	9:22–7
The Transfiguration	17:1–8	9:2–8	9:28–36
Healing the demoniac child	17:14–21	9:14–29	9:37–42
Second prediction of the Passion	17:22–3	9:30–32	9:43–5
Lesson on humility	18:1–14	9:33–7	9:46–8

On the contrary, if people were being asked to commit themselves to a faith that might well lead to the fate suffered by the founder, it would be odd if they were told nothing or asked nothing about him.

It is true that, apart from confirmation in non-biblical sources that Jesus was crucified during the governorship of Pontius Pilate,[4] there is no information about Jesus's life and teaching other than in the Gospels. On the other hand, if an explanation is sought as to how the churches came into existence that is mirrored, for example, in Paul's genuine letters, then the account of the life of Jesus in Mark's Gospel provides that explanation. Both Paul (1 Corinthians 2:1–4) and Mark's Gospel (Mark 14:50, 66–72) emphasize that the Gospel exists in spite of rather than because of the followers of Jesus. Mark's Gospel also records disputes with Jesus and the Jewish teachers about the important Pauline theme of the interpretation and status of the Jewish law (Mark 2:15–3:6, 7:1–13).

These similarities, in fact, probably point to an origin for Mark's Gospel in an area where Pauline churches were established. The purpose of the Gospel was to provide instruction for believers as well as material for preaching, in a situation where it became desirable to record the events of Jesus's life and his teaching, as the distance in time since the crucifixion lengthened, and there was no return of the Lord in glory. The date of writing is usually placed after the destruction of Jerusalem in 70 CE because that event is thought to be alluded to at Mark 13:2; and the two stages of composition of the Gospel may be dated in the decade 70–80 CE.

1 Peter

As with Mark's Gospel, the traditional place of authorship of 1 Peter is Rome, especially on account of the reference to Babylon, taken to be a code-name for Rome, at 1 Peter 5:13. Indeed, that verse, which also contains a reference to Mark, has been one of the factors that traditionally associated Mark's Gospel with the teaching of Peter, imprisoned in Rome. Modern critical scholarship has mostly rejected Petrine authorship, for a number of reasons.

First, although the author claims to have been a witness to the sufferings of Christ (5:1; the phrase, however, can also mean that he witnesses to Christ by his own sufferings), at no point in the letter is there any personal reminiscence of Peter's close relationship with Jesus during the latter's earthly ministry. Second, the writer is obviously someone for whom Greek is a first language and who has an extensive knowledge of the Old Testament in Greek. The disciple Peter's first language was Aramaic, and although it would be wrong to regard him as illiterate or unintelligent, it is unlikely that he could have produced so polished a writing. Defenders of Petrine authorship meet this point by crediting Silvanus (5:12) with the actual writing of the letter, thus conceding that Peter did not produce it in the form in which we have it. Third, the theology of the letter is said to contain certain Pauline traits (some important Pauline themes are also missing) and that the letter is best placed in Asia Minor towards the end of the 1st century CE. This latter view will be followed here.

Although the letter begins and ends with the greetings and farewells typical of a letter, and although it contains advice to slaves, wives and elders, it lacks any of the personal touches to be found, for example, in Galatians and the Corinthian letters. Such is the content that it has sometimes been described as a sermon, of which parts (1:3– 4:11) have been identified as a sermon preached at a baptism. Attempts at sustaining this type of argument, as well as attempts to place the letter in a particular situation of persecution, have not won universal acceptance. It is probably best to regard the letter as a general composition addressed to churches that were experiencing misunderstanding and hostility from the outside world.

In this situation, the writer reminds his readers/hearers that they have a hope, based upon the resurrection of Jesus Christ (1:3– 5), namely, a heavenly inheritance. This hope is meant to sustain them in their present troubles, just as the example of Jesus in his sufferings on the cross is meant to encourage them. Indeed, their sufferings are a sign of, and a participation in, God's graciousness. They must therefore live out, as a community, the new life which God has made possible through Jesus Christ.

The letter is replete with references to the Old Testament and draws upon a stock of Christian tradition. Although there are many echoes of other New Testament writings, actual dependence upon or knowledge of these writings cannot be demonstrated. Thus 1 Peter is evidence for a widespread diffusion of teachings in the early Church, in oral as well as in written form, upon which a skilled and educated writer could draw in addressing a group of churches.

THE CHURCH IN ANTIOCH (?)

Matthew

Traditionally, Matthew's Gospel was held to be an eye-witness gospel, the eye-witness being the tax or customs officer Matthew (whose name is given as Levi in Mark and Luke), who was called to be one of the twelve disciples (Matthew 9:9). The view of modern critical scholarship is that the work could not have been that of an eye-witness, given that it is largely dependent upon other sources. It has been calculated that, of the roughly 1070 verses in Matthew, around 600 are closely paralleled in Mark, while around 230 come from a collection of sayings of Jesus that scholars have named Q (from German *Quelle*, meaning 'source').

Although some scholars doubt the existence of Q as a source for the sayings of Jesus, it is generally accepted as a working hypothesis that the source can be reconstructed from material common to Matthew and Luke that is not found in Mark. One of the problems is that in some cases, for example the story of the temptations of Jesus, the verbal identity between Matthew and Luke is so high (although they have the temptations in a different order) that a common written source can be assumed. In other cases, verbal identity is slight (as in the Lord's Prayer), suggesting the use of oral rather than written tradition. It has also been argued that Q had a Passion narrative, but this view has not gained widespread support. On the assumption that Luke has preserved the original order of Q, which Matthew has broken up so as to include different parts in his five great discourses, the following is roughly the content:

Description	Luke	Matthew
Preaching of John the Baptist	3:7-9, 16-17	3:7-12
Temptations of Jesus	4:2-12	4:2-10
The Beatitudes	6:20-27	5:3-12
Command to love enemies	6:27-36	5:39-48
Command not to judge	6:37-8	7:1-2
The beam and the speck	6:41-2	7:3-5

The tree and the fruit	6:43–5	7:18–19
The wise and foolish builders	6:47–9	7:24–7
Healing of the centurion's servant	7:2–3, 6–10	8:5–10
The questions of John the Baptist and Jesus's reply	7:18–35	11:2–19
The demands of discipleship	9:57–62	8:19–22
The mission of the disciples	10:1–12	9:37–8, 10:7–16
The doom of the unrepentant cities	10:13–15	11:21–3
The Father's revelation of the Son	10:21–2	11:25–7
The disciples' privilege	10:23–4	13:16–17
The Lord's Prayer	11:2–4	6:9–13
The importance of persistence of prayer	11:9–13	7:7–12
Proof that the Kingdom of God has drawn near	11:14–23	12:22–30
Parable of the House of the Unclean Spirit	11:24–6	12:43–5
The sign of Jonah	11:29–32	12:39–42
The eye and the lamp	11:34–5	6:22–3
Woes to Pharisees and lawyers	11:39–52	23:23–36
What is hidden will be uncovered	12:2–3	10:26–7
God's care for those who acknowledge Him	12:4–9	10:28–33
God's support in times of persecution	12:11–12	10:19–20
Teaching on not being anxious	12:22–31	6:25–33
Disposing of possessions	12:33–4	6:19–21
Parable of the Returning Householder	12:39–40	24:43–4
Parable of the Wise Steward	12:42–6	24:45–51
Jesus as cause of division	12:51–3	10:34–6
Signs of the times	12:54–6	16:2–3
The need for right judgement	12:57–9	5:25–6
Parable of the Leaven	13:20–21	13:33
The wide and narrow gates	13:23–4	7:13–14
Jerusalem loved and rejected	13:34–5	23:37–9
Parable of the Reluctant Wedding Guests	14:16–24	22:1–10
Taking up the cross	14:26–7	10:37–8
Parable of the Lost Sheep	15:4–7	18:10–14
Parable of the Pounds/Talents	19:12–26	25:14–30

If Matthew is largely based upon material from elsewhere, this is not to say that it is an unoriginal composition. On the contrary, it is very distinctive; and the fact that it contains teaching of Jesus divided into five great discourses (5:1–7:29; 10:5–11:1; 13:1–53; 18:1–19:1; 23:1–26:1) of which the fifth contains the parables of the Wise and Foolish Virgins, and the Sheep and the Goats (both found only in Matthew), made it the favourite of the four Gospels in the early Church.

The setting and purpose of the Gospel can be deduced from its content. Important clues include, first, constant reference to the fulfilment of Old Testament prophecy, second, particularly harsh judgements on the Jewish scribes and Pharisees (see especially 23:1–32) and third, the presentation of Jesus as though he were a new Moses giving a new law to Israel (cp. 5:1 where Jesus ascends to a mountain and gives the Sermon on the Mount).

These, and other clues, indicate that Matthew was written in a setting in which the Church was in dispute with the local Jewish community. The Gospel's account of the virgin birth of Jesus may have been a response to Jewish claims that Jesus was illegitimate; while the passage in Matthew 27:62–6, which represents the Pharisees as suggesting that the disciples of Jesus might steal the body of Jesus and claim that he has risen from the dead, could be a response to a Jewish claim that the resurrection was a fraud. The constant reference to the fulfilment of Old Testament prophecy in the life and ministry of Jesus, and the promulgation by Jesus of a new law, carry the implicit claim that the Matthean Church, not the Jewish community, is the true inheritor of God's purposes revealed in the Old Testament. It is also the case that Matthew has a greater eschatological emphasis than the other Gospels, in that it contains parables about the future judgement that individuals and nations will face (see the Parables of the Wise and Foolish Virgins, the Talents, and the Sheep and the Goats in chapter 25). This heightened stress on future judgement may arise from contact with Zoroastrianism in northern Syria.

The setting of Matthew's Gospel, then, is a church community in dispute with a Jewish community and defending itself against criticism. But the Gospel also has a positive purpose, that of instructing new believers about the life and teaching of Jesus. The Gospel ends with a commission of the risen Christ to the apostles to make disciples, to baptize them and to teach and observe what Christ has taught them (28:19–20). The Gospel of Matthew is meant to contain the teaching that is to be taught. Thus, its presentation of the life and teaching of Jesus is refracted through the apologetic and missionary task of the church in which it was written. A likely place for this is widely held to be Antioch, with a date about 80–90 CE.

'THE LUKAN HISTORY'

Luke, Acts of the Apostles

Luke and the Acts of the Apostles are unique in the New Testament in at least two ways. First, they are two treatises by the same author, in which the later work, Acts, refers back in its preface to the former work, Luke (Acts 1:1). Second, both works are dedicated to an otherwise unknown Theophilus (Luke 1:3–4; Acts 1:1). Traditionally the author was held to be the Luke mentioned at Colossians 4:14 and 2 Timothy 4:11, although neither the Gospel nor Acts contain any information about their author. On the basis of several sections in Acts in the first person plural ('we' sections, e.g. Acts 16:10–18) it was surmised that Luke had been Paul's travelling companion for at least some of his journeys. The mention of him being a physician (Colossians 4:14) stimulated a search for details in the Gospel that might indicate a medical interest.

When the two works are compared, a startling fact emerges. Although Acts presents the story of the beginnings of the Church and its expansion in the Roman empire, it makes little reference to the portrait of Jesus found in the Gospel. This statement must be qualified, of course, by the accounts of the preaching of Peter in Acts 2:14–36, 3:12–26 and 10:34–43, all of which mention Jesus. Yet only the latter speech deals in any detail with the ministry of Jesus, while the other two longer speeches concentrate largely on the Old Testament and mention Jesus only as the one whose sufferings and resurrection are foretold there. Again, the long speech of Stephen in Acts 7 is a summary of Old Testament history emphasizing the failures of Israel to obey God. Only in the penultimate verse is there a reference to those who betrayed and murdered the Upright One (i.e. Jesus). If the preaching of Paul in Acts is examined, a similar phenomenon is found. Paul's speech at Antioch in Pisidia (13:16–41) is largely a rehearsal of the Old Testament, whose climax is the resurrection of Jesus through whom forgiveness of sins is promised. On other occasions Paul rehearses the story of his own conversion, including his encounter with the Risen Christ on the road to Damascus (22:3–21, 26:2–23).

The speeches in Acts attributed to Peter, Stephen and Paul are probably, according to the conventions of the time of Luke (as it is convenient to call the author), free compositions which most likely represent the preaching with which Luke was familiar. This being so, the circles in which Luke moved saw Jesus primarily as a focal point in an historical process which began in the Old Testament and which now continued in the life of the Church – the era of the Holy Spirit. Thus, some interpreters have spoken of Luke's concern with salvation history, while others have attributed this interest in the present as a continuation of what began in the Old Testament, to the fading of the expectation of the immediate return of Jesus in glory. It is entirely consonant with this interest in history that Luke should, as stated in the preface to his Gospel, 'have undertaken to compile a narrative of the things which have been accomplished among us' (1:1).

What were Luke's sources? For the Gospel he used Mark (probably in a shorter form than the extant Gospel of Mark; see above), the collection of sayings known as Q (see above) and material from his own collection including well-known parables such as the Good Samaritan (Luke 10:30–37) and the Prodigal Son (15:11–32). The Passion narrative of Luke differs significantly from that in Mark and Matthew, but scholars are not agreed about whether Luke had access to a source other than Mark for this account.

The sources of Acts are harder to determine. On the whole, critical scholarship does not accept that Luke knew or travelled with Paul. The reason for this is that it is not easy to reconcile Luke's account of Paul's ministry with the autobiographical details in the genuine Pauline letters. Further, Luke does not appear to be familiar with Paul's letters. For the early chapters of Acts a possible source was popular stories about Peter, who is the dominant figure among the apostles. It is also possible that Luke had access to a chronicle of events in the Church in Antioch, the Church which is prominent in commissioning Paul (Acts 13:1–3). For Paul's work, Luke probably used popular stories about Paul and about his conversion. It is likely that Luke travelled around seeking material for his work from local churches, and it has been suggested, on the basis of the uneven narrative structure of Acts, that Luke compiled written sources as he went, and then combined them to form Acts.

The date of Acts is usually put at around 90 CE. The place and author are unknown. The dedicatee, Theophilus, was most likely the patron of a local congregation; but this does not mean that the books were meant only for his personal use. However, Luke/Acts is an example of the many and different reasons that lay behind the writing of what became the New Testament. Undoubtedly originating in an area where Pauline churches flourished, it interpreted their existence in terms of an historical scheme going back to the Old Testament, with the ministry of Jesus as the point which began a new era. Whether these churches were also experiencing hardship is difficult to say. It has long been recognized that Luke's Gospel is especially sensitive to the poor and to women, and that it emphasizes that following Jesus entails hardship.

THE CHURCH IN EPHESUS

John

The Gospel of John is strikingly different from the other three Gospels. It begins not with stories of the birth of Jesus (as in Matthew and Luke) nor with John the Baptist (as in Mark), but with a prologue which identifies Jesus as the pre-existent Word (*Logos*) who participated in the creation of the universe and who became a human being, allowing his glory to be seen by those closest to him. The Gospel then proceeds to recount a ministry of Jesus in both Jerusalem and Galilee (the other Gospels have no record of a visit of the adult Jesus to Jerusalem except at the end of his life), structured around seven signs (miracles) and seven discourses. The teaching in the discourses is of a completely different style compared with the parables in the other Gospels, while some of the signs – turning water into wine at Cana (John 2:1–10), healing the lame man at the pool of Bethesda (5:2–9), giving sight to the blind man in Jerusalem (9:1–8), the raising of Lazarus (11:1–44) – are found only in John.

This outline may wrongly give the impression that John is a carefully constructed composition. In fact, scholars have noted many unevennesses in the narrative, and the NJB Study Bible, for example, notes that 'the sequence of chapters 4, 5, 6, 7:1–24 is awkward' (p. 1739). The conviction has grown that the Gospel was not written by a single author, but is the outcome of a long process of growth in which the distinction between author and redactor/editor was not clear (see chapter 2 above). This conclusion militates against the traditional view that the author was the apostle John, the son of Zebedee, and the disciple whom Jesus loved (John 13:23).

The sources and purpose of the Gospel have been much disputed. A good case can be made for its familiarity with and use of Mark and Luke. The fact that it contains details about a Jerusalem ministry of Jesus together with a setting in south Palestine has led some commentators to suggest a source close to the apostles. It has been argued that part of the Gospel is based upon a source in Aramaic. Another approach has drawn attention to the number of sharp disputes in the Gospel between Jesus and 'the Jews', not so much on the question of the Jewish law, but on Jesus's claim to be the Son of God. It has been suggested that these disputes mirror the hostility between Jewish and Christian groups in the area of the Gospel's genesis.

This last suggestion draws attention to an important point. However John's Gospel may have reached its present form, it contains material that presents Jesus very differently from the other Gospels. Generally speaking, Jesus can be described in those Gospels as the witness of faith, urging his followers and hearers to believe in God. In John's Gospel he has become the object of faith, and his discourses urge his hearers to have faith in him as the one sent by his Father.

John's Gospel is a work whose apparent simplicity conceals many depths of possible meaning. It originates from a developed Christianity which uses the occasion of relating the ministry of Jesus to combine description and interpretation, attaining in the process a level of sophistication that is matched elsewhere in the New Testament only by Paul at his very best. A date at the very end of the 1st century CE is usually proposed.

1, 2 and 3 John

Of the three so-called letters of John, only the latter two contain the greetings and concluding formulae that letters are expected to contain. These two letters are also very brief, amounting to thirteen and fifteen verses respectively (fifteen according to the numbering adopted in some translations). The first letter is in fact a theological tract of five chapters addressed to readers who are variously described as little children and beloved. (The RSV and NJB have 'dear friends'.)

The occasion for writing these letters is clear. There is dissension in the church or churches to which the letters are addressed (assuming, as is likely, that the three letters have a common author). In 3 John the dissension appears to be a matter of clash of personalities. A certain, and otherwise unknown, Diotrephes has been opposing the author of the letter and has been refusing to welcome workers sent by him. The author addresses another unknown person, Gaius, asking him to welcome Demetrius, who is presumably the bearer of the letter. The author describes himself as 'the elder'.

The same 'elder' addresses 'the elect lady and her children' in the second letter, meaning a local church and its members. A warning is given against 'deceivers' who do 'not abide in the doctrine of Christ', and who therefore do 'not have God'. This problem is spelled out more fully in 1 John where it is stressed that 'No one who denies the Son has the Father' (1 John 2:23). The identity of the 'deceivers' who, according to 1 John 2:19, have left the Church, has been much discussed. An ancient view with modern supporters is that Christians with Gnostic* tendencies are meant. These are people who would question the physical nature of the incarnation of the Word in Jesus Christ, provoking the testimony in 1:1 that the 'word of life' had been 'touched with our hands'. Another view is that the deceivers had denied that access to God the Father could be had only via Jesus. Whether these were Jewish Christians or believers seeking some kind of religious pluralism is disputed. That the matter was not merely an intellectual dispute is shown by the strong ethical content of the letter. The author maintains that victory over 'the world' is possible only through being grasped by the love that God has displayed by sending his Son to be an expiation for sins (1 John 4:10). In turn, this love is to be manifested in practical terms in the Christian community, especially in sensitivity to the needs of the poor.

If, as most scholars believe, the letters were addressed to the Church mirrored in John's Gospel, the situation is one of internal dispute over fundamental doctrines. The Church is unsettled, not only by those who have left, but by visiting prophets (4:1). The purpose of the letter is to restate the fundamentals of Christian doctrine, and their practical importance in enabling believers to experience here and now the implications of the victory over sin and evil won by Christ.

Revelation

This work, whose author names himself as John (Revelation 1:4), and which is addressed to seven churches in the Roman province of Asia, falls into two main parts. In chapters 2–3 each of the seven churches is addressed in turn, and particular problems are highlighted, albeit in allusive language. These problems include internal disputes about doctrine, persecution by the civil authorities, altercations with Jewish communities and complacency. Chapters 4–22 are a series of visions, whose climax is the appearance of New Jerusalem coming from heaven. The genre of these visions is apocalyptic (see chapter 4 above).

Although the vision is said to be experienced on the island of Patmos on the Lord's day (1:9–10), the work is one of considerable literary complexity. Not only are there rich allusions to the Old Testament; the book is structured in a series of seven main acts, within which the action is also seven-fold. Thus, for example, there is a scroll with seven seals (5:1) which are opened in turn, and there are seven angels who blow trumpets to usher in new happenings. There are seven bowls of the wrath of God (16:1).

Inevitably, such mysterious and symbolic detail has made Revelation a happy hunting ground for those forecasting the future and the end of the world. This is a pity, because Revelation contains the largest number of Christian hymns of any book in the New Testament, and gives a glimpse of the worship of the early Church. It is no accident that Handel's *Messiah* concludes Parts 2 and 3 with choruses the words of which come from this book. They are the 'Hallelujah Chorus' (19:6, 11:15) and 'Worthy is the Lamb' (5:12, 7:12).

It is generally agreed that the book was written around 95 CE in response to the persecution of the Church by the emperor Domitian. It gives hope to its readers/hearers by seeing events from a heavenly perspective, and reassures martyrs that they will share the triumph over evil that has been won by Christ's death and resurrection. The identity of the author is not known. Its erratic Greek makes it unlikely that the author is the same as the 'author' of the Gospel and letters.

MISCELLANEOUS BOOKS

Jude and 2 Peter

These two books can be linked, in that 2 Peter 2:1–3:13 appears to be dependent on Jude, and has in common the following themes: warning against false teachers (2 Peter 2:1, Jude verse 4); the sinning of angels (2 Peter 2:4, Jude verse 6); Sodom and Gomorrah (2 Peter 2:6, Jude verse 7); the error of Balaam (2 Peter 2:15, Jude verse 11). However, 2 Peter has used Jude creatively and not slavishly, as a reading of 2 Peter 2 and Jude will indicate.

Jude claims to be written by Jude the brother of James, and on the basis of Matthew 13:55 ('Is not this the carpenter's son . . . And are not his brothers James and Joseph and Simon and Judas') this Jude was traditionally identified as a brother (or half-brother) of Jesus. Modern critical scholarship dates the book at around 100 CE, noting how verse 17 refers to the teaching of the apostles of Jesus, so as to suggest that the generation of original apostles has passed away. The letter is noteworthy not only for its references to the Old Testament (the Exodus, Sodom and Gomorrah, and Balaam) but to two Apocryphal works not included in the Old Testament Apocrypha, the Assumption of Moses* and the Book of Enoch. From the former is taken the tradition that the archangel Michael disputed with the devil for the soul of Moses (Jude verse 9). From the latter is a quotation of the words of Enoch based on Enoch 1:9.

The purpose of the letter, which contains no details about who is being addressed, is to warn the readers/hearers against false teaching. Exactly who the false teachers are cannot be determined from the text, except that they attend the fellowship meals of the community. The letter stresses that among the Israelites who were saved from Egypt by the Exodus were those who refused to believe or who rebelled, and who were punished (Jude verses 5, 11). The same fate will befall false teachers and godless sinners in the Church.

2 Peter is generally reckoned to be the latest book in the New Testament, dated 120–40 CE. Although claimed to be by Simon Peter the apostle, it not only is dependent upon Jude, but knows 1 Peter (2 Peter 3:1) as well as some of the Pauline letters. Paul's letters are mentioned in 3:15–16, in which 'there are some things ... hard to understand, which the ignorant and unstable twist to their own destruction, as they do the other scriptures'. This is a noteworthy reference to Paul's letters as being regarded as on a par with the Old Testament Scriptures.

Given that 2 Peter uses material from Jude, its purpose is similar to that of Jude, and like Jude it contains no specific addressee. An additional factor is the need to answer the complaint that despite the life, death and resurrection of Jesus, the world carries on as before (3:3–4). There is no return of Jesus in glory, nor punishment of wickedness. The writer urges faithfulness. God has punished wickedness in the past, and will do so in the future when the day of the Lord comes unexpectedly like a thief, and the world is destroyed by fire.

James

This letter of five chapters, written by 'James, a servant of God and of the Lord Jesus Christ' (James 1:1), was traditionally ascribed to James the brother (or half-brother) of Jesus (cp. Mark 6:3). It has no specific address other than to 'the twelve tribes in the dispersion' (James 1:1), no concluding personal details and no hint of being a response to a problem or controversy in a local congregation. In fact, it is a series of ethical and religious discourses in which the following themes are prominent: the importance of humility and patient endurance (1:9–15), the need for positive Christian action rather than passive hearing or gossip (1:22–7), the implications of God's impartiality for one's treatment of rich and poor (2:1–7), the need for faith to be expressed in works (2:14–26), the dangers of slander and gossip (3:1–12), outer action as springing from the inner life (4:1–12), the perils of riches (5:1–6) and the efficacy of prayer (5:13–18).

The book contains echoes of the teaching of Jesus as recorded in the Synoptic Gospels without it being possible to demonstrate direct dependence, and the theme of 'wisdom' is pervasive (James 1:5–7, 3:13–18). A much-discussed question is whether 2:18–26 is an attack upon the Pauline doctrine that people are justified before God by faith alone. It is noteworthy that both Paul (Romans 4) and James (James 2:21–3) refer to Abraham and to Genesis 15:6 – 'Abraham believed God, and it was reckoned to him as righteousness'. Yet if James is trying to correct Paul or a misapplication of Paul, this is not done in a polemical way, and the argument can be contained within James's insistence that Christian living is bound up with practical help to the poor members of the Church (2:14–17).

Modern critical scholarship dates the book in the period 70–100 CE and has no agreed solution about the author or his place of writing. If it is correct to find in James allusions both to the teaching of Jesus and to Paul's doctrine of the importance of faith, then the letter is an important witness to the way in which a Christian teacher familiar with the Jewish and Hellenistic 'wisdom' traditions could creatively adapt different streams of Christian teaching for the edification of a local church or churches. It is difficult to identify the James of this letter with the James portrayed in Galatians 2:12, whose emissaries persuaded Peter not to eat with non-Jewish Christians.

Hebrews

The AV heads this book of thirteen chapters as 'The epistle of Paul the Apostle to the Hebrews', thereby recording a view of the authorship and address of the book that the Church embraced from around the 4th–19th centuries. The view that the work was Pauline derives from the closing verses (13:22–5) which speak of the release (from prison) of 'our brother Timothy' and which promises that the author and Timothy will soon visit those who are addressed. That the addressees were 'Hebrews' is nowhere stated in the book, and this early designation is derived from the considerable use of argument from Old Testament texts that the work contains. In view of the clear and implicit claim to Pauline authorship in 13:22–5 (the reference to 'our brother Timothy'), it is interesting to note that Pauline authorship was disputed by early Christian scholars such as Clement of Alexandria (born *c.* 150 CE), Origen (*c.* 185–254) and Tertullian (*c.* 160–*c.* 225).

Modern scholarship agrees that the work was not by Paul; but its concerns can be said to fit well within those of Paul. As was argued earlier in this chapter, Paul regarded the coming of Jesus as both a fulfilment of the Old Testament Scriptures, and as a setting aside of their legal provisions as far as non-Jews who became Christians were concerned. The position of the law is also the major preoccupation of Hebrews; but it is worked out in relation to the sacrificial system of the Old Testament, and in particular in relation to the ceremony of the Day of Atonement*.

The writer draws upon a theme which is known from the Dead Sea Scrolls to have been important in the Judaism of the time, namely, the significance of the high priest Melchizedek. In Genesis 14:18, Melchizedek king of Salem greets and blesses Abram after the latter has defeated Chedorlaomer and his allies; in Psalm 110 the king is declared to be a 'priest for ever after the order of Melchizedek' (verse 4). The writer of Hebrews applies this verse to Jesus (Hebrews 5:6) and this enables him to describe the significance of Jesus in priestly terms even though Jesus could not have been a priest, not coming from a priestly family. In chapters 7 to 10 Jesus is seen as both fulfilling and making unnecessary for evermore the sacrificial arrangements under the old covenant whereby sins were cancelled by the offering and the blood of sacrificial animals. Annually on the Day of Atonement the high priest had to enter the Holy Place to sprinkle blood on behalf of the people, first having purified himself by means of a sacrifice. Jesus, on the other hand, through the shedding of his own blood has entered once and for all into the heavens where he acts as a mediator on behalf of those who believe in him (9:15–28).

This bold and imaginative use of the Old Testament, which is of interest in its own right, caused the letter to develop a very high Christology: that is, the work of Jesus is understood in cosmic terms. Jesus is involved in the creation of the universe (Hebrews 1:1–14), and is the one to whom all creation is subject (2:1–9). He is the great high priest through whom a New Covenant has been established (8:8–13). Yet along with this high Christology there is also stress on the incarnation of Jesus culminating in his sufferings. This means that the great high priest of Christian faith has become in every respect like those whom he represents (2:17). Because he himself has suffered and been tempted, he is able to help those who are tempted (2:18).

Hebrews, then, is one of the most creative and important theological works in the New Testament, and possibly derives from Pauline circles sometime after 70 CE. From its content it may be addressed to a situation of persecution or backsliding. Examples are taken from the Old Testament of the fate of those who rebelled against God's grace (3:1–13) and the point is made that rebellion against such a new manifestation of God's grace as has occurred in Jesus is all the more fraught with danger. Again, in chapter 11 there is a splendid roll-call of Old Testament heroes and heroines of faith beginning with Abel. These great examples of loyal devotion to God before the coming of Christ are a great 'cloud of witnesses' (12:1) who should inspire believers in their pilgrimage as they look to follow Jesus, who has gone on ahead. A final chapter enjoins hospitality, faithfulness in marriage, avoidance of love of money and obedience to leaders in the Church.

THE MAKING OF THE NEW TESTAMENT AS A WHOLE

This chapter has tried to outline why the individual books of the New Testament were written. How did they become the collection that we know? Nobody, in fact, made the conscious decision that there should be a New Testament. What happened was that collections of books were made by various churches, with these collections gradually adding up to something like the New Testament as we know it. An early such collection is found in the Chester Beatty papyrus P[46], which is usually dated around 200 CE and which contains the Pauline letters from Romans 5:17 to 1 Thessalonians 5:28, with Hebrews following Romans. This is evidence that the Pauline letters (including Hebrews!) were regarded as a special corpus. Another early collection was of the four Gospels and Acts in the 3rd-century Chester Beatty papyrus P[45].

These collections helped to begin to delineate what books were to be regarded as Scripture, a process that was assisted by the Christian adoption of the codex (leaves fastened at the left-hand end) rather than the scroll. The number of pages of a codex had to be fixed in advance, and thus its contents had to be planned.[5] As Elliott remarks, the gospels that lay outside the four-fold collection were never bound together, with any or all of the four. 'There are no manuscripts that contain say Matthew, Luke and Peter*, or John, Mark and Thomas*'.[6] The number four may also have been helped by the early identification by Irenaeus (*c.* 130–*c.* 202) of the Gospels with the four living creatures of Ezekiel 1:4–25: the man (Matthew), the lion (John), the ox (Luke) and the eagle (Mark).[7]

The Gospels, Acts and Pauline letters constitute the bulk of the New Testament, to which were added collections such as the so-called Catholic Epistles (James, 1 and 2 Peter, Jude, 1, 2 and 3 John). From the 3rd or 4th centuries attempts were made to define the scope of the New Testament, a notable example being the so-called Muratorian* canon. However, this brings the book to the point where the next chapter needs to consider the question of the canon of the Bible.

CHAPTER 6

The Canon of the Bible

In earlier chapters mention has been made of the canon, or more accurately, the various canons of the Bible adopted by different churches. The subject of canon requires at least a book in its own right, and what follows will necessarily be impressionistic.[1] At the same time, the subject will be approached differently from treatments in the standard works, and will consider a question that is not usually asked: what is the relation between canon and power?

Whatever the connection may be between the English word 'canon' and the Greek word from which it derives, a canon is an official list of books that designates those books as normative or authoritative for a particular community. This sense needs to be distinguished from the practice of designating certain books as normative or authoritative by publishing them in a particular format. As far as I am aware, no technical term exists for this practice; but since it is important for the argument of this chapter, the term 'canonical format' will be used to designate it. A final point is that the words 'canon' and 'canonical' are sometimes used as though their meaning was constant throughout the history of the Church (and of Judaism). The present chapter will assume that the meaning of 'canon' has not been constant, but that it has depended upon the interests of those using it at any particular time.

The discussion can most usefully begin by addressing the question why there are several canons of the Bible and not one. As the preceding chapters have shown, there are the following possibilities, among others, with regard to the Old Testament, or, for the Jewish community, the Hebrew Bible:

1. For Jews and Evangelical Protestants the twenty-four books in Hebrew are alone recognized.

2. For Anglicans the twenty-four books are canonical Scripture but the Apocrypha can be read 'for example of life and instruction of manners' (Article VI of the 39 Articles).[2]

3. For Roman Catholics the twenty-four books are canonical and the Apocryphal books (minus 1 Esdras, Prayer of Manasseh, Psalm 151 and 3 Maccabees) are deuterocanonical, but are equally authoritative.

4. For the Greek Orthodox Church the twenty-four books are canonical and the Apocryphal books (including those omitted by Roman Catholics) are deuterocanonical, and all are equally authoritative.

5. The Ethiopic Church accepts the Book of Enoch as canonical.

With regard to the New Testament, some of the variations include the acceptance of 1 and 2 Clement as canonical by the Coptic Church, and the similar acceptance of 3 Corinthians at least for some of their history by the Ethiopic and Syriac churches.

The reason for this diversity is obvious. There has been no single body with power over all these churches to designate or enforce a single canon. What we have are individual decisions of religious communities whose different canons are an expression of localized power, with the decisions in some cases taken precisely in order to distinguish one community from other communities. A case in point would be the decision of the Westminster Assembly of Divines in 1648 to reject the Apocrypha for use in the Church of God.

A useful comparison can be made here with the situation in Islam, where, according to the traditional understanding, there was a ruler who had the authority to introduce the Qur'an in such a way that not only were its contents without any variation, but its text also. This ruler was the third caliph, Uthman (*c.* 577–656, caliph from 644). According to Islamic tradition, the collection of the material for the Qur'an was undertaken by Zayd ibn Thabit, Mohammed's secretary, at the instigation of the first caliph, Abu Bakr (*c.* 573–634, caliph from 632). Uthman is credited with standardizing the text, although oral traditions persisted about how it should be recited. These, together with questions arising from the vocalization of the text (the adding of vowel signs to the consonantal text), became the basis for discussions about interpretation; but the text established by Uthman resulted in a standard edition without parallel in Christianity.[3] How did the question of power affect the canon of the Bible?

Undoubtedly the most potent power in modern times, in the form of what I have called 'canonical format', has been that of publishing decisions. As already mentioned in chapter 1, the British and Foreign Bible Society took the decision early in 1827 not to include the Apocrypha in its Bibles. The result was that the Apocrypha has become virtually unknown even to Anglicans who regularly worship and/or read the Bible in spite of the fact that Article VI of the 39 Articles recommends it 'for example of life and instruction of manners' and the fact that Handel based oratorios on Judith and Maccabees. It comes as a surprise to devotees of the Authorized or King James Version to discover that this was usually published with the Apocrypha until the 19th century.[4] Similarly, the deliberate non-inclusion of the Apocrypha in the NIV is an instance of canonical format. Luther also used canonical format to indicate his view that certain books of the New Testament fell below the rest in value. He placed Hebrews, James, Jude and Revelation after 3 John and, unlike the other New Testament books, did not number them.

A good example of the importance of civil and ecclesiastical power in the matter of canon is found in the 39 Articles of the Church of England which were drawn up in the reign of Elizabeth I in 1562 and issued by authority of the queen as Supreme Governor of the Church of England. Article VI lists the 'names and number' of the canonical books 'of whose authority was never any doubt in the Church'. In the list that follows, Ezra and Nehemiah are called the First and Second Books of Esdras and the concluding books of the Old Testament are 'Four Prophets the greater, Twelve Prophets the less'. Lamentations is not mentioned explicitly. The 'other Books' are the Apocrypha as found in traditional English language translations, e.g. the AV, RV, NEB, REB – books which were represented in the lectionaries of the Prayer Books of 1549 and 1551 (i.e. Tobit, Judith, Wisdom, Ecclesiasticus, Baruch), but distinguished from the Old Testament because the Church (i.e. the Church of England) does not 'apply them to establish any doctrine'.

This last comment represents the theological interest behind the issuing of the authoritative list. Article VI begins with the theological statement that

Holy Scripture containeth all things necessary to salvation: so that whatsoever is not read therein, nor may be proved thereby, is not to be required of any man, that it should be believed as an article of the Faith, or be thought requisite or necessary to salvation.

The purpose of defining the canon is therefore to delimit the books to which appeal can be made if there is a dispute about the necessity of an article of faith. There is also the intention to distinguish the Church of England from the Roman Catholic Church, which justified belief in the efficacy of prayers for the dead, for example, from the 'other Books' listed by Article VI.

An instance is 2 Maccabees 12:38–45 which tells how it is discovered that members of the army of Judas Maccabeus who had been killed in a battle had been wearing 'the idols of Jamnia' – quasi good-luck charms dedicated to foreign gods. Judas and his men pray that God will forgive this sin of their dead comrades-in-arms and he also collects a sum of money to finance a sin-offering in the Jerusalem temple on behalf of the fallen. The sober and scholarly Roman Catholic NJB Study Bible comments that 'this text expresses the conviction that prayer and expiatory sacrifice are efficacious for the remission of sins for the dead' (p. 741). But this view was repugnant to the Anglican (and other) Reformers for whom salvation could be obtained only by the 'Name of Jesus Christ' (Article XVIII of the 39 Articles). In contrast to Reformation statements such as those that would appear in the 39 Articles, the Roman Catholic Council of Trent had, in April 1546, declared the deuterocanonical books to be of equal value with the canonical books of the Old Testament, and had pronounced an anathema (an exclusion order) upon 'anyone who does not receive these entire books, with all their parts, as they are accustomed to be read in the Catholic Church and are found in the ancient edition of the Latin Vulgate, as sacred and canonical'.[5]

Clearly both sides were engaging in a certain amount of rationalizing in this debate. There had been discussion in the Western Church at least since the time of Jerome in the late 4th century CE about whether to regard the smaller Hebrew canon or the larger Greek canon as canonical. The result was that both sides could claim historical precedent for the position that they adopted. But the final decision was not determined by historical research but by doctrinal positioning, with each side adopting the canon that best supported its doctrinal stance. An implication of this fact is that, in the West, the canon was not fixed once and for all until the combination of doctrinal dissension and ecclesiastical and political power in the 16th century led to the fixing of the respective canons.

These considerations will be taken back into the earlier period shortly, but before this is done, another canonical factor will be considered, that of what I shall call 'canonical text form'. It was noted in chapter 4 on the Apocrypha that, in modern translations, books such as Tobit and the Wisdom of Jesus ben Sirach (Ecclesiasticus) exist in differing versions. Also, the Hebrew and Greek versions of books such as Jeremiah show considerable divergence. This textual diversity contrasts signally with the Qur'an in Islam, where there are no significant textual variations.

Who decides which text of a writing is canonical (in the loose sense of authoritative)? Nowadays, such decisions are taken by groups of scholars who are usually working under the auspices, but not control, of various churches, and financed by publishers or independent bodies such as the Bible Societies. Although they do not consciously decide that their textual decisions will become authoritative for churches, in practice this is what happens, because their texts are used as the basis for translations, or their translations become the Bible available to particular communities.

It has not always been so. In the era immediately after the invention of printing, official Church permission and financial patronage were usually required by any printer who wanted to produce Bibles. Because the invention of printing raised, not for the first time, the question of the accuracy of texts as representing what the biblical writers wrote, the 16th and 17th centuries saw the production of Polyglott* Bibles, which gave the biblical text in many versions as an aid to textual criticism. All the major Polyglott Bibles were sponsored by powerful interests. The Complutensian Polyglott (1514–17) was produced by Cardinal Ximenes de Cisneros, Archbishop of Toledo, and its revision, the Antwerp Polyglott (1569–72), was produced by Arias Montano under the patronage of Philip II of Spain. The Paris Polyglott, conceived as an extended edition of the Antwerp Polyglott (1629–45), was financed by a parliamentarian, while the London Polyglott (1653–7) was edited by Brian Walton, later Bishop of Chester. The Polyglotts included versions in Aramaic, Syriac, Samaritan and Arabic, and in some cases provided the earliest printed editions of the text.

Before the invention of printing, when all copies had to be hand made, the situation was clearly different; yet, arguably, the canonical considerations that have been identified from the modern period still operated in their own way. In what follows, several selected, but important, issues will be discussed in the light of these considerations.

THE JEWISH CANON

A popular view of the formation of the Jewish canon has been that there was a council held at Jamnia (Javneh) after the destruction of the temple in 70 CE at which the extent of the Hebrew canon was fixed. This suggestion, which goes back to Heinrich Graetz in 1871, has fallen out of favour, and attention has centred upon rabbinic discussions about books which 'defiled the hands' on account of their sacredness.[6] These books included Ecclesiastes and the Song of Songs, over whose 'canonicity' there was evidently some difference of opinion.

However, I intend to approach the matter from a different angle, by connecting the problem of canon (the list of authorized books) with that of canonical text form. It is well known from the discoveries at and near Qumran since 1947 that the Dead Sea Community (assuming that it was a community and that the bulk of the discoveries came from its 'library') not only regarded books such as Ben Sirach and Jubilees as authoritative, but that it possessed biblical books in different textual versions. In contrast, the texts discovered at Wadi al Murabba'at which date from early in the 2nd century CE display mostly only what has come to be the standard text of the Hebrew Bible. Again, discoveries at Nahal Hever provide evidence that in the middle of the 1st century CE corrections to, or marginal comments on, the Greek version of Old Testament texts were seeking to approximate these closer to the Hebrew.

It seems to be too much of a coincidence that evidence should come from different quarters that work was in progress in Jewish circles in the

1st–2nd centuries CE on standardizing the Hebrew text and bringing Greek versions into line with it; and further evidence for this process may be found in the so-called Letter of Aristeas, especially if a date in the 1st century CE is preferred.[7] The 'Letter' contains a legendary account of the origin of the Septuagint according to which seventy-two translators produced, in seventy-two days, an official translation of the Pentateuch into Greek under the auspices of the Egyptian Ptolemy II (Philadelphos, 285–246 BCE). Whatever else this writing indicates, it shows the existence of the belief that a sacred text should have an official, authorized and standardized translation. It also recognizes the part played in such a process by political authority.

For present purposes, the importance of this line of argument is as follows. A standardized text implies the existence of a canon, in the sense of an approved list or corpus of writings. The Letter of Aristeas may be evidence only for a movement to produce a standardized translation, and presumably a standardized Hebrew text, of the Pentateuch. Taken together with the evidence from Wadi al Murabba'at and Nahal Hever it indicates activity whose aim was eventually to produce a standardized text for a fixed corpus of writings regarded as sacred (i.e. the Hebrew Bible). Such activity does not happen spontaneously. It requires either political power, as in the case of the Qur'an, or the activity of a group sharing a common aim and working through scribal outlets. Although no direct evidence exists to identify such a group, a reasonable guess would be that this work was carried out by those within 'Pharisaism' who later became dominant in Judaism after the destruction of the temple in 70 CE. This suggestion is not meant to deny that, by the 1st century BCE, most of the books of the Hebrew Bible had come to be regarded as sacred. It is meant to address the vexed question of how and when the canon of the Hebrew Bible was fixed. The view taken here is that this process was bound up with the belief that sacred texts should exist, as far as possible, in a standard textual form.

THE SEPTUAGINT

In a much-quoted text from his foreword to the Books of Chronicles, Jerome noted that in his day (late 4th century CE) the Septuagint existed in three versions: the version in Alexandria and Egypt owed its form to Hesychius,[8] while in Antioch and Constantinople the version of Lucian (*c.* 240–312) held the field. The Palestinian province used a version based on the work of Origen. Sufficient is known about the activity of Origen to comment on Jerome's opinion.[9]

Origen (*c.* 185–254) enjoyed patronage and secretarial support in Caesarea that would make a modern academic envious. He was able, as a result, to compile a massive 6,000-page Hexapla in which various editions of the Septuagint were placed in parallel columns alongside the Hebrew. One of the columns contained a revised text of the Septuagint, complete with asterisks and other diacritical marks indicating revisions. One of the reasons for Origen's work was that there were disputes between Jews and Christians about passages in the Old Testament relating to Christ, and said by the Jews to be insertions and by the Christians to be omissions. A famous instance is the phrase 'he reigns from the tree' in the Greek of Psalm 95:10 but absent from the Hebrew of Psalm 96:10. These disputes highlight another important factor in canonizing processes. If texts become the basis of arguments about the nature of divine revelation, then it becomes important to define not only which books are authoritative, but also which textual editions are authoritative. In Origen's case, his aim was apparently to produce a Greek version that approximated as closely as possible to the Hebrew. Whether this was also the aim of Lucian, presumed to be a martyr in Antioch around 311 CE, is disputed. What is clear is that he undertook or initiated a revision of the Septuagint that preferred those manuscripts that were thought to be of greatest authority.

Judging from the diversity of text types of manuscripts of the Septuagint and modern attempts to classify them into text types, the diversities observed by Jerome were never consolidated into a standard text.[10] Presumably this was because no political or ecclesiastical authority could impose its will upon the Eastern churches to the degree required to produce a standard text. Printing would, to some extent, change this situation.

THE VULGATE

The interesting thing about Jerome's project, begun around 380, to produce a standard Latin text of the Bible, is that it was commissioned by Pope Damasus. It thus represented an official attempt to produce order out of the chaos of the existence of popular Latin versions.[11] Initially, the so-called Old Latin versions were revised on the basis of the Septuagint, but when Jerome became aware of the unsatisfactory state of the existing versions of the Septuagint, he undertook a translation directly from the Hebrew. It can be no accident that work that began with the project of what I have called canonical text form eventually led to discussion of the limit of the canon itself, with Jerome wanting to restrict the canon to those books that belonged to the Hebrew canon.

Despite its official sponsorship, Jerome's Vulgate found it hard to oust the Old Latin versions. Latin manuscript Bibles were produced with mixed Vulgate and Old Latin texts. An attempt at some form of standardization was made by Theodulf and Alkuin, who worked in the 9th century CE under the patronage begun by Charlemagne. In the 20th century there have been large-scale projects to re-establish the original text of Jerome's Vulgate.

THE NEW TESTAMENT

With minor exceptions noted at the beginning of the chapter, the extent of the New Testament canon was not a matter of dispute from at least the 4th century CE, although important codices of the Bible such as Sinaiticus and Alexandrinus contain between them non-New Testament books such as 1 and 2 Clement, Barnabas and the Shepherd of Hermas. The text of the New Testament also began to show some uniformity beginning in the 4th century CE, with the majority of extant manuscripts exhibiting some form of what has been called the Byzantine or 'Majority Text'. This text may have received official support from the Christian Byzantine empire; but its widespread use may also have depended upon the comprehensive nature of its readings. This Majority Text served as a sort of standard Greek text for nearly 1,000 years, and was the basis for the earliest printed Greek New Testaments, as well as of translations such as the AV. Ironically, modern research has deemed it to be an inferior text. Chapter 1 gives instances of cases where modern translations have departed from readings based upon the Majority Text.

PRINTING

To conclude the chapter, the impact of printing will be considered once more, since it radically affected the canonical text form. It has just been noted that the printing of the Majority Text became the basis of 16th- and 17th-century translations of the New Testament. This was an unconscious instance of canonical text formation. A deliberate instance followed the decree of the Council of Trent in 1546 about the canon of the Bible. It led to the production in 1592 of a standard edition of the Vulgate under the authority of Clement VIII. Printing also led to quasi-authoritative editions of the Septuagint and the Hebrew Bible.

CONCLUSION

No attempt has been made in this chapter to answer the probably unanswerable questions of where, when and by whom the books of the Old and New Testaments and Apocrypha were canonized. Instead, the attempt has been made to link canonization with what I have called canonical format and canonical text form. It has also been argued that these inter-linked processes have been affected by various considerations. These include (a) the belief that sacred writings should have a standard text, (b) the need to establish, in the face of controversy, what writings are authoritative and in what version, and (c) the importance of ecclesiastical and political power in promoting canonical processes.

It has been noted that Christianity has been less successful than Islam and Judaism in achieving a canonical text form. The fates of the Old and New Testaments indicate opposing fortunes. The unanimity that began to be established with the Byzantine or Majority Text of the New Testament was shattered by scholarly researches from the 19th century. While a new, scholarly-imposed, general agreement has emerged in the form of printed Greek New Testaments issued under the imprint of various Bible societies, it is perhaps a fragile unity preserved by theological interests. G. D. Kilpatrick produced most of a new edition of the Greek New Testament for the British and Foreign Bible Society using quite different principles from those governing Nestle-Aland and United Bible Societies editions (see chapter 1), and yielding different results. The edition was abandoned when the British and Foreign Bible Society joined the United Bible Societies project.[12]

On the Old Testament front, there has been a movement from diversity to uniformity. Before printing, the Bible in Greek existed in various editions and, after the Reformation, the western churches based their translations of the Old Testament on the Latin if they were Catholics and the Hebrew if they were Protestants. The modern position in the West is that Catholics and Protestants accept the Hebrew text as the basis for translation, with readings based on the Septuagint and other versions only being accepted where the Hebrew is manifestly corrupt. It is strange, if not significant, that there has been no attempt to produce an eclectic text of the Old Testament based equally on the Hebrew and Greek versions. The textual situation of the Apocryphal books remains fluid, as indicated in chapter 4. This shows that while, in theory, these books are regarded as equally inspired as the other Old Testament books in some churches, in practice there is no wish or will to move towards anything like a canonical text form.

Some readers may be alarmed at the implications of this chapter, which further confirms there is not so much a thing as *the* Bible, but rather, Bibles in various shapes and forms. Does this undermine the 'authority' of 'the Bible'? The answer is no. For even if there were a single standardized Bible comparable in its format to the Qur'an, this would not necessarily result in an agreed interpretation of it, accepted at all times and in all places. The fluidity of the extent and textual character of the Bible can be seen as part of the wider matter of its interpretation and use – the subjects of the remaining two chapters.

CHAPTER 7

The Study of the Bible

The ways in which the Bible can be used in interpretation, if not infinite, vary considerably in number. Presumably, the greatest use and interpretation of the Bible has been in sermons in churches all over the world. The number of such sermons must run into millions; and this use has been going on for nearly 2,000 years, although not always on the scale of today. The vast majority of these sermons have been, and will be, forever lost. Before the invention of printing, only the sermons of great figures such as Augustine of Hippo (354–430 CE), John Chrysostom (c. 350–407) and Pope Gregory I (c. 540–604) were recorded for posterity. After the invention of printing, it became common for sermons to be published individually, and there must be hundreds of thousands of such pamphlets in the libraries of Europe and North America. In the 19th and 20th centuries famous preachers published volumes of sermons. Although there have been studies of preachers and preaching, this aspect of the use of the Bible is virtually unknown.

It should not be supposed that the Christian tradition has had a monopoly on the interpretation of the Bible. Within Judaism, the Hebrew Bible has been commented on in the great Midrashim* and Talmudim* and, as will be indicated later in this chapter, the Middle Ages saw the emergence of outstanding Jewish commentators such as Abraham Ibn Ezra, Rashi, Kimhi and Maimonides.

The Bible has been one of the greatest influences on the arts in the Western world, and the study of this is a growing area of interest in current biblical studies. The recent *Dictionary of Biblical Tradition in English Literature* fills an important gap in previous knowledge of part of this use.[1] An amateur, but serious, interest of the present writer is in the interpretation of the Bible in Bach's church cantatas. Bach composed over 200 such cantatas, most of which employed librettos based upon the New Testament readings for each Sunday morning of the Lutheran calendar. Other areas where the Bible has been influential include the fine and applied arts (dress, sculpture, jewellery, architecture), not to mention its influence on Western culture including education and politics.

The point of this introduction is to indicate that no one writer can do justice to the many ways in which the Bible has been used, and certainly not in two chapters of an introductory book. What follows will therefore be selective, and based upon my own interests and previous researches. Chapter 8 will concentrate upon the use of the Bible in ethics. The present chapter will be structured as follows:

The study of the Old Testament, with special reference to scientific matters and to biblical criticism.

The use of the Apocrypha in literature, art and music.

The story of the New Testament, with special reference to the life of Jesus.

Fundamentalism.

Recent developments in biblical studies: literary readings, feminism, Liberation Theology.

THE OLD TESTAMENT, WITH SPECIAL REFERENCE TO SCIENTIFIC MATTERS AND TO BIBLICAL CRITICISM

The Study of the Bible has always been critical, in the sense that human rationality and scientific knowledge of the world have naturally been applied to interpreting the biblical text, as they have to all areas of human experience.[2] An early instance of this is the problem created by the Hebrew of 1 Samuel 13:1. Translated literally, the Hebrew means: 'Saul was one year old when he began to reign, and he reigned for two years.' Faced with this obvious absurdity which contradicted knowledge of human growth and development as well as other information about Saul, e.g. that he had a son Jonathan (1 Samuel 13:2), the translators of the Septuagint either omitted the verse or supplied the figure '30'. Early Jewish interpreters took the phrase to mean that Saul was as free from sin as a one-year-old child when he became king. The influential medieval Jewish interpreter Rashi (1040–1105) took the phrase to refer to Saul's first year as king, and the two years to refer to a period after which he chose the men of Israel.[3] This interpretation was followed by the AV: 'Saul reigned one year; and when he had reigned two years over Israel, Saul chose him three thousand men of Israel . . .'

An early example of wrestling with questions raised by common sense and by science can be found in Augustine's great work the *City of God* (413–26). In the opening chapters of Genesis, light is created before the sun (1:3, cp. 1:14–19), the universe is created in six days, before the Flood people live to be over 900 years (Genesis 5) and do not begin to have children until they are over 100 years old. Genesis 6:4 says that there were giants on the earth 'in those days' while in order to escape from the Flood Noah brings all the animals into the ark 'two by two' (7:9). Augustine felt the need to deal with all of these matters as 'difficulties' (see Books 11–15).

According to Augustine, the light and the days of Genesis 1 were different from what we understand by light and days; but the same was not true of the years lived by people before the Flood. Those years were the same as our years, and it was possible that the people concerned matured more slowly than we do. The offspring mentioned as being born when the parent was over 100 may not have been the first-born – thus introducing the possibility that the information in Genesis 5 might be selective and thus incomplete. That there were giants in earlier ages could be substantiated by the very large tombs or statues that existed of earlier rulers, as well as the existence in recent times of very tall people. Augustine instanced a woman in Rome shortly before its fall in 410 who towered above all the other inhabitants.

On the Flood, Augustine made many concessions to common sense. It was not, in fact, necessary for all creatures to enter the ark. Those that lived normally in water would not need to do so (we are tempted to ask how these creatures would be destroyed by a Flood!), nor was it necessary for there to be male and female of creatures such as bees. Because the earth had produced animals in Genesis 1:24, it was likely that it did so again after the Flood, especially in remote islands. Whatever we may think of Augustine's solutions, he did not accept the text literally, but approached it using common sense as well as his (to us) rudimentary knowledge of science, history, botany and archaeology.

The next landmark to be considered is the influence of the rediscovery of Aristotle upon biblical interpretation. This influence was mediated to Christianity and Judaism by Muslim civilization, which was well in advance of the West in the 8th and following centuries CE. Aristotle, the 4th-century BCE Greek philosopher, was studied in Muslim Spain from the 8th century CE, where the great Jewish philosopher Maimonides (1138–1204) grew up. His masterpiece, *The Guide of the Perplexed*, was written in Arabic in around 1190, and was translated into Latin about thirty years later, whence it influenced Christian thinkers such as Aquinas (see the next chapter).[4] Maimonides believed that Aristotle had correctly described the nature and functioning of the universe, and that biblical interpretation had to start from the world as it was. In *The Guide* he expressed this view as follows:

I shall say to you that the matter is as Themistus puts it. That which exists does not conform to the various opinions, but rather the correct opinions conform to that which exists (*Guide*, Book I, chapter 71).

One of the results of Maimonides's approach is that he did not always take the accounts of miracles literally. Basing himself on Genesis 15:1, 'the word of the LORD came to Abram in a vision', Maimonides argued that no divine communication took place with humans except through a dream or vision of prophecy; and that where the vision was not mentioned explicitly in the text, it had to be assumed. Thus, to mention two famous and notoriously difficult passages, Jacob wrestling with the unknown assailant who is at the very least an angel (Genesis 32:22–32) and Balaam's she-ass that spoke to her master (Numbers 22:28), Maimonides maintained that both were visions of prophecy, and not events that occurred while Jacob and Balaam were in their normal state.

The 'rationalizing' of Maimonides was not unique in medieval Jewish scholarship, but was nowhere better anchored in philosophical and theological theory than in his writings. Another Jewish interpreter, David Kimhi (*c.* 1160–*c.* 1235), who was a prolific and profound commentator, also applied much common sense to the biblical text. Commenting on

Genesis 1:1, the creation of the light before the sun, he maintained that the sun and moon were created on the first day, but that they did not shine on the earth until the fourth day. His long discussion of Genesis 3:1, in which the serpent speaks to Eve, is most informative. He is worried by the literal meaning, that an animal spoke, but cannot accept the view ascribed to Sa'adia Gaon (882–942) that neither the serpent spoke, nor Balaam's ass. If the serpent did not speak, why was it punished? He is similarly worried about the view that the serpent merely gestured. How would the woman understand him? Kimhi advances no really satisfactory answer; but his discussion indicates a sharp critical awareness.[5]

All these Jewish interpreters were concerned with what was called in Judaism *peshat**, that is, the interpretation of the plain meaning of the text. In Christian interpretation, while it would be wrong to suggest that there was no interest in the plain meaning, there had developed the doctrine of the four-fold sense of Scripture – the literal, the moral, the Christological* and the analogical (i.e. what was concerned with ultimate salvation). This to some extent diverted interest from the plain sense. It also enabled interpreters to maintain a unity between the Old and New Testaments, especially through finding references to or types of Christ in the Old Testament.

The Reformation marks a high point in the history of the study of the Bible. The Reformers had at their disposal printed editions of Bibles in Hebrew and Greek (New Testaments) and there was a revival of Christian Hebrew scholarship, which was deeply indebted to Jewish scholarship. Because the Reformers emphasized the primacy of the Bible over the authority of the Church, great effort was devoted to translations into the main languages of Europe, and to commentaries on the Bible. Although the Reformers did not entirely abandon the four-fold scheme of interpretation, they paid most of their attention to the plain meaning of the text. Out of the mass of material that could be mentioned, what follows will highlight the attitudes of Luther and Calvin to critical and scientific matters.[6]

It has already been noted that Luther used his published Bible to indicate his low opinion of James, Peter, Jude and Hebrews (see chapter 6). Although he did not rearrange the Old Testament books, he had little regard for Esther, and gave no lectures on Joshua, Samuel, Kings and Chronicles. He regarded the Pentateuch as 'Mosaic' rather than as necessarily all written by Moses, and held that there was no coherent order of material in books such as Isaiah, Jeremiah and Hosea. On the other hand, he had a particular liking for the story of Samson in the Book of Judges. He evidently identified with Samson's lone stand against the Philistines, comparing it with his own stand against the Roman Catholic Church of his day. Also, the fact that, after all his failings, Samson had his final prayer answered by God and found his strength restored, was a sign that God's forgiveness could extend to even the least promising situations.

Calvin was a much more systematic, if less interesting, commentator than Luther; and yet some of his positions were more critical than those of orthodox commentators of the 19th century. In his lectures on Genesis, Calvin held that Genesis 1 was not a scientific account of the origin of the universe, but a description from the point of view of an Israelite of the Old Testament period. Genesis 1:14–19 implies that the sun and moon are the two great lights in the heavens. Calvin knew that the moon was much smaller than the other planets of the earth's solar system. He concluded that the statements of Genesis 1:14–19 were not statements of scientific fact; as he said of the waters above the firmament (Genesis 1:6): 'He who would learn astronomy, and other recondite arts, let him go elsewhere.' For Calvin, then, what was important about Genesis 1 was not its science but its theology.

It is now necessary to try to sketch the movements that led to the emergence of biblical criticism as we know it today, bearing in mind that this was a gradual rather than an abrupt development. Of the many and complex factors, the following can be mentioned. First, there was a concentration upon the plain or historical meaning of the Old Testament text that placed the Old Testament in its setting as work originating in specific circumstances in ancient Israel rather than as a work that could be read mystically or spiritually in connection with the New Testament. This historicizing of the Old Testament led, secondly, to a reduced willingness on the part of interpreters to make moral allowances for Old Testament characters. That the behaviour of characters from Abraham onwards raised moral questions had long been recognized. Thus, in the

City of God (Book 16 chapter 25), Augustine defended Abraham's action in producing a son through his wife's servant Hagar, and maintained that it had been done without lust. It was not, however, a permissible action for Christians. Luther's affection for Samson has been noted. How did he justify Samson's acts of slaughter of his enemies? By making the distinction between what Samson did in his office as a judge and what he did as a private person. As a judge, he was entitled to defend his people against the Philistines. A similar strategy defended David who, although described as a future king after God's own heart (1 Samuel 13:14), would commit adultery and engineer murder (2 Samuel 11). In support of David it was said that his dubious moral actions were committed as a private person, and that he was punished by God for them. In his office as king, however, he was a man after God's heart.

As interpreters became less willing to make such allowances, the Old Testament looked increasingly like the literature of a barbaric people. For the English deists* of the 18th century, for whom religion was primarily a matter of reason, and for whom morality was one of the most important aspects of religion, the Old Testament was an embarrassment on account of its moral content. However, the deists did not contribute directly to the development of modern biblical criticism.[7]

The foundations of modern biblical criticism were laid in Protestant Germany in the latter part of the 18th century. Whereas there were only two universities in England at the time, at neither of which was theology taught (there were, however, five universities in Scotland and some fine dissenting academies in England), Germany possessed some twenty Protestant theological faculties which began to put the study of the Bible on a professional basis. This involved having an established career structure for academics as well as scholarly outlets, especially academic journals. By the end of the 18th century a body of critical knowledge about the Old Testament had begun to be assembled. Parts of the Book of Genesis had been divided into two sources – Jehovah and Elohim – depending primarily on which divine name was used in the text (see chapter 2), it had been proposed that Isaiah 40–66 had been written by an unknown prophet in Babylon 200 years later than the 8th-century Isaiah of Jerusalem, it was questioned whether Zechariah was a unity, and whether chapters 9–14 were not a separate, later work from chapters

1–8; and the unity of the Book of Daniel had been questioned. Many of these, and other results, were embodied in an *Introduction to the Old Testament* by J. G. Eichhorn, whose first edition appeared in 1780–83.

A major step forward was the publication, in 1806–7, of W. M. L. de Wette's *Contributions to Old Testament Introduction*.[8] This work used source* and other criticism to argue that the picture contained in the Old Testament of the course of ancient Israel's religious development was inaccurate. Against the Old Testament picture that Moses had given to Israel a fully developed system of law, sacrifice and priesthood at the beginning of its life as a people after the Exodus from Egypt, de Wette argued that these things had developed gradually over the course of Israel's history. He contrasted the injunction in Deuteronomy that sacrifice should only be offered at a single, central sanctuary (12:5–14) with the practice of characters such as Samuel in 1 Samuel who offered sacrifices at Mizpah (7:5–11), Gilgal (11:14–15) and an unnamed city in the land Zuph (9:5–14). There was also the complaint of Elijah (1 Kings 19:10) that the Israelites had destroyed altars, something that is *commanded* in Deuteronomy 12:1–3! After some initial support, de Wette's work was forgotten and needed to be repeated later in the 19th century when, as the result of the labours of K. H. Graf in Germany, A. Kuenen in the Netherlands and William Robertson Smith in Scotland, a classic statement of a newly emerging scholarly consensus about the history, literature and religion of ancient Israel was published in J. Wellhausen's *Prolegomena to the History of Israel* (1883).[9] Despite attempts to disprove or undermine it, this synthesis has been the starting-point for all subsequent Old Testament scholarship.

While this debate within Old Testament studies was proceeding, scholarship was having to come to terms with scientific discoveries that challenged traditional interpretation. J. Ussher had worked out, on the basis of the biblical chronology, that the world had been created in 4004 BCE.[10] Geologists in the 1830s maintained that the world was much older than this. Again, Darwin's *Origin of Species* (1859) and *Descent of Man* (1871) challenged the view that there had been a 'Fall' of the human race.[11] While orthodox churchmen attacked Darwin's position, other more liberal-minded thinkers saw no incompatibility between Darwin and Genesis. Thus, the newly appointed professor of Hebrew at Oxford,

S. R. Driver, preached a sermon in 1883 entitled 'Evolution Compatible with Faith', and in his commentary on Genesis (1904) he sought to interpret Genesis in accordance with science, biblical criticism and archaeology.[12] Another scholar who sought to show that Christians had nothing to fear from biblical criticism or science was the Primitive Methodist layman and first Rylands Professor of Biblical Criticism and Exegesis at the University of Manchester, A. S. Peake.[13]

Roman Catholic scholarship began to appreciate the necessity of biblical criticism through the work of M.-J. Lagrange of the École Biblique, founded in Jerusalem in 1890.[14] After some setbacks, Roman Catholic biblical criticism was positively encouraged by the 1943 Papal Encyclical *Divino afflante Spiritu* and by the Second Vatican Council (1962–5). Today, there is no difference between the critical methods used by Protestant and Catholic scholars, and the latter are a large and creative factor in international biblical criticism.[15]

The scholarly study of the Old Testament is divided up into various branches, each of which has become a life-long field of study in its own right. These include textual criticism (the study of the history of the text of the Hebrew, Greek, Latin and other Bibles), source, form and redaction criticism (the study of the growth of biblical literature from simple forms to completed narratives), social and historical criticism (the study of the history and social structure of ancient Israel using the Old Testament, other literary evidence and archaeology), and religious and theological study of the Old Testament. Newer approaches will be discussed in the last section below.

Within Judaism, orthodox believers have continued to hold that God revealed the law to Moses on Mount Sinai. They have therefore been totally opposed to the conclusions of (Christian) critical biblical scholarship. However, in Reform and Liberal Judaism there has been a cautious welcome for critical methods; and Jewish and Israeli scholars have made notable contributions to the study of the Hebrew Bible in areas such as textual criticism, archaeology, literature and poetics.[16]

THE USE OF THE APOCRYPHA IN LITERATURE, ART AND MUSIC

The large-scale ignorance of the Apocrypha, at least among Anglicans and other Protestants, contrasts with its prominence in the liturgies of various churches, as well as its use in art, literature and music. In the Orthodox churches, quotations from and allusions to the Books of Tobit, Judith, Wisdom of Solomon, the Wisdom of Jesus ben Sirach (Ecclesiasticus) and the four Books of Maccabees are to be found in the Liturgies of Basil of Caesarea and John Chrysostom and the services of Baptism, Chrism, Marriage and Holy Unction. In the Orthodox services of Vespers (the service preparatory to the Eucharist) which commemorate major saints, the most widely quoted of all Old Testament/deutero-canonical books is the Wisdom of Solomon.[17]

The popularity of the Wisdom of Solomon is easy to understand. Whereas the Old Testament is virtually silent about the fate of the wicked and the righteous in the after-life (the New Testament is not very much more explicit!), the Wisdom of Solomon deals with the subject in chapters 2–3, culminating in the passage:

But the souls of the righteous are in the hand of God, and no torment will ever touch them. In the eyes of the foolish they seemed to have died, and their departure was thought to be an affliction, and their going from us to be their destruction; but they are at peace (3:1–3).

That this reading was used at Orthodox commemorations of major saints and in Roman Catholic requiems is not surprising. And even the Church of England Prayer Books of 1549, 1552 and 1662 included the passage for Mattins on All Saints Day, while the *Alternative Service Book* of 1980 included it among the possible readings for Holy Communion 'At a Funeral'.

Another book to feature prominently in liturgies has been the Wisdom of Jesus ben Sirach (Ecclesiasticus). Verses such as 24:9: 'From eternity, in the beginning, he created me, and for eternity I shall not cease to exist,' and 24:3: 'I came forth from the mouth of the Most High . . .'

have been used in Roman Catholic liturgies of the Virgin Mary. In the Church of England, passages from Sirach are included for Communion services for 'Group Commemorations' (2:10–18 or 44:1–15), 'A Teacher' (39:1–10) or 'Any Saint' (2:1–6). In the Prayer Book of 1549 there was a charming reference in the Marriage service to the Story of Tobias:

> Looke, O Lord, mercifully upon them from heauen, and blesse them: And as thou diddest sende thy Aungell Raphaell to Thobie, and Sara, the daughter of Raguel, to their great comfort; so vouchsafe to send thy blessyng upon these thy seruauntes . . .

In the 1552 Prayer Book, this allusion to the Apocrypha was replaced by reference to Abraham and Sarah. It has already been noted that Church of England prayer books since 1549 have included a substantial part of the Song of the Three Young Men (an addition to Daniel 3:23) as the canticle 'Benedicite' at Mattins (see chapter 4).

Regarding the use of the Apocrypha in literature and art, the popular stories of Tobit, Judith, Susanna and Bel and the Dragon were sufficiently well known for writers such as Chaucer and Shakespeare to refer to them. Shylock's exclamation in *The Merchant of Venice* (IV.i), 'a Daniel come to judgement', is a reference to the Susanna story. Chaucer referred to Tobit and Tobias in the *Parson's Tale* (10.905–10), and themes from Tobit are found in paintings by Rembrandt, and at least ten other artists. The story of Judith is also much cited.[18]

On the musical front, Handel composed three oratorios using libretti based on the Apocrypha – *Judas Maccabaeus* (1747), *Alexander Balus* (1747–8) and *Susanna* (1748). In accordance with the political and theological use of the Bible in 18th-century England these oratorios had considerable political importance.[19] The year 1745 had seen a serious attempt of the Catholic House of Stuart to topple the Protestant Hanoverian royal house of England, and in 1747 England was at war with Catholic France. Preachers of the time equated the rejection of the house of Saul in the Old Testament with the ousting of James II in 1688, and Catholic Europe was equated with the Philistines. *Judas Maccabaeus*, which celebrated the Jewish victory over the Seleucids in 164 BCE, both reminded hearers of the recent victory of the Duke of Cumberland over the Jacobite rebels, and expressed anxiety in the time of war with France. Daniel, the hero of the Susanna story, and her deliverer, had long been regarded as a type or anticipation of Christ according to the Christological interpretation of the Old Testament.

As these brief comments indicate, it is only possible here to hint at aspects of a branch of study that has hardly begun to be explored seriously.

THE NEW TESTAMENT, WITH SPECIAL REFERENCE TO THE LIFE OF JESUS

The New Testament is a more sensitive area than the Old Testament and Apocrypha. Even very traditional Christian believers can accept that large parts of the Old Testament are not applicable to them, for example, the parts dealing with animal sacrifices. The New Testament, however, is central for Christian believers, containing as it does the accounts of the life and teaching of Jesus, and portraits (not always flattering ones) of the early Church. In the early centuries, the main arguments centring on the New Testament revolved around the development and articulation of the distinctive doctrines of Christianity, especially the Trinity, the divinity of Christ, and Christology with special reference to the relation between the human and the divine in Jesus.[20] The arguments were philosophical, theological and speculative, because the main challenges to Christian orthodoxy came either from Jewish circles that denied the divinity of Jesus or from Gnostic-type speculations that denied the humanity of Jesus. The one serious critical challenge came from Marcion of Pontus (*c.* 85–160) who, because he believed that the God of the Old Testament was different from the God revealed by Jesus, rejected the Old Testament and parts of the New Testament that contained or echoed the Old Testament. His canon of the New Testament therefore consisted of one Gospel (Luke) and ten Pauline letters, edited to remove 'Jewish' elements.

Once Christian orthodoxy had been largely established, the study of the New Testament centred upon such things as attempts to reform the

Church and Christian life in accordance with the simplicity of the life of Jesus, and in various monastic movements and revivals, and speculations about the end of the world, based upon the Book of Revelation. At the Reformation, the discovery or rediscovery of Paul's teaching on Justification by grace or faith profoundly affected the Church and theology.

It was not until the 17th century that an orthodoxy that had prevailed for more than a millennium began to be disturbed. The first disturbers, and then only indirectly, were the deists, for whom religion was not something supernaturally revealed, but something accessible to human reason, with special reference to morality. Furthermore, salvation depended upon following the moral dictates of reason. This, in effect, made the New Testament witness to Jesus superfluous. At best, Jesus was a moral authority who had been, or who was, obeyed by people who could not or did not use reason to discern what was right.

The philosopher Immanuel Kant (1724–1804), while not himself a deist, was a powerful exponent of the importance (and limitations) of human reason, and his verdict on aspects of the New Testament in his *The Conflict of the Faculties* (1798) well expresses some of the thinking of the times.[21] Accepting the distinction between the necessary truths of reason (i.e. truths that are true in any circumstances) and the contingent truths of history (i.e. truths limited to particular times and places, and which could be superseded), Kant subjected the New Testament (which he considered to be contingent) to investigation from the standpoint of necessary truths. Thus, Jesus was best understood as a fully moral human being who had done all that God could expect of him. Only if viewed in this way did it make sense to say that Jesus was an example to other human beings. Jesus did not expect to be resurrected after his death. If he had done so, he would have prepared his disciples better than he did for this eventuality, he would not have founded a memorial meal and would not have cried despairingly from the cross.

Kant's type of approach was embraced enthusiastically by some theologians. The young theological student W. M. L. de Wette who was later to be a pioneer in biblical criticism heard lectures in Jena in Germany in which the Gospels were stripped of their miraculous and supernatural elements, and Jesus was presented as a Kantian moral sage. So far, this did not involve any radical criticism of the Gospels themselves, but rather a rationalizing rereading of them in terms of contemporary philosophical understanding. However, the historical investigation of the Gospels was beginning in the 18th century with speculation about the oral and written sources behind the Gospels, and about the relation of the first three Gospels to each other. Matthew and John, the two supposed eye-witness Gospels, were the foundation for understanding the life of Jesus.[22]

This position was overturned towards the middle of the 19th century by the emergence of the view that Mark was the earliest gospel, and that Matthew and Luke were dependent upon Mark and upon a collection of sayings of Jesus, usually referred to as Q (see chapter 5) and which could be broadly reconstructed from material common to Matthew and Luke but not in Mark. At the same time, the reliability of John's Gospel was fiercely attacked by D. F. Strauss in his *Life of Jesus* (1835), a most radical work which left only the barest outlines of the life of Jesus intact. Strauss represented an extreme of criticism, and although his general position was not influential, his work had the effect of producing a consensus that lasted for over a century, which amounted to the view that Mark and the collection of sayings of Jesus (Q) did provide a reasonable basis for recovering the historical Jesus.

The remainder of the 19th and the first part of the 20th century proceeded to produce portraits of Jesus that were based on roughly the same evidence, but different according to the outlook and interest of the scholars involved. The so-called liberal Jesus of the late 19th century, who was primarily a teacher of the fatherhood of God and the brotherhood of man, was succeeded by the apocalyptic and eschatological Jesus represented in Albert Schweitzer's *Quest of the Historical Jesus* (1906). This Jesus expected the imminent end of the world and tried to induce its coming by dying on the cross. In the 1930s the eschatological aspect of Jesus's teaching was interpreted as 'realized eschatology'. It was not so much that Jesus expected an imminent end as that he proclaimed that the end was already present and that his ministry was a manifestation of this. C. H. Dodd's *The Parables of the Kingdom* (1935) was a classic statement of this view, and engendered a discussion that lasted for over twenty-five years in which realized eschatology was refined into such categories as 'proleptic eschatology' (the view that the end was present, but only in anticipation of a final consummation).

While this was going on in Germany and Britain, the form critical investigation of the Gospels in German was suggesting that far less could be known about Jesus than had been supposed. Form criticism analysed Gospel stories and sayings into basic components such as miracle stories and confrontation stories, and suggested that situations in the life of the early Church rather than in the ministry of Jesus had produced these elements as we have them in the Gospels. It also noted how material was grouped thematically rather than chronologically in the Gospels; for example, all the parables of Jesus in Mark's Gospel are collected together in chapter 4. This approach was long resisted in Britain and the United States, with the method being compared to cutting the string of a necklace and allowing the stones to scatter. As part of an emerging deal in England between the state and the churches in the 1940s, in which the state would take over the Church schools in return for religious instruction being a compulsory subject in state schools, it was believed that a moderate criticism of the Gospels would produce a reliable picture of a non-ecclesiastical Jesus who could be the basis of religious instruction in the secular setting of state schools. It is significant that Rudolf Bultmann's *The History of the Synoptic Tradition*, a classic work of form criticism first published in Germany in 1921, did not become available in English translation until 1968.

The discovery of the Dead Sea Scrolls beginning in 1947 shed new light on the Jewish matrix from which Christianity emerged, and further stimulated research into the historical Jesus. Earlier in the century it had been suggested that Jesus had been an Essene*, and it was now even suggested that he had been a member of the Qumran community. On the whole, such attempts to link Jesus with Qumran have failed, although recent New Testament scholarship has interpreted Jesus against his Jewish background, seeing him, to take one example, as actively opposed to the temple in Jerusalem and to its wealth and power.[23]

R. P. C. Hanson wrote some years ago that

the Church's interpretation of Jesus is inexplicable if we can know nothing about the historical Jesus and that the significance of the historical Jesus is irrecoverable if we reject the Church's interpretation of him.[24]

What he meant was that it would be incredible if Christianity as portrayed in the New Testament bore no relation to, or was a profound misunderstanding of, the historical Jesus; and that to say that there can be no access to the Jesus of history via the New Testament is to take scepticism to an extreme. On the other hand, the impact that Jesus has had on the history and civilization of the world has been via the Church and is the only impact of significance that there has been or is likely to be; and reconstructions of his life that differ radically from the broad lines of the Church's understanding are likely to be curiosities.

This is not to say that research on the Gospels should not be carried out, or that everything that the Church says about Jesus should be accepted uncritically. On the contrary, the figure of Jesus as studied critically by research into the New Testament sources and their background can speak powerfully to the modern world, as indicated by South American and other liberation* theologies which have drawn much strength from Jesus's solidarity with the poor and his opposition to the power structures of his day.

FUNDAMENTALISM

Fundamentalism is a diverse phenomenon with many different roots. Strictly speaking, it is a movement that began in the United States in the late 19th and early 20th centuries and which reads the Bible according to a particular interpretative scheme. But it has many looser forms, as well as roots that go back to what is known as Protestant scholasticism of the 16th and 17th centuries.

It has been pointed out earlier in the chapter that the study of the Bible has always been critical, that its difficulties in regard to science have been recognized for at least 1,500 years, and that medieval Jewish commentators suggested that some of the miracles, for example, that of Balaam's speaking she-ass, took place in visions rather than normal consciousness. Yet many ordinary readers of the Bible today still find it difficult to approach the Bible in a critical frame of mind. It is still widely held that the Bible is holy, and therefore must not in any way be questioned; and this reverent reading of the Bible is reinforced by devotional reading of the Bible as a guide to daily life, as well as the way it is used in worship in churches and in sermons. Consequently, fundamentalism in a loose sense has an abiding appeal and a ready-made constituency of adherents, such that highly intelligent people can apply to the Bible an unthinking literalism that they would not dream of applying to their own area of professional expertise.

It is not the intention of the preceding paragraph to poke fun at or pour scorn on the devotional use of the Bible, or its use by the Church in worship and evangelism. It is, however, my experience that many people are unhappy at being told that they must either accept everything that the Bible says or reject it altogether, and that there is no in-between position. They are often relieved, and can even be liberated, by discovering that the study of the Bible has always been critical and that it is no sin to ask intelligent questions about problems raised by the biblical text.

One of the reasons for this loose type of popular fundamentalism is ignorance of the way that 'books' were 'written' in the ancient world. It goes against modern experience to be told that a book such as Genesis was not written by one author but that it was composed in various stages by different authors/editors, and that some of the sources used can be more or less isolated from the final form of the text. Or, to highlight a different problem, it comes as a shock to people whose religious faith has been nourished on a text such as John 14:6: 'Jesus said to him, "I am the way, and the truth, and the life; no one comes to the Father, but by me,"' to learn that modern scholars, including ones who are convinced and practising Christians, hold that the words attributed to Jesus in John's Gospel are interpretations of his teaching rather than his actual words. Thus, unless ordinary readers of the Bible are given help in understanding why the Bible is studied critically in academic circles and what the reasons are for saying that John 14:6 does not record the actual words of Jesus, they will be potential recruits for the philosophy of 'either accept everything in the Bible or reject it completely'.

There is also another piece of history that needs to be accurately recorded, alongside the fact that the study of the Bible has always been critical. It is natural to suppose that the academic study of the Bible is conducted almost solely in secular university departments. It is then easy to blame these secular institutions for being divorced from the life and needs of the Church, and to accuse them of studying the Bible in the light of secular rather than theological principles. All would be well, it is implied, if the study of the Bible could be reinstated as the study of Holy Scripture in theological institutions.

This overlooks some important points. The modern critical method originated in Protestant German theological faculties and is today carried on in Protestant and Catholic faculties in countries such as Germany, France, the Netherlands, Austria and Switzerland. In Britain up to the beginning of the Second World War most of the academic study of the Bible was undertaken in England in theological colleges, not university departments. If the balance has now swung away from Church theological colleges to secular university departments in England and Wales (but not Scotland), this does not mean the isolation of the latter from needs pertinent to the churches. In fact, the university departments have been much more open to developments such as Liberation Theology than have the churches, and it is secular university departments that have pioneered and offered courses to clergy in pastoral theology and industrial theology. Again, in the United States and Australia, the great bulk of critical biblical scholarship is done in theological institutions rather than state universities.

So far, the discussion has centred on what can loosely be called 'popular fundamentalism', that is, a kind of gut reaction against the findings of biblical criticism arising, as much as anything, from ignorance of the history and development of the study of the Bible. Fundamentalism takes on sharper lines when it is encountered in its theological forms. Two strands will now be followed. The first goes back to the aftermath of the Continental Reformation and its residual effects in Britain, the second concerns the rise of Fundamentalism proper in the United States and its influence in Britain.

In the aftermath of the Reformation, with Protestant churches needing to defend themselves against the Roman Catholic Church and against each other, rigid doctrinal positions were developed which depended upon proof texts taken from the Bible. Among the doctrinal positions adopted was the view that the Bible was verbally inspired by God and that it was therefore infallible and free from error. By verbally inspired was meant that God, through the Holy Spirit, had been involved in the process of writing in such a way that God could be said to be the author of every word. If God was the author of every word, it follows that the Bible could contain no errors. This position naturally left scope for discussion about whether the biblical writers were simply dictating machines whose personalities were overruled in the composition process, or whether God used their individual gifts and styles to achieve the final outcome.

Statements embodying such views of the inspiration and infallibility of the Bible were embodied in Articles and Confessions of various churches. Interestingly, the 39 Articles of the Church of England stated only that the Bible contained 'all things necessary to salvation' and made no observations about its inspiration or infallibility. The same was not true of the Westminster Confession of Faith drawn up during Puritan rule of England in 1648. This listed the books of the Bible, not including the Apocrypha, adding: 'All of which are given by inspiration of God to be the rule of faith and life.' The Confession added statements about 'our full persuasion and assurance of the infallible truth and divine authority of the Bible', and also stated:

The Old Testament in Hebrew, and the New Testament in Greek, being immediately inspired by God, and, by his singular case and providence, kept pure in all ages, are therefore authentical.[25]

This Confession was adopted by the Church of Scotland and by various synods in America in the 17th and 18th centuries.

However, we are not simply dealing here with a view of the inspiration of the Bible. The various Confessions also contained doctrines about the Fall of Mankind through the agency of the devil, and of redemption only by faith in the vicarious death of Christ on the cross, who had borne the penalty of sin, and opened access to God. The coming of the suffering and atoning Messiah was prophesied in the Old Testament, and the Old Testament also contained types that pointed towards the coming of Christ. Further, as will be shown in the final chapter, the Old Testament in particular was believed to be binding upon Christians at least as far as its moral laws were concerned. Belief in the infallibility of the Bible was part of a particular way of reading the Bible and of understanding Christian doctrine, and was not an end in itself.

Biblical criticism in its modern, late 18th-century, sense originated in Lutheran Germany because there developed in Germany a tradition of a speculative philosophy and theology that was willing to be adventurous and creative in interpreting Christianity in the post-Enlightenment world. The British tradition of philosophy was analytic rather than speculative, and its theological tradition was rigid rather than adventurous. Thus, although the deists of 17th- and 18th-century Britain had a low estimate of the Old Testament, they contributed nothing directly to biblical criticism. Further, 19th-century Church life in England was strongly influenced by two conservative movements – an Evangelical revival which went back to 18th-century Methodism and the Catholic movement within the Church of England known as the Oxford Movement*.

When it first began to be known in Britain, German biblical criticism was rejected because it seemed to undermine belief in the infallibility of the Bible as well as some aspects of received Christian doctrine. Several different types of anxiety can be identified. First, if biblical books came about through long and complex processes of editing and redaction, how could they be said to be inspired by God? Beliefs such as those embodied in the Westminster Confession implied that God had directly inspired particular writers, whom tradition identified as Moses, Joshua, Samuel, David, Isaiah, Matthew, John and Paul, to name some. Thus, suggestions that biblical books were not written by individuals identified in tradition were seen as an indirect attack on belief in their inspiration and authority.

A second anxiety was that if biblical criticism was correct about the authorship of the Pentateuch, then Jesus was wrong. In Mark 10:3 Jesus explicitly attributes Deuteronomy 24:1–4 to Moses. If he was wrong, did not that impugn his divinity? A third anxiety was that biblical criticism undermined the prophetic links between the Old and New Testaments. The traditional Christian scheme of biblical interpretation said that Isaiah 52:13–53:12 was a prophecy of the vicarious death of Christ on the cross. Biblical criticism said that the figure referred to was an Israelite of the time of Isaiah chapters 52–3 (mid-6th century BCE) or possibly the prophet himself.

One of the reasons why popular fundamentalism continues to be a factor in churches today is that the doctrinal position with which belief in biblical infallibility was bound up continues to be taught in churches. While biblical criticism gradually won acceptance in Britain from the 1860s in intellectual and academic circles, the doctrinal position with which infallibility was connected continued to be taught even in churches which were open to biblical criticism. Indeed, there is not necessarily a contradiction between accepting the results of biblical criticism, and according high authority to the Bible and some of the traditional ways of interpreting it. However, such a position requires sophistication, and clergy are often not able or willing to embrace such sophistication. They often prefer to deal with congregations at the level of 'simple faith', ignoring in the process the considerable desire of 'simple believers' to ask radical questions and to have them answered.

There is also another factor, which brings this section to the second strand, that of the influence of 'genuine' American fundamentalism, which has also influenced, and continues to influence, British Church life via evangelistic crusades, books and satellite radio and television programmes. George Marsden has identified several factors that were crucial in the development of American fundamentalism.[26] The first was the common sense philosophy that regarded the Bible as a datum rather like the natural phenomena investigated by physics. It was no more legitimate to question the Bible than it would be to question light.

Second, the threats of Darwinism and of German biblical criticism engendered a pessimistic mood in American evangelicalism that saw post-millennianism replaced by pre-millennialism. Post-millennianism was the optimistic view that the present age (millennium) was one in which Satan was being defeated and that it would culminate in the return of Christ once the process was complete. Pre-millennialism saw the present age more pessimistically and believed that Christ would return to defeat Satan and then inaugurate the millennium. These positions were based upon interpretations of the latter parts of Daniel and of Revelation, and they also divided history in general and biblical history in particular into dispensations. The third factor was the rise of holiness and pentecostal* movements with their emphasis on individual conversion experience, growth in holiness and evangelistic outreach. An interesting piece of cross-fertilization from England to America was the Keswick* Holiness Movement. As Marsden observes, the importance of the holiness and pentecostal movements was that they accepted, in accordance with pre-millennialism, that the present age was the site of a cosmic struggle between good and evil at national and international levels, but that at the personal, individual level, the Holy Spirit was being poured out upon those who turned to God and who obeyed his laws. The moral code for holiness was supplied by the Old and New Testaments. From the 1870s to the 1980s there were periodic but regular evangelistic campaigns conducted in Britain by American evangelists, and while it would be wrong to say that all these evangelists held identical beliefs, they were all fundamentalists in the sense that they preached a gospel of individual salvation based upon doctrines that included the inerrancy of the Bible. Also, the Keswick Movement in Britain, which continues to this day, maintained a tradition of holiness preaching involving obedience to God's laws as revealed in the Bible.

The term 'fundamentalism' is derived from a series of paperback volumes published from 1910 to 1915. Although the volumes covered a number of subjects, something like a third of the articles that appeared defended the Bible against biblical criticism. But fundamentalism was (or is) not simply about the infallibility of the Bible. This belief was bound up with other doctrines, and was re-expressed in terms of individual salvation and holiness which in turn were set within a framework of understanding a world history in which the Holy Spirit was active now in anticipation of the return of Christ to defeat Satan. As has been indicated in this section, American fundamentalism did not invent belief in the Bible's infallibility, nor should what I have loosely called 'popular fundamentalism' in Britain be necessarily equated with it, even though it may in some times and at some places be affected by American fundamentalism. Ultimately, 'fundamentalism' is a complex and varied phenomenon with many causes. It often springs from a basic human need, in a violent and ambiguous world, to hold on to something firm, which makes sense of life, and which gives hope. This is also why fundamentalism is no longer simply a western phenomenon but the major understanding of the Bible among black churches in Britain and North America, and in countries such as Korea, Central and Latin America, and parts of Africa, where the Protestant churches in their pentecostal form are growing rapidly. These churches, untouched by the Enlightenment in Europe and thus by biblical criticism, have mostly been founded by fundamentalist missionaries from Europe and North America, and clearly meet the needs of the particular cultures in which they flourish.

RECENT DEVELOPMENTS IN BIBLICAL STUDIES

The fundamentalist reaction to biblical criticism is a reaction to the Enlightenment world view that gave birth to biblical criticism in its 18th–20th-century form. This Enlightenment view made human reason the touchstone for judging the truth or falsity of things, including the Bible and the traditional doctrines of Christianity. The Enlightenment view has been subjected to severe criticism in recent decades, for two reasons. First, although the primacy of human reason has given many benefits to humankind, especially in the conquering of diseases and medical conditions that were once fatal, it has also produced movements such as Stalinist totalitarianism and Nazi fascism, not to mention acquisitive capitalism, all of which have oppressed rather than liberated humankind. Second, the Enlightenment reason that was the touchstone of truth was the reason of European and North American intellectual males who were in positions of power. It did not include women or non-whites or the oppressed and underprivileged.

Two of the most important developments in recent biblical studies have emerged from questionings of the Enlightenment view of reason, and although they have been dependent upon biblical criticism as it has been outlined in this book, they have also criticized it. Liberation Theology has emerged from the struggles of the poor against powerful right-wing regimes in Central and Latin America and from the opposition of black and coloured people to apartheid in Southern Africa. Feminism, on the other hand, has come from intellectual white women in North America and Europe. On the face of it, there is a contradiction between this statement about Central and Latin America and Southern Africa and what was said above about fundamentalism in these countries. In fact, the leading theorists of Liberation Theology have been people trained in the western tradition of critical scholarship and, in Latin America, they have been Catholics rather than Protestants.

In spite of their diverse origins, Liberation Theology and feminism have several things in common. First, they are critical of the western, male and privileged version of reason that has been responsible for biblical criticism. Second, they both exist in several versions, ranging from the view that the Bible can be used positively to support feminist and liberation aims, to the view that the Bible's only value, since it was produced by males in positions of power, is to show how men and women have been oppressed by males.[27] In practice, the two approaches have emphasized different methodologies among those available within biblical studies.

A starting-point of Liberation Theology is that the authentic voice of the Bible can be heard only in solidarity with the poor and oppressed. Attention is drawn to the Exodus story in which God liberated the Hebrews from slavery in Egypt, and to the critiques by the prophets of social injustice and oppression in ancient Israel. An implication of this is that terms such as 'salvation' in the Bible, which were traditionally held to apply only to the after-life, are seen to relate to today's world, and oblige Christians actively to oppose poverty and injustice. With regard to the New Testament, Liberation Theology emphasizes Jesus's solidarity with the poor and understands incidents such as the cleansing of the temple (Matthew 21:12–13 and parallels), when Jesus drove out the traders and money-changers, as an attack on a political and financial system that enabled powerful interests in Jerusalem to exploit the ordinary people.

Liberation Theology has mostly used the tools of biblical criticism in its work, and especially archaeology, historical criticism and social theory, in an attempt to reconstruct the social realities of ancient Israel and the early Church. In the process, light has been thrown on passages that were often neglected by biblical scholarship. For example, it is well known that the sin of Sodom was an attempted public homosexual orgy (Genesis 19:4–11). But liberation theologians have drawn attention to another passage that defines the sin of Sodom, that at Ezekiel 16:49: 'Behold, this was the guilt of your sister Sodom: she and her daughters had pride, surfeit of food, and prosperous ease, but did not aid the poor and needy.'

A New Testament instance of a type of Liberation Theology (called socio-materialist theology by some) is the German New Testament scholar Louise Schottroff's treatment of the Parable of the Labourers in the Vineyard (Matthew 20:1–16).[28] The story concerns a householder who engages day labourers to work at an agreed rate for twelve hours gathering the grape harvest. Additional workers are employed at the third, sixth, ninth and eleventh hours and, to the amazement and annoyance of those who worked for twelve hours, all the workers receive the same wage. The usual, theological, interpretation of the parable is that the workers all receive the same wage because, in the Kingdom of Heaven, the love of God cannot be divided up into portions according to length of service. Schottroff interprets the parable in the light of the unfavourable employment conditions for day labourers in the time of Jesus, where employers could drive hard bargains and employ casual labour for next to nothing.

In practice, Liberation Theology has arrived at a more positive estimate of the recoverability of the history and social background to the Old and New Testaments than some of the more established biblical criticism. For example, the figure of Jesus emerges solidly. Also, Liberation Theology has to privilege certain parts of the Bible as against other parts, although this has been standard practice in the Church as the final chapter will indicate. Thus, accounts such as 1 Kings 4:22–8, listing the lavish food provision for Solomon's court without any criticism, are hardly suitable material for supporting the struggle of the poor, and the whole language about kingship as applied to God is not a helpful mode of expression. There can be no doubt, however, that Liberation Theology has made a profound and lasting impression upon biblical studies.

The same is true of feminist criticism. This has not entirely ignored historical and sociological methods: and one line of feminist investigation had been to recover the lost or suppressed story of women in ancient

Israel and the early Church. Much feminist criticism has, however, worked with the final form of the text and has used literary methods related to character, plot and genres such as tragedy to approach the text from a feminine angle. Much attention has been focused upon the opening chapters of Genesis, given that they have been understood to endorse the superiority of male over female in according with 1 Timothy 2:13−15.[29] Feminist approaches that hold that the text can still be meaningful for Christian women readers have argued that Genesis 1−2 indicates the essential equality and complementarity of the sexes; and there have been sympathetic studies of Old Testament women including Hagar, Ruth, Miriam and Deborah. In studies of the New Testament it has been argued that Jesus was virtually unique in Judaism in having women disciples (Luke 10:39 and 8:1−3), and that he showed solidarity with women as well as with the poor.

An interesting recent development is that feminism has been accused of being anti-Jewish. It is a commonplace of feminist Old Testament writing that Old Testament society was patriarchal and oppressive to women, and that the women who gain prominence in the Old Testament do so only on male terms. The charge that this is anti-Jewish has been particularly keenly felt in Germany, for obvious reasons, and steps have been taken to try to discover a feminism that is not anti-Jewish.[30]

The final development to be considered in this section is the use of new literary methods. Whereas biblical criticism as it developed from the late 18th century became concerned with how the Bible had reached its final form from small units of tradition and larger literary sources, the new literary criticism has concentrated upon the final form of the text. Again, whereas biblical criticism saw discovering the original intention of the biblical writers as the starting-point of responsible interpretation, the newer criticism has used notions such as presumed author, narrator and presumed reader, taken from modern literary criticism, as a key to interpretation.[31] Traditional biblical criticism concerned itself with the text; newer approaches have investigated readers of texts and reading processes, noting that how a text is read depends on who is doing the reading and according to what interest. At this point there is some contact with liberation and feminist approaches, since these are readings from the standpoint of clearly identified interests.

Two simple illustrations will give the flavour of the newer approaches. First, it was noted above that the study of the Synoptic Gospels concluded that Mark was the earliest gospel, and that Matthew and Luke used Mark and a Sayings of Jesus source. The attempt to penetrate back to the historical Jesus tended sometimes to treat these Gospels not as texts in their own right but as containers of traditions whose only value was as possible evidence for the historical Jesus. The newer criticism would take a Gospel such as Matthew, and treat it as a text in its own right, looking for literary markers and patterns within it as a clue, not so much to the author's intention, as to the meaning of the text. Such an approach differs from what is called redaction criticism, which attempts to discover the author's intention by comparing Matthew with its source Mark, and seeing what changes were made by Matthew and why.

A second example can be taken from the Exodus story in Exodus 7–12. In these chapters there are verses that say that God hardened the heart of Pharaoh so that he would not let the Israelites go (cp. 7:3, 14, 8:19, 9:12, 10:1, 10:20, 27, 11:10), while other verses say that he hardened his own heart (cp. 8:15, 32, 9:34). Traditional biblical criticism has regarded such apparent inconsistencies as evidence for the existence of different sources, which it has then tried to isolate. The newer criticism, taking the final form of the text, would see the differences not as inconsistencies, but as a wrestling within the text with the problem of human freewill and divine providence. One of the implications of newer literary approaches is that God in the Old Testament and Jesus in the New Testament are not extra-linguistic realities to whom the text refers, but characters in pieces of literature. This does not mean that such readings are anti-theological; and they are almost always illuminating. It does mean, however, that they raise questions about the relationship between texts and the world, which must not be overlooked.

This chapter has tried to indicate something of the enormous diversity of the study of the Bible, a diversity that derives from the many sub-cultures in which it is used. These sub-cultures include ordinary church-goers, mainstream academic critical scholars, members of fundamentalist (e.g. evangelistic, charismatic and holiness) churches, feminist theologians, liberation theologians, practitioners of various literary approaches. It says much for the Bible that, having been subjected to minute critical analysis that no other text, let alone a religious text, has had to suffer, it continues to receive so much attention from so many different quarters.

CHAPTER 8

The Use of the Bible

Readers of this chapter who have heard or seen radio and television debates which have included representatives of churches, may well have got the impression that all that one has to do in using the Bible in ethics is to discover an appropriate text and apply it to the matter at hand. Indeed, the impression is often created, whether intentionally or not, that this rather mechanical way of using the Bible in ethics is the only one that is 'true' to the Bible; and at the level of what I have called in the previous chapter 'popular fundamentalism', many ordinary Christians find it difficult to resist the argument that if something is commanded in the Bible then it should be obeyed or observed.

The aim of the present chapter is to set the debate about how the Bible might be used in ethics in an historical context. Just as the study of the Bible has always been critical, so its use in ethics has always been sophisticated. Recognition of this is a necessary prerequisite for contemporary positive use of the Bible, an outline of which will conclude the chapter.

Because it comes from the ancient world, the Bible says nothing about many contemporary problems. Those who seek guidance on whether it is legitimate to manufacture weapons of mass destruction as a deterrent, or whether building an airport runway is more important than preserving the habitat of threatened species of wildlife, will get no direct help from the Bible. This is no surprise. What does come as a surprise to some people, however, is that within its own setting in the life of ancient Israel and the early Church, the Bible did not address many issues that needed resolution. The laws in the Old Testament say nothing about marriage, divorce, adoption, or how to gain redress against a physician for injuries received during medical treatment, or redress against the builder of a faulty house or defective boat. All of these matters are dealt with in the laws of Hammurabi* (*c.* 1,800 BCE). It is true that divorce is mentioned in Deuteronomy 24:1–4, but this is only in passing, the main point being that a man may not remarry his divorced wife who in the meantime has re-married and has then been divorced or widowed.[1]

In orthodox Judaism the problem of the inadequate coverage of Old Testament law for regulating a society is met by the belief that two laws were delivered to Moses by God on Mount Sinai: a written law embodied in the Pentateuch, and an oral law passed down by a chain of teachers from Moses to the present day. The oral law, hints of which can be found in the Bible outside the Pentateuch, is contained in the Mishnah*, the Tosephta* and the Babylonian and Jerusalem Talmuds*, and, as interpreted today by experts in conjunction with the written law, it enables an observant orthodox Jew to regulate every aspect of daily life in accordance with what is believed to be the will of God.[2] The situation in Roman Catholicism is not dissimilar. Catholic ethical teaching combines what there is in the Bible with natural law, that is, the belief that God has revealed through natural human institutions and social arrangements principles that can be applied to modern ethical problems.[3] The point that is underlined by these two examples is that if the Bible can be applied directly to ethical problems, this can only be done for a limited number of topics.

However, it is now necessary to note that, apparently, the New Testament writers handled the laws in the Old Testament with a good deal of freedom. The outstanding instance of this is Acts 15, which records decisions of a meeting in Jerusalem between Paul and Barnabas on the one hand, and Peter and James the leaders of the Jerusalem Church, on the other hand. The issue was whether non-Jews who became Christians should observe the Jewish law, and the decision was that they should observe only three 'necessary things'. They should abstain from what had been sacrificed to idols, from blood (i.e. they should eat only meat from which the blood had been drained at the time of the slaughter of the animal – what is today called 'kosher' meat), and from unchastity (Acts 15:20, 29).[4]

Whether or not this meeting actually took place is immaterial.[5] The writer of Acts believed that it had taken place, and that it had been decided that non-Jews who became Christians were not required to observe the Old Testament laws. An interesting question arising from Acts 15 is whether Christians who use the Bible as a guide to life should eat only kosher meat. In my experience of teaching many students from conservative church backgrounds, this is a question that they have never been required to face, and which causes them some embarrassment. It is, in fact, an instance of what is often the case with modern conservative churches, that they have adopted secular middle-class values generally, and concentrate their concern to be faithful to the Bible selectively on matters of private, usually sexual, morality. Yet Acts 15 has been taken seriously in the history of the Church, as binding upon Christians. Adam Clarke, in his commentary on the New Testament of 1817, devoted no fewer than seven pages to extensive quotations from P. Delany's *Revelation examined with candour* of 1745–63, in which Delany defended the injunction of Acts 15 against eating blood with the flesh of creatures as a prohibition 'expressly assigned by God himself', and summed up as 'A command given by God himself to Noah, repeated to Moses, ratified by the apostles of Jesus Christ'.[6]

Another interesting instance of New Testament handling of Old Testament laws concerns the matter of slavery. Laws in Deuteronomy 15:12–18 require that male and female slaves should be released after six years unless they agree to serve for life, with their decision being publicly witnessed (cp. Exodus 21:5–6). Another law in Deuteronomy 23:15–16 makes it an offence to return an escaped slave to his master. In all that is said about slavery in the New Testament, no mention is ever made of the obligation that slaves should be released after six years. Slave owners are simply told to treat their slaves as servants of a God who shows no partiality (cp. Ephesians 6:9). Furthermore, if the interpretation of Philemon is correct, according to which Paul sent back the slave Onesimus to his master (cp. Philemon 16), then he was ignoring the injunction at Deuteronomy 23:15–16. These are, of course, arguments from silence, but the inconsistencies at least raise questions that need to be answered.[7]

Attention can also be drawn to the attitude of Jesus to Old Testament law, as presented in the Gospels. If John 7:53–8:11 is part of the Bible (it is not present in the earliest papyri and manuscripts and is variously placed by others after Luke 21:38, John 7:36 or 21:24), it shows Jesus abrogating the law in Deuteronomy 22:23–4, which prescribes stoning as the penalty for a betrothed virgin caught in the act of adultery. By saying that only those without sin can carry out the stoning, Jesus says, in effect, that the sentence cannot be carried out. Again, whereas the Old Testament allows a man to divorce his wife, the Church, rightly or wrongly, has taken Mark 10:2–12 to mean that Jesus taught that there should be no divorce.[8] In Matthew 5:17–48, Jesus replaces the Old Testament law of 'An eye for an eye' with 'Do not resist one who is evil' (5:38), and by redefining murder in terms of anger and adultery in terms of lust, makes it impossible for any normal person not to break these commandments.

Turning to the positive ethical teaching of the New Testament, in Romans 12:1–13:14 there are various ethical injunctions drawn from the Old Testament and other sources that command generosity, hospitality, forgiveness, obedience to lawful authority and observance of parts of the Ten Commandments, summed up in the golden rule: 'You shall love your neighbour as yourself.' This teaching can be fairly described as oriented towards individuals who are urged to be generally law-abiding citizens whose behaviour will not bring Christianity into disrespect.

The story of the use of the Bible in ethics up to the Reformation can be summed up under several headings.[9] First, there is a general reliance upon ethics and law as developed in Greek philosophy (especially Stoicism) and Roman law, with attention to 'natural law', that is, what can be deduced from human institutions and arrangements. Second, the particular contribution of the New Testament is to provide a model of discipleship based upon the life of Jesus, and emphasizing the supreme importance of love. When the persecution of the Church ceased in the early 4th century, the ideal of Christian discipleship passed from martyrdom (the imitation of Christ's death on the cross) to asceticism and monasticism (the imitation of Christ's poverty). Third, the use of the Old Testament law underwent a change from almost complete neglect to one of partial rehabilitation, that became important for a section of the Reformation. This issue will now be addressed in slightly more detail.

Granted that the Old Testament contains far more regulations than the New Testament, even if its coverage is far from complete, it was almost totally neglected in the post-New Testament era in treatises on Christian living. There may have been several reasons for this. First, there was the fear initially that converts might be attracted to Judaism. Secondly, early Christian interpreters of the Old Testament allegorized it, seeing its meaning as lying below the surface. The Epistle of Barnabas, for example, takes the prohibition of eating certain kinds of meat (cp. Leviticus 11:2–47, Deuteronomy 14:3–21) as a command not to associate with certain types of human beings.[10] Also, in one regard, and perhaps for the reasons just given, the early Church deliberately ignored the clear command and creation ordinance of Exodus 20:8–11 that the sabbath (i.e. Friday evening to Saturday evening) should be kept holy.

When, from around the 5th–6th centuries CE, there was a shift back towards taking some Old Testament laws seriously in the Christian Church, this was done according to dispensational schemes. One such was to distinguish between laws given before the incident of the Israelites making the Golden Calf (Exodus 32) and laws given after this time. The great bulk, though not all, of the laws on sacrifice and priesthood occur after Exodus 32, and thus it was argued in the *Apostolical Constitutions** that the laws given after Exodus 32 were given because of and to remedy Israel's apostasy in making the Golden Calf. Thus, laws before Exodus 32 could be binding upon Christians, but that those given after Exodus 32 were not.[11] Another form of dispensationalism, found in Cyril of Alexandria (c. 380–444), was based upon Leviticus 19:23–5. This law prohibits the eating of the fruit of a newly planted fruit tree for its first three years. In the fourth year it must be used as an offering of praise to God. Only from the fifth year may the fruit be eaten. The three years are taken to mean the period of Moses, Joshua and the Judges, while the fourth year represents the purification of the law by the prophets prior to the fifth year, representing the law of Christ. This view seems to value the moral teaching of the prophets more highly than that of the Law in the Old Testament.[12]

In the later Middle Ages, and because of renewed contact between Christian biblical scholars and Jews in Europe, a more positive view of the value of the Old Testament laws began to emerge. An important influence was that of Maimonides (see chapter 7) who, among other things, proposed a rational basis for the laws as excellent instances of hygiene, and as instruments for preserving the Israelites from paganism. Maimonides's works were studied by Christian theologians, including Aquinas (*c.* 1225–74).

Two aspects of Aquinas's use of the Bible will be mentioned: first, his treatment of the sacrificial laws of the Old Testament; second, his application of natural law.[13] Following Maimonides, Aquinas regarded the Old Testament laws as perfectly fitted for what they were intended to do, namely, to preserve Israel from paganism and idolatry and to engender reverence for God. Because, for Christian belief, the death of Christ had rendered sacrifices unnecessary, Old Testament laws on this subject were not binding on Christians; but this did not mean that Christians should ignore or lightly regard them. They were important in their own right as God's provision for Israel, and they also pointed forward, typologically, to Christ's death. Aquinas's work entailed that, although the spiritual senses of the Bible were not assailed, the literal sense was granted more respect.

On natural law, Aquinas divided the Old Testament laws, as had been done before him and was to be done after him, into three classes: moral, ceremonial and civil. The moral laws of the Old Testament embodied natural law, and to that extent were universally binding. The civil and ceremonial laws could also be seen as particular applications of natural law, directed to the specific situation of ancient Israel. In their particularity they were not universally binding, although the principles of natural law that they enshrined would be binding. This approach to using the Bible was, therefore, highly sophisticated and based upon a general theory of ethics, Aquinas's understanding of natural law going back ultimately to Aristotle.

The distinction between moral, civil and ceremonial laws was taken in to sections of the Reformation and officially expressed in the 39 Articles of the Church of England as follows:

Although the Law given from God by Moses, as touching Ceremonies and Rites, do not bind Christian men, nor the Civil precepts thereof ought of necessity to be received in any commonwealth; yet notwithstanding, no Christian man whatsoever is free from the obedience of the Commandments which are called Moral (Article VII).

However, this kind of distinction assumes that it is possible to distinguish between the different types of law. That this was not so easy can be illustrated from attitudes to the sabbath law among the Reformers.

Is the sabbath law a moral commandment or a ceremonial commandment? If it is the latter, then it is not binding upon Christians according to the representative formulation in the 39 Articles. This appears to have been the view of the main Reformers, who also rejected the view that the Catholic Church had the power to substitute Sunday for the sabbath. Tyndale is quoted as saying:

we be lords over the Saboth and may yet change it into the Monday, or any other day, as we see need . . . Neither needed we any holy day at all, if the people might be taught without it.[14]

Calvin similarly held that it was up to the local church to decide which day of the week should be the Lord's day, and is reported to have played bowls on a Sunday. Luther regarded any ecclesiastical coercion to regard a particular day as holy as an affront to Christian liberty.[15]

So far, the view that the sabbath law was a ceremonial law has been considered. But what if it was taken to be a moral law? Where the Bible was believed to be the supreme authority and it was believed that no church had the power to alter its teaching, those who took the sabbath commandment to be a moral law (and a creation ordinance) held that it should be obeyed to the letter, and that God required the sabbath (i.e. Friday evening to Saturday evening) to be honoured. Thus there emerged early in the 17th century in England a Seventh-day Sabbatarian movement which was also taken by English non-conformists to America later in the century.[16] The debate over the interpretation of the sabbath law continued throughout the 17th century in England and produced, on the anti-sabbatarian side, some surprisingly liberal responses. Thus, Gabriel Towerson stressed that the sabbath, whenever it was observed, should have a social aspect:

take away all Recreation, and you make the Sabbath to afford little Refreshment to Servants, and other such Labouring People, for whose Benefit we find it to have been in a great measure design'd.[17]

If this sounds very much at odds with Sunday Sabbatarianism as it later developed, especially in parts of Scotland, this is because the Reformation in Britain proceeded along Reformed (i.e. Calvinist) lines rather than along Lutheran lines. Lutheranism stressed that the Bible was not primarily a law book but a witness to the Gospel; and there was always the fear that observance of biblical laws would become a form of justification by works. The other side of the Reformation saw things differently. Martin Bucer (1491–1551), for example, while accepting that

we being free in Christ are not bound by the civil law of Moses any more than by the ceremonial laws given to ancient Israel as they pertain to external circumstances and elements of the world,

went on to say that

since there can be no laws more honorable, righteous, and wholesome than those which God, himself, who is eternal wisdom and goodness, enacted, if only they are applied under God's judgement to our own affairs and activities, I do not see why Christians, in matters which pertain to their own doings, should not follow the laws of God more than those of any men.[18]

The implication of this was that Bucer wished to legislate as much of the Old Testament as possible upon 16th-century Protestant England, with the death penalty prescribed for capital offences, blasphemy, violation of the sabbath (Sunday), adultery, rape and false testimony.

Another type of thinking that conditioned the approach to using the Bible was the covenant theology in Britain of the 16th–17th centuries. According to this, there were two covenants: a covenant of works and a covenant of grace. The first was made by God with Adam at creation and was binding on all mankind. However, the fall of humankind and the entry of sin into the world made it impossible for the covenant of works to be fulfilled. To remedy this, the covenant of grace was given, the effect of which was to redeem mankind from sin and to make it possible for the covenant of works to be effective. Thus, the Old Testament in particular indicated how God wished human society and daily life to be ordered.[19]

This covenant theology does not differ in essence from the position maintained today by evangelicals, with the important difference, as will be illustrated later, that it is possible to enforce much less of the Old Testament on society in the 20th century than it was in the 17th. Thus, the view known as 'creation ethics' holds that the Bible reveals God's will for his creation as a kind of 'maker's instructions'.[20] Among the creation ordinances cited by creation ethics is Genesis 2:24: 'Therefore a man leaves his father and his mother and cleaves to his wife, and they become one flesh.' This is held to reveal God's will for human relationships – 'one man-one woman – for keeps' as one writer has put it.[21] From a New Testament angle, passages such as Ephesians 5:22, 'Wives, be subject to your husbands, as to the Lord', are taken to teach the 'headship' of husbands over wives, and to indicate a leading role for males, especially in the Church.

In what follows, it will be argued that this way of using the Bible is unsatisfactory, and that it detracts from, rather than does justice to, the ethical content of the Bible.

The first reason for rejecting the creation ethics approach is that it fails to take seriously the social and historical setting of the Bible. Old Testament society was polygamous, and if Genesis 2:24 teaches 'one man-one woman – for keeps' then many prominent Old Testament figures either did not know or did not observe the injunction. Among figures with more than one wife, and without any condemnation in the Bible, are Abraham, Jacob, Elkanah (father of Samuel), David and Solomon, while it could be argued that Moses had more than one wife (Numbers 12:1, cp. Exodus 2:21) and that the various minor judges (Judges 10:3–4, 12:8–15) with thirty sons and thirty daughters also had more than one wife. It can be argued, of course, that in Mark 10:2–9 Jesus affirmed Genesis 2:24 as the pattern for human relationships; but it then has to be asked whether the saying would have been understood in terms of monogamy. Judaism has never formally repudiated polygamy, although Western Jews observe the temporary abrogation of polygamy by Gershom ben Judah of Metz around *c.* 1000 CE.[22] The 17th-century opponents of Seventh-day Sabbatarianism were certainly sensitive to the issue of polygamy versus monogamy, with one writer saying that the

Judaizing practice of observing the seventh day should cease 'unless a Woman may lawfully have two Husbands at the same time'.[23]

A second reason for rejecting the modern conservative use of the Bible in ethics is that while it claims to uphold biblical standards against the encroaching tide of secularism, it does not in practice do this, but conforms gradually to secular ethics. Several examples can be given. First, the death penalty for capital offences can be said to be a creation ordinance (Genesis 9:6), and advocates of the death penalty have appealed to the passage. Yet many countries have abolished the death penalty, regarding it as inappropriate in a civilized society. The death penalty for capital offences has thus joined other parts of the Old Testament, such as those advocating the death penalty for striking or cursing one's parents (Exodus 21:15,17), violating the sabbath (Numbers 15:32–6) or committing adultery (Deuteronomy 22:23–4) as injunctions no longer suitable in a civilized society.

A second instance of the Bible being conformed to secular values regards marriage between a man and his deceased wife's sister. Such marriage was long regarded in the Church as contrary to God's law as contained in Leviticus 18 and 20. The 'Table of Kindred and Affinity' that was printed at the conclusion of the Book of Common Prayer listing those who were 'forbidden in Scripture and our laws to marry together' included as number 17, 'Wife's sister'. The theory was that because people who married became 'one flesh' (Genesis 2:24), forbidden sexual relationships needed to include close relatives of a person to whom anyone was married. In the late 19th century, a move to have this particular law changed was bitterly opposed in Parliament by the Church of England as an attempt to legislate something contrary to the law of God. Eventually, the law was changed in 1907 in spite of ecclesiastical opposition, and civil law and Church law remained in conflict until the latter was revised after the Second World War to allow a man to marry his deceased wife's sister.[24] Books of Common Prayer published after that date contained a revised 'Table of Kindred and Affinity' which not only omitted 'wife's sister' from the prohibited degrees of marriage, but any reference to the prohibited degrees being 'forbidden in Scripture'.

A third reason for rejecting the modern conservative approach is that it is selective in its use of biblical material. Reference has already been made to the fact that Acts 15 clearly teaches that Christians should eat kosher meat, that is, meat killed so that the blood is drained, yet I have never met a conservative Christian who takes this teaching seriously. The usual response is to cite Acts 10:9–16 in which Peter is commanded in a vision to kill and eat the flesh of unclean animals. This, of course, misses the point, which has nothing to do with which animals may be eaten, but rather that their blood must have been drained.

Another instance of selectivity concerns interest. For most of its history the Church believed that it was wrong to charge interest on loans. This view was based on texts such as Exodus 22:25: 'If you lend money to any of my people with you who is poor, you shall not be to him as a creditor, and you shall not exact interest from him.' Also, the teaching of Jesus and his example of poverty were held to exclude interest. A text referred to was Luke 6:35: 'But love your enemies, and do good, and lend, expecting nothing in return.' It was only from the 12th century onwards that the views on interest began to be relaxed. Yet, as late as the end of the 16th century, in Shakespeare's *The Merchant of Venice*, the Christian merchant Antonio could be distinguished from the Jewish merchant Shylock in that the Christian did not charge interest whereas the Jew did.[25] In today's world it is Islam that takes seriously the prohibition of interest, in accordance with Qur'an sura 2, verse 279:

Believers, have fear of God and waive what is still due to you from usury, if your faith be true; or war shall be declared against you by God and His apostle.[26]

I have never met a conservative or 'Bible believing' Christian who felt any embarrassment about taking out a loan; and the income of some churches depends upon their involvement in the stock-market.

The chapter so far has been deliberately negative in attempting to set the use of the Bible in ethics in an historical context, in order to emphasize the point that such use is not just a matter of finding, and applying, appropriate texts. What can be said positively?

First, the use of the Bible in ethics cannot and should not be separated from ethics as a whole and Christian theological involvement in ethics. The Christian tradition has always recognized that ethics is not a concern confined to religions or religious people, and it has always drawn upon philosophically informed ethics as well as what can be called 'natural morality'.[27] These points can be illustrated from the Bible. It has already been noted how the New Testament and the early Church appealed to the ethical values of their society and then added to them distinctive teachings about the need for mutual love in the Christian community (see chapter 5).

In the Old Testament it is taken for granted that there is a 'natural morality', especially in the opening chapters of Amos where various foreign nations are condemned for committing what today would be called war crimes or crimes against humanity. Also, the laws about damages to persons and property in Exodus 21–3 can be paralleled from non-biblical laws such as the laws of Hammurabi, indicating that the Old Testament laws are Israel's share of a wider heritage of law in the ancient Near East.

If it can be accepted that much of what the Old and New Testaments contain by way of laws is not divinely revealed instructions to be applied to today's world (in the few, and diminishing, number of cases where this might be possible), but that these laws are instances of natural morality, there will be two gains. First, it will be possible to understand why so much of what the Bible contains on ethics cannot be applied to today's world. The fact is that as humanity gets older its natural morality in some areas becomes more sensitive. That is why injunctions demanding the death penalty for cursing or striking one's parents, and suchlike, sound barbaric to us today. That is also why both the Old and New Testaments tolerated the institution of slavery which is officially outlawed in today's world, and why the subordinate position of women in the biblical texts is no longer tolerable. Unfortunately, the fact that humanity has become more sensitive to moral matters does not mean that the human race has become more moral or humane, as the ghastly history of the 20th century has shown and continues to show. This latter consideration then leads to the second gain, which is to concentrate attention in the Bible not on its ethical injunctions but on the driving forces at work in and behind them.

At the beginning of the chapter it was noted that the laws in the Old Testament cover relatively few areas of life. What they do cover, however, may be significant. It has been observed, for example, that the collection of non-religious laws in Exodus 21 begins with regulations about the release of slaves, and that it also includes laws which protect the poor (22:25-7), and widows and orphans (22:21-4). In Exodus 23 there is concern for wild animals, who are specifically included among the beneficiaries of the sabbath year when fields are not sown and vineyards and olive orchards are not harvested, with their produce being available only for the poor and the wild animals. At 23:12 the observance of the sabbath day as a day of no work is enjoined, 'that your ox and your ass may have rest, and the son of your bondmaid, and the alien, may be refreshed'. It is striking that the main beneficiaries of the sabbath day's rest are the domesticated animals who would be vulnerable to exploitation. This strong compassionate stance can be found elsewhere, and a famous instance is the Jubilee law of Leviticus 25, which designates the fiftieth year as a year when property is returned to original owners, slaves are released and debts are cancelled.

What can be seen in these laws is an attempt to legislate compassion; to construct what I have called elsewhere 'structures of grace', that is, social and administrative arrangements designed to allow humans to be free and to live their lives responsibly and creatively in regard to each other and to the created order. Things that hinder such freedom: slavery, debt, poverty and exploitation of animals are attacked in this Old Testament legislation; and the reason why they are attacked is that they are perceived to be contrary to God's intention in freeing the Israelites from slavery in Egypt (cp. Exodus 23:9; Deuteronomy 15:15).

It can be objected against this approach that the Old Testament contains 'structures of oppression' as well as structures of grace. An example would be the injunction in Deuteronomy 7 and 9 to destroy utterly the nations who already possess the land of Canaan. Again, if the story of the Exodus is a driving force behind the attempts to legislate compassion, if it is what I call an 'imperative of redemption', then it has to be admitted that this story has its objectionable sides. The divine treatment of the Egyptians in the inflicting of plagues upon them fits the popular idea of the God of the Old Testament as a God of anger.

There is no point in trying to deny that these negative points exist. However, they are only an embarrassment if it is being claimed that the Old Testament is a propositional revelation of God's character; and that is not the view adopted in this chapter. What is being argued is that the Old Testament contains ancient Israel's 'natural morality', a morality with many features that are objectionable to the modern world. Within that morality, however, can be found strands that attempt to legislate and establish compassion, for animals as well as humans. These impulses come from a more profound understanding of what it means to be human in relation to other humans and the created order, and in relation to God. The structures of grace cannot be legislated on to today's world, because human society has changed so much. What remains of value is that the Old Testament challenges contemporary readers to devise appropriate structures of grace for today's world, to legislate compassion as a profound way of understanding humanity, the world of nature and divinity.

The same approach can be applied to the New Testament. In discussing Ephesians 5:22–3, the passage which begins: 'Wives, be subject to your husbands', Andrew Lincoln has no hesitation in saying that the passage's view of marriage is 'conditioned by the cultural assumptions of its time'. He sees the best way of approaching the passage as via its attempt to bring the Pauline understanding of the Gospel to bear on the household structures of its society, so as to produce 'a distinctive adaptation of those structures'. He continues:

Contemporary Christians can best appropriate it by realizing that they are to attempt to do something similar in their own setting – to bring to bear what they hold to be the heart of the Christian message on the marriage conventions of their time. Those who consider love and justice to be the central thrust of the Bible's ethical teaching will, therefore, want to work out a view of marriage where both partners are held in equal regard, where justice will require that traditional male dominance cannot be tolerated . . . and where love will ensure that the relationship does not degenerate into a sterile battle over each partner's rights to his or her own fulfillment . . .

Instead of assigning love to the husband and submission to the wife, a contemporary appropriation of Ephesians will build on the passage's own introductory exhortation (v. 21) and see a mutual loving submission as the way in which the unity of the marriage relationship is demonstrated.[28]

To sum up this first, and lengthy, positive point, the Bible contains indications of driving forces that seek to transform the natural morality and social arrangements of biblical times into structures of grace. In the Old Testament these structures of grace concentrate upon neutralizing things such as slavery, debt, poverty and exploitation, including the exploitation of animals. In the New Testament the impetus is more personal and private, inviting Christians to allow the love of Christ to transform personal relationships and their social embodiment. Because in these cases the structures of grace are located in specific historical and social conditions they cannot be simply transferred to modern society. But the processes at work in creating structures of grace can be appropriated in today's world and can be the impetus for devising structures of grace for modern situations. It goes without saying that such activity requires knowledge and skills beyond the competence of biblical scholars and theologians.

The second positive point – much shorter – is that the Bible contains a good deal of moral debate and that it recognizes that ethical decisions are not easy to reach in some instances. For example, the absolute command in Exodus 21:12, 'Whoever strikes a man so that he dies shall be put to death', is immediately modified by allowing that such killing may be accidental, in which case the 'killer' can seek a place of refuge where he will be free from the death penalty. This distinction between homicide and manslaughter must have resulted from ethical discussion. Again, the injunction to observe the sabbath posed a problem for those who resisted the attempt of Antiochus IV to ban Judaism in 168–167 BCE. They were pursued by the king's officers and troops and because they would not violate the sabbath by fighting on it they were brutally killed. Mattathias, the father of Judas Maccabeus, decided with his supporters that they would *have* to fight against anyone who came to attack them on the sabbath (1 Maccabees 2:39–41).

In 2 Samuel 14:4–7, a woman comes to David with the following dilemma. She is a widow with two sons, one of whom has killed the other. The murderer is thus liable to the death penalty; but if it is carried out the woman and her deceased husband will have no heir and their 'name' will be extinguished – a tragedy from the ancient Israelite point of view. Whether or not the incident is historical, it is evidence for an awareness of moral dilemmas, and that however desirable it may be to have moral absolutes, they have to be applied to particular circumstances, something which is not necessarily straightforward.

In the New Testament there is a moral debate about whether Christians should eat food which has been offered to idols (1 Corinthians 8:1– 11:1). This was a practical matter because most food on sale in Corinth had not been killed so as to drain the blood (although Paul never mentions Acts 15 in this connection) and it had probably come on to the market via a pagan temple.[29] The debate is complex, and Paul's part in it is subtle. For example, he advises a Christian who is invited to a meal by a non-Christian, to eat what is set before him and only to refuse to do so if the host explicitly says that the meat has been sacrificed to idols. The reason for refusing will not be to do with any scruples that the Christian may have about eating such meat, but so as not to offend or disturb the conscience of the non-Christian! (see 1 Corinthians 10:27– 9). One of the principles that Paul invokes in the discussion (what I would call an imperative of redemption) is that Christian behaviour should not be such as to harm the faith of another Christian (1 Corinthians 8:11–12), and that one should 'Give no offence to Jews or to Greeks or to the church of God' (10:32).

These examples do not provide rules for using the Bible in ethics, but they show that reaching ethical decisions is not a simple matter of enforcing absolutes. The Pauline handling of the food question is especially illuminating in this regard, and is driven by respect for the integrity and moral worth of people who may not share his opinions, and by the overriding concern not to hinder the progress of the gospel.

The third positive approach to using the Bible is based upon A. D. Lindsay's book, *The Two Moralities*, published in 1940.[30] In it, Lindsay contrasts what he calls 'the morality of my station and its duties' with 'the morality of grace'. The first morality is an inescapable duty for all citizens, including the duty to see that it conforms to the highest standards of justice. It is confronted, however, by the morality of grace which, in its formulation in the Sermon on the Mount, both undermines and goes far beyond 'the morality of my station'. For example, the injunctions not to resist evil and to turn the other cheek (Matthew 5:39) undermine the necessity for 'the morality of my station' to defend itself and potential victims against injustice backed by force. Yet at the same time they point to an imperfection in 'the morality of my station', namely, its need to use force to uphold justice. Lindsay therefore sees the function of the morality of grace as providing a constant challenge to 'the morality of my station'. It also nurtures prophets and poets who give new moral insights to the world; and, ideally, it should in the Church display a model of communal life that transcends 'the morality of my station'.

No doubt Lindsay is over-optimistic in what he hopes for the Church:

The actual life lived in the Church ought in itself to be a living, effective, and constructive witness against the evils and failures of society. It is also the function of the Church to produce prophets, and the evidence of its vitality will be the fact that it is a school of the prophets: that the men and women who show us what society might do, who correct our blindness and indifference to evils, are inspired by the Church's fellowship. The Church ought to go a long way to encourage liberty of prophesying, to be prepared to face all the scandal to which liberty of prophesying is bound to give rise. But prophecy itself is an individual responsibility. Prophets speak in the name of God who gives them their individual message. They may expect and hope that the Church will hear them and support them. But however much they draw, and ought to draw, their inspiration from the Church, they and not the collective Church must give the message. To hope or ask for anything else is to confound the institutional and prophetic functions of the Church.[31]

The portrait given here of the Church may well be unrecognizable; but Lindsay's words are a profound description of the forces that produced the Bible. The Old Testament is not the national literature of ancient Israel, but a prophetically driven set of questionings about the nature of humanity and God, that was prepared to see the disappearance of the Israelite states rather than their preservation on the foundation of injustice (see especially Micah 3:1–3, 9–12). The Old Testament is also a prophetic vision of what a redeemed world might look like, with a created order and a humanity at peace with themselves (Isaiah 65:17–25). It is also an utterly realistic appreciation of human nature and structures, that makes the prophets' hopes counter-factual. The New Testament, again, is the record of an individual whose totally unconventional view of God defined greatness in terms of servant-hood, reached out to outsiders and the non-religious people of his day, and who summed up his work by dying a criminal's death. His influence on Paul was such that Paul was compelled to throw over all that had been dearest to him in the religion of his fathers in order to work out in theory and practice the implications of what he believed God had done in Jesus Christ (see Philippians 3).

The most profound use that can be made of the Bible is not to treat it as a law book, but to seek to hear and act in accordance with its prophetic voice, a prophetic voice that is disturbing and unconventional, and which can never be content with the world as it is.

Glossary

Annalistic Chronicles, records of events occurring in each year of the reign of a king.

Apostolical constitutions, a 4th-century CE Christian writing that gives guidance on which Old Testament laws are binding on Christians and which are not.

Ark of the Covenant, a portable shrine believed to symbolize the warlike presence of God during Israel's wanderings from Egypt to the promised land after the Exodus, and which contained the tablets of the Ten Commandments.

Assumption of Moses, a Jewish work composed in the early years of the Common Era which is an attack, among other things, on the Maccabean priest kings of Judah, and which looks forward to the end time and the establishment of God's rule.

Barnabas, Epistle of, an early Christian writing from the 2nd century CE which allegorizes the Old Testament and was possibly regarded by some parts of the Church as Scripture.

Chester Beatty Papyri, papyri acquired by A. Chester Beatty from dealers in Egypt in 1931, of which the best known are P^{45} and P^{46}. The former contains parts of the Gospels and Acts, the latter the Pauline letters from Romans to 1 Thessalonians including Hebrews. The papyri date from the 3rd century CE.

Chrism, the sacrament of chrismation administered immediately after baptism in the Eastern Orthodox Church. The newly baptized are anointed with oil that has been blessed by a bishop or patriarch.

Christological interpretation of the Old Testament is a method of study which tries to see in the Old Testament either explicit references to Christ as the coming Son of God and dying saviour, or which sees Old Testament characters and institutions as 'types' of Christ, that is, as anticipations of his work.

Clement, 1 and 2, Christian writings of the late 1st and mid-2nd centuries CE and traditionally ascribed to Clement, an early Bishop of Rome.

Codex, a volume of pages bound together at one side so that the pages can be turned, as in a modern book.

Covenanters, those who had joined the community based at Qumran by taking part in a ceremony in which they pledged themselves to observe the community rules.

Covenant laws, laws accepted by a people as part of their obligation to a covenant made usually with a superior party.

Day of Atonement, an annual ceremony of confession and forgiveness described in the Old Testament in Leviticus 16.

Decapolis, a term found in the New Testament and designating ten Greek cities mostly in what today is Jordan and Syria.

Deists, intellectuals who were active particularly in Britain in the 17th and 18th centuries, and who believed in a universal natural religion that was confirmed by reason. This included belief in God as creator, immortality and rewards for the righteous and punishments for the wicked. They were critical of what they took to be the moral crudities of the Old Testament, and its apparent lack of belief in immortality.

Deuterocanonical, a term used by Catholics and Orthodox to denote books regarded by Protestants as belonging to the Apocrypha. Literally it means 'second canon' but books in this category are regarded as having an equal status with the other books of the Bible.

Douay Version of the Bible, a translation into English from Latin for use by Catholics, produced at the English College at Douai, northern France (founded in 1569; from 1578–93 the college was in Rheims). The New Testament appeared in 1582, and the Old Testament (including the deuterocanonical books) in 1609–10.

Doxology, a prayer of thanks to God.

Ecstatic Prophets, groups living on the margins of society in ancient

Israel whose behaviour was characterized by trance-like states, nakedness and exuberant movements.

Enoch, Book of, a collection of five booklets extant in its entirety only in Ethiopic, regarded as Scripture by the Ethiopian Church, and pseudonymously attributed to Enoch. Its earliest parts date from the 3rd century BCE. At least three of the booklets in Aramaic have been found at Qumran among the Dead Sea Scrolls. It contains speculations about the future history of the world and the afterlife as well as interpretations of past history. Its immense popularity is indicated by the number of copies found at Qumran.

Eschatology, from the Greek *eschatos* meaning 'last', is the doctrine of the last things, including the final defeat of evil, the last judgement and resurrection.

Essenes, a religious group within Judaism from *c.* 150 BCE to 100 CE, described by Classical and Jewish writers and commonly identified with the community at Qumran and the Dead Sea Scrolls. They seem to have been very strict observers of the law, pacifists, celibate and to have practised community of goods. However, there may have been Essenes who did not observe all these principles.

Exile, exilic, terms describing the period 587–540 BCE when the most important of the inhabitants of Judah and Jerusalem were exiled to Babylon.

Exodus, The, a term for the departure of the Hebrews from slavery in Egypt as described in Exodus 12–15. Critical scholarship has traditionally dated the Exodus to the early part of the 13th century BCE.

Gilgamesh, Epic of, put together possibly in the 18th century BCE from various stories about a king of Sumer and his search for eternal life. Tablet XII contains an account of the Flood which parallels that in the Bible in Genesis 6–8.

Gnosticism, a complex set of teachings found in the Graeco-Roman empire from the 2nd century CE, emphasizing the importance of secret knowledge (Greek, *gnosis*) as the way to salvation. Gnostic systems stressed that the material world is evil and that the spiritual world alone is good.

Halakah, a Hebrew word from the verb *halakh*, 'to walk or go'. As a
   general term it denotes a method of interpretation of laws which
   gives guidance on how one should live. As a particular term it
   denotes a certain legal ruling.

Hammurabi, ruler of Babylon for 43 years in the late 18th and early
   17th centuries BCE, whose laws discovered in Susa in 1901–2 are
   an important source for our knowledge of law in the ancient Near
   East, with important parallels with Old Testament laws.

Jews, a term used, rightly or wrongly, in academic scholarship to describe
   the adherents of Judaism after the Babylonian exile (597–540 BCE).

Jubilees, a popular pseudepigraphical work dating from the mid-2nd
   century BCE, which is an interpretation of Old Testament history
   and law and which advocates a solar calendar of 364 days. Some
   fifteen or sixteen copies were found at Qumran among the Dead
   Sea Scrolls.

Judges, the principal characters in the Old Testament Book of Judges.
   Although, according to the narratives, some of them exercised
   judicial functions, others were also military leaders, while Samson
   was a highly individualist opponent of Israel's enemies.

Keswick, a small town in the Lake District of north-western England at
   which an annual convention is held, whose speakers stress that
   Christians should live holy lives based upon biblical principles.

Knox translation of the Bible, a translation for Catholics based on the
   Vulgate. The New Testament was published in 1945 and the
   translation of the complete Bible appeared in 1955.

Levitical, as in the Book of Leviticus.

Liberation Theology, a movement originating in mostly Catholic circles
   in Latin and Central America in the 1960s and spreading to other
   parts of the world where poor communities were oppressed by
   dictatorial governments. It criticizes the view that salvation is
   simply something that occurs in the hereafter, and preaches the
   need for social justice and economic and political liberation in this
   life.

LXX, see Septuagint.

Manuscript, handwritten copy of a text, usually on leather or vellum
   (parchment prepared from the skins of calves).

Midrash, a method of biblical commentary in Judaism, which gave rise
to the great biblical commentaries or Midrashim, of which the
most famous is the Midrash Rabbah on the first five books of the
Bible.

Mishnah, a collection of Jewish laws traditionally believed to have been
compiled by Rabbi Judah the Prince in *c.* 220 CE.

Muratorian Canon, named after L. A. Muratori who, in 1740, published
a fragmentary account in Latin of the canon of the New Testament.
It may be based on a Greek original and is dated around 200 CE.

Oxford Movement, a movement within the Church of England which
began in Oxford in the 1820s, and associated especially with John
Keble, E. B. Pusey, and J. H. Newman. It sought to recover the
Catholic roots of the Church of England, and initially perceived
biblical criticism to be a threat to traditional Christianity.

Papyrus, papyri, the equivalent of paper in the ancient Near East, made
from reeds glued together. Papyrus was used for letters and official
documents, and the letters of Paul were written on papyrus.

Passover, an annual commemoration of the Exodus from Egypt whose
institution is described in Exodus 12.

Pastoral Epistles, a name given to the letters of Paul to Timothy and
Titus, and so called because of their content. Modern critical
scholarship does not believe them to have been written by Paul.

Pentecostal, an adjective describing churches that believe that the gifts
of the Holy Spirit described in the New Testament, such as
speaking in tongues, prophecy and healing, should be practised in
today's churches. Churches belonging to traditional denominations
such as the Church of England or the Baptists, that stress the gifts
of the Spirit, are usually called charismatic churches.

Peshat, a method of Jewish commentary on the Bible which aims at
straightforward explanation of the text.

Peter, Gospel of, referred to by Christian writers of the 3rd–4th
centuries CE of which fragments were discovered in Egypt towards
the end of the 19th century. The extant material is an account of
the Passion of Jesus.

Polyglott Bibles, Bibles which contain parallel versions in several
languages.

Prophetic movements, groups of people living on the margins of society in ancient Israel who were fervently religious. Their leaders, such as Elijah, did not hesitate to intervene in the politics of Israel and neighbouring countries. See 1 Kings 17–2 Kings 10.

Proto-canonical, the Roman Catholic designation for the Old Testament books that are in the Jewish canon.

Pseudepigrapha, pseudepigraphical, terms relating to Jewish writings of the period roughly 200 BCE–100 CE which are not in the Bible or the Apocrypha. Examples would include Jubilees and the Testaments of the Twelve Patriarchs.

Satan, the (in the Book of Job), not the developed figure of later Jewish and Christian angelology, but one of the sons of God whose task is to keep watch over human affairs. In Zechariah 3:1 Satan is portrayed as a heavenly accuser.

Semites, Semitic, a term derived from one of Noah's sons Shem who, according to Genesis 10:21–31, was the ancestor of various nations. In modern usage it denotes the ancient and modern users of the family of Semitic languages, which includes Akkadian, Aramaic and Syriac, Hebrew and Arabic. A narrower use of Semitic in the combination anti-Semitic refers to the persecution of Jews.

Septuagint, also called the LXX, a loose term covering several things including the translation of the Old Testament into Greek by Jewish scholars beginning in the 3rd century BCE, and the Greek Bible of the early Church. LXX is derived from a legend according to which seventy (or seventy-two) translators produced a translation of the first five books of the Bible for the Egyptian ruler Ptolemy II (Philadelphus) 285–246 BCE.

Shepherd of Hermas, a 2nd-century CE Christian writing of instruction in the Christian life that was regarded as Scripture in some parts of the early Church.

Source criticism, a method of study of biblical texts which seeks to discover and reconstruct the literary sources used by biblical writers.

Talmud, a general term derived from the Hebrew verb *lamad*, 'to learn'. As applied to the Babylonian and Jerusalem Talmudim it denotes two compilations of Jewish law and discussion completed towards the end of the first millennium CE, and containing the Mishnah and subsequent commentary on the Mishnah, called the Gemara.

Temple accounts, administrative records of acquisition or disposal of temple properties (see 2 Kings 18:13–14).

Thomas, Gospel of, containing a collection of sayings, parables and rules attributed to Jesus and best preserved in a Coptic version discovered at Nag Hammadi in Egypt in 1945. It was probably written in Greek around 200 CE and has Gnostic tendencies.

Tosephta, a collection of laws complementary to and additional to those in the Mishnah.

Transformational grammar, the theory that speech and writing on the 'surface level' are transformations of kernels in a 'deep structure'. It is used in the translation theory underlying the Good News Bible.

Tyndale, William (1494–1536), pioneer translator of the Bible into English who published the New Testament in 1526 (revised in 1534) but who did not complete the Old Testament before he was betrayed in Antwerp and later executed because his translation work was deemed to be illegal.

Vassal treaties, agreements between an overlord and a subject people stipulating the obligations of the latter to the former. The vassal treaties of the Assyrian king Esarhaddon (681–669 BCE; see Pritchard, *ANET*, pp. 534–41) indicate the kind of treaty to which Judah may have been subject while a vassal state of the Assyrians in the 7th century BCE.

Vulgate, a term given to describe the translation of the Bible into Latin by Jerome in the late 4th and early 5th centuries CE. An edition issued in 1592 by Pope Clement VIII, known as the Clementine edition, became the official text of the Roman Catholic Church.

Westminster Confession of Faith, The, a statement of belief and doctrine promulgated in 1648 by Puritan divines meeting at Westminster (London) from 1643–9.

'Wisdom' literature, a term used since the late 19th century to designate the Old Testament Books of Job, Proverbs and Ecclesiastes, as well as other material in the Old Testament and books in the Apocrypha such as the Wisdom of Solomon and the Wisdom of

Jesus ben Sirach (Ecclesiasticus). Wisdom was once thought to originate from the scribal and diplomatic schools employed in temples and palaces in the ancient Near East, but this view is now contested.

YHWH, the four consonants in Hebrew that indicate God's special name in the Old Testament. They are thought to have been pronounced 'Yahveh'. Many translations in English use LORD (in capitals) to indicate the Hebrew.

Zoroastrianism, the religion of followers of the Iranian prophet Zoroaster (*c.* 1400 BCE) which from the 6th century BCE to the 7th century CE was the official religion of three successive Iranian empires. Its stress on the defeat of evil, and on heaven, hell, resurrection and judgement, had an influence on Judaism after Judah became part of the Persian empire (540–333 BCE) and on Christianity where the latter spread into northern Syria and Mesopotamia.

Abbreviations

ANET	*Ancient Near Eastern Texts Relating to the Old Testament*
AV	Authorized Version, or King James Version
CCB	*The Cambridge Companion to the Bible*
GNB	Good News Bible
JB	Jerusalem Bible
JBL	*Journal of Biblical Literature*
JSNT	*Journal for the Study of the New Testament*
JSOTSS	*Journal for the Study of the Old Testament*, Supplement Series
NAB	New American Bible
NEB	New English Bible
NIV	New International Version
NJB	New Jerusalem Bible
NRSV	New Revised Standard Version
OTW	*The Old Testament World*
REB	Revised English Bible
RSV	Revised Standard Version
RV	Revised Version
SBL	Society of Biblical Literature
TRE	*Theologische Realenzyklopädie*
ZTK	*Zeitschrift für Theologie und Kirche*

Bibliography

Bibles and Editions of Bibles

Authorized Version: The Holy Bible containing the Old and New Testaments and Apocrypha (Cambridge: Cambridge University Press n.d.).

Good News Bible: with Deuterocanonical Books/Apocrypha. Today's English Version (London: British & Foreign Bible Society; Collins/Fontana 1979).

D. Martin Luther. Die gantze Heilige Schrifft (Munich: Deutscher Taschenbuch Verlag, 1974, 3 vols).

The New English Bible with the Apocrypha (Oxford: Oxford University Press, Cambridge: Cambridge University Press 1970).

The New International Version Study Bible (London: Hodder & Stoughton 1996).

The New Jerusalem Bible, Study Edition (London: Darton, Longman & Todd, new edn 1994).

The New Revised Standard Version Reference Bible with the Apocrypha (Grand Rapids: Zondervan 1993).

The Oxford Annotated Apocrypha of the Old Testament, Revised Standard Version, ed. B. M. Metzger (New York: Oxford University Press 1965).

The Parallel Apocrypha, ed. J. R. Kohlenberger III (New York: Oxford University Press 1997).

The Revised English Bible with Apocrypha (Oxford: Oxford University Press, Cambridge: Cambridge University Press 1989).

Revised Standard Version, containing the Old and New Testaments (New York & Glasgow: Collins 1971).

Revised Version, with the Books called Apocrypha (Cambridge: Cambridge University Press n.d.).

Tyndale's New Testament: a modern-spelling edition of the 1534 translation with an introduction by D. Daniell (New Haven: Yale University Press 1989).

Dictionaries and Companions to the Bible

The Anchor Bible Dictionary, ed. D. N. Freedman (New York: Doubleday 1992, 6 vols).

Lexikon Arabische Welt, eds G. Barthel, K. Stock (Darmstadt: Wissenschaftliche Buchgesellschaft 1994).

The Cambridge Companion to the Bible (CCB), eds H. C. Kee et al. (Cambridge: Cambridge University Press 1997).

A Dictionary of Biblical Tradition in English Literature, ed. D. C. Jeffrey (Grand Rapids: Eerdmans 1992).

General Works and Articles

P. Addinall, *Philosophy and Biblical Interpretation. A Study in Nineteenth-century Conflict* (Cambridge: Cambridge University Press 1991).

R. Alter and F. Kermode, *The Literary Guide to the Bible* (London: Collins 1987).

G. Auld, *Kings without Privilege: David and Moses in the Story of the Bible's Kings* (Edinburgh: T. & T. Clark 1994).

H. R. Balz, 'Anonymität und Pseudepigraphie im Urchristentum', in *ZTK* 66 (1969), pp. 403–36.

O. Barclay, 'The Nature of Christian Morality', in B. N. Kaye, G. J. Wenham (eds), *Law, Morality and the Bible* (Leicester: Inter-Varsity Press 1978).

C. K. Barrett, *The First Epistle to the Corinthians*, Black's New Testament Commentaries (London: A. & C. Black 1968).

J. Barton, *The Spirit and the Letter. Studies in the Biblical Canon* (London: SPCK 1997).

G. K. A. Bell, *Randall Davidson, Archbishop of Canterbury* (London: Oxford University Press, 3rd edn 1952).

A. W. F. Blunt et al., *Helps to the Study of the Bible* (London: Oxford University Press, 2nd edn n.d.).

C. Brown, *Jesus in European Protestant Thought 1778–1860*, Studies in Historical Theology 1 (Durham, North Carolina: Labyrinth Press 1985).

F. F. Bruce, *The English Bible* (London: Methuen 1963).

M. Bucer, *De regno Christi*, Library of Christian Classics, vol. 19 (London: SCM Press 1959).

M. C. Callaway, 'The Apocryphal/Deuterocanonical Books: An Anglican/Episcopal View', in The Parallel Apocrypha.

B. D. Chilton, *The Temple of Jesus. His Sacrificial Program within a Cultural History of Sacrifice* (Pennsylvania: Pennsylvania State University Press 1992).

A. Clarke, *The New Testament of Our Lord and Saviour Jesus Christ; containing the Text taken from the most correct copies of the present Authorised Translation, including the Marginal Readings and Parallel Texts with a Commentary and Critical Notes designed as a Help to a Better Understanding of the Sacred Writings* (London: 1817).

A. Y. Collins, *Feminist Perspectives on Biblical Scholarship*, SBL Centennial Publications 10 (Chico: Scholars Press 1985).

J. J. Collins, 'The Apocryphal/Deuterocanonical Books: A Catholic View', in The Parallel Apocrypha.

D. J. Constantelos, 'The Apocryphal/Deuterocanonical Books: An Orthodox View', in The Parallel Apocrypha.

P. R. Davies, 'Was there Really a Qumran Community?', *Currents in Research* 3 (1995), pp. 9–35.

S. R. Driver, *Sermons on Subjects Connected with the Old Testament* (London: 1892).

— *The Book of Genesis*, Westminster Commentaries (London: Methuen 1904).

— *Introduction to the Literature of the Old Testament* (Edinburgh: T. & T. Clark, 9th edn 1913).

J. D. G. Dunn, *The Epistles to the Colossians and to Philemon*, New International Greek Testament Commentary (Grand Rapids: Eerdmans 1996).

J. K. Elliott, 'Manuscripts, the Codex and the Canon', in *JSNT* 63 (1996), pp. 105–23.

E. J. Epp, 'Textual Criticism (NT)', in *The Anchor Bible Dictionary*, vol. 6.

G. P. Fogarty, *American Catholic Biblical Scholarship. A History from the Early Republic to Vatican II* (San Francisco: Harper & Row 1989).

P. Gerlitz, 'Pseudonymität I', in *TRE* XXVII (1997), pp. 659–62.

N. K. Gottwald (ed.), *The Bible and Liberation. Political and Social Hermeneutics* (Maryknoll: Orbis Books 1983).

L. L. Grabbe, *Judaism from Cyrus to Hadrian*, vol.1: *The Persian and Greek Periods* (Minneapolis: Fortress Press 1992).

M. Green et al., *The Church and Homosexuality. A Positive Answer to the Current Debate* (London: Hodder & Stoughton 1980).

S. L. Greenslade, 'English Versions of the Bible, 1525–1611', in *Cambridge History of the Bible*, vol. 3: *The West from the Reformation to the Present Day* (Cambridge: Cambridge University Press 1963).

G. Gutierrez, *A Theology of Liberation. History, Politics and Salvation* (London: SCM Press 1974).

R. P. C. Hanson, Introduction to *The Pelican Guide to Modern Theology*, vol. 3 by R. Davidson and A. R. C. Leaney (Harmondsworth: Penguin Books 1970).

T. H. Horne, *An Introduction to the Critical Study and Knowledge of the Holy Scriptures* (vol. II, London: 1825).

L. Jacobs, *Principles of the Jewish Faith. An Analytical Study* (London: Vallentine, Mitchell 1964).

D. C. Jeffrey (ed.), *A Dictionary of Biblical Tradition in English Literature* (Grand Rapids: Eerdmans 1992).

S. Jellicoe, *The Septuagint and Modern Study* (Oxford: Clarendon Press 1968).

W. C. Kaiser Jr, *Toward Old Testament Ethics* (Grand Rapids: Zondervan 1983).

D. Katz, *Sabbath and Sectarianism in Seventeenth-Century England*, Brill's Studies in Intellectual History 10 (Leiden: E. J. Brill 1988).

H. C. Kee et al. (eds), *The Cambridge Companion to the Bible* (*CCB*) (Cambridge: Cambridge University Press 1997).

B. Kienast, 'Bibliothekswesen I/1', in *TRE* 6, pp. 410–11.

David Kimhi, *Perush Rabbi David ben Qimhi 'al Hatorah* (Jerusalem: Mossad Harav Kook 1970).

The Koran, translated with notes by N. J. Dawood, Penguin Classics (Harmondsworth: Penguin Books, 5th revised edn 1997).

A. Krausz, *Short Digest of Jewish Literature in the Middle Ages* (Sheffield: Naor Publications 1984).

W. G. Kümmell, *The New Testament. The History of the Investigation of its Problems*, New Testament Library (London: SCM Press 1973).

M.-J. Lagrange, *Père Lagrange. Personal Reflections and Memoirs* (New York: Paulist Press 1985).

A. T. Lincoln, *Ephesians*, Word Biblical Commentary 42 (Dallas: Word Books 1990).

B. Lindars, 'The New Testament', in Rogerson et al., *The Study and Use of the Bible*.

A. D. Lindsay, *The Two Moralities. Our Duty to God and to Society* (London: Eyre & Spottiswoode 1940).

R. Loewe, *The Position of Women in Judaism* (London: SPCK 1966).

Moses Maimonides, *The Guide of the Perplexed*, translated by S. Pines (Chicago: University of Chicago Press 1963, 2 vols).

G. M. Marsden, *Fundamentalism and American Culture. The Shaping of Twentieth Century Evangelicalism 1870–1925* (New York: Oxford University Press 1980).

E. M. Meyers and J. W. Rogerson, 'The Old Testament World', in *CCB*.

G. F. Moore, 'Tatian's *Diatessaron* and the analysis of the Pentateuch', in Tigay (ed.), *Empirical Models for Biblical Criticism*. The original article appeared in *JBL* 9 (1890), pp. 201–15.

J. R. Moore, *The Post-Darwinian Controversies* (Cambridge: Cambridge University Press 1979).

R. Morgan, *Biblical Interpretation*, Oxford Bible Series (Oxford: Oxford University Press 1988).

M. Müller, *The First Bible of the Church. A Plea for the Septuagint, JSOTSS* 206 (Sheffield: Sheffield Academic Press 1996).

E. A. Nida, *Toward a Science of Translating, with Special Reference to Principles and Procedures involved in Bible Translating* (Leiden: E. J. Brill 1964).

E. A. Nida and C. R. Taber, *The Theory and Practice of Translation*, Helps for Translators vol. VIII (Leiden: E. J. Brill 1969).

D. Novak, *Law and Theology in Judaism* (New York: Ktav Publishing House 1974).

A. C. Partridge, *English Biblical Translation* (London: André Deutsch 1973).

A. S. Peake, *The Bible. Its Origin, Its Significance and Its Abiding Worth* (London: Hodder & Stoughton 1913).

A. S. Peake (ed.), *Peake's Commentary on the Bible* (London: Thomas Nelson 1919).

E. Plümacher, 'Bibliothekswesen II', *TRE* 6, pp. 413–26.

J. B. Pritchard (ed.), *Ancient Near Eastern Texts Relating to the Old Testament (ANET)* (Princeton: Princeton University Press, 3rd edn 1969).

K. Rahner (ed.), *Encyclopedia of Theology. A Concise Sacramentum Mundi* (London: Burns & Oates 1975).

Rashi (Rabbi Solomon ben Isaac) in *Mikra'ot G'dolot, N'vi'im R'ishonim* (Jerusalem: Shoken 1959).

A. E. J. Rawlinson, *The Gospel According to St Mark*, Westminster Commentaries (London: Methuen 1925).

F. Robinson, 'Knowledge, its Transmission, and the Making of Muslim Societies', in F. Robinson (ed.), *The Cambridge Illustrated History of the Islamic World* (Cambridge: Cambridge University Press 1996).

N. Robinson, *Discovering the Qur'an. A Contemporary Approach to a Veiled Text* (London: SCM Press 1996).

N. H. G. Robinson, *The Groundwork of Christian Ethics* (London: Collins 1971).

J. Rogerson, 'An Outline of the History of Old Testament Study', in J. Rogerson (ed.), *Beginning Old Testament Study* (London: SPCK 1983; revised 1998).

— *Old Testament Criticism in the Nineteenth Century. England and Germany* (London: SPCK 1984).

— 'The Old Testament', in J. Rogerson, C. Rowland and B. Lindars, *The Study and Use of the Bible* (Basingstoke: Marshall Pickering, Grand Rapids: Wm. B. Eerdmans Publishing Co. 1988).

— *Genesis 1–11*, Old Testament Guides (Sheffield: Sheffield Academic Press 1991).

— *W. M. L. de Wette, Founder of Modern Biblical Criticism. An Intellectual Biography*, *JSOTSS* 126 (Sheffield: Sheffield Academic Press 1992).

J. Rogerson, P. Davies, *The Old Testament World (OTW)* (Cambridge: Cambridge University Press, Englewood Cliffs: Prentice-Hall 1989).

H.-P. Rüger, 'Apokryphen I', *TRE* 3, pp. 294–5.

Sa'adia, *Perush Rabbenu Sa'adia Gaon 'al Hatorah* (Jerusalem: Mossad Harav Kook 1963).

L. Schottroff, 'Die Güte Gottes und die Solidarität von Menschen. Das Gleichnis von den Arbeitern im Weinberg', in W. Schottroff, W. Stegemann (eds), *Der Gott der kleinen Leute. Sozialgeschichtliche Auslegungen* (Munich: Chr. Kaiser Verlag, Gelnhausen: Burckhardthaus-Laetare Verlag, vol. 2 1979).

L. Schottroff and M.-T. Wacker (eds), *Von der Wurzel getragen. Christlich-feministische Exegese in Auseinandersetzung mit Antijudaismus*, Biblical Interpretation Series 17 (Leiden: E. J. Brill 1996).

R. Smith, *Handel's Oratorios and Eighteenth-Century Thought* (Cambridge: Cambridge University Press 1995).

W. R. Smith, *The Old Testament in the Jewish Church* (1st edn, Edinburgh: 1881, 3rd edn, London: A. & C. Black 1926).

J. Stevenson, *A New Eusebius* (London: SPCK 1957).

J. H. Tigay, 'The Evolution of the Pentateuchal Narratives in the Light of the Evolution of the *Gilgamesh Epic*', in Tigay (ed.), *Empirical Models for Biblical Criticism*.

J. H. Tigay (ed.), *Empirical Models for Biblical Criticism* (Philadelphia: University of Pennsylvania Press 1985).

E. Tov, 'The Composition of 1 Samuel 16–18 in the Light of the Septuagint Version', in Tigay (ed.), *Empirical Models for Biblical Criticism*.

E. E. Urbach, *The Sages – Their Concepts and Beliefs* (Jerusalem: Magnes Press 1975).

J. Ussher, *The Annals of the World* (London: 1658).

James C. Vanderkam, *The Dead Sea Scrolls Today* (London: SPCK, Grand Rapids: Eerdmans 1994).

G. Vermes, *The Complete Dead Sea Scrolls in English* (London: Allen Lane, The Penguin Press 1997).

J. Wellhausen, *Prolegomena zur Geschichte Israels* (Berlin: 1883); English translation, J. S. Black and A. Menzies, *Prolegomena to the History of Israel* (Edinburgh: 1885).

G. West, *Biblical Hermeneutics of Liberation. Modes of Reading the Bible in the South African Context* (Pietermaritzburg: Cluster Publications 1991).

W. M. L. de Wette, *Beiträge zur Einleitung in das Alte Testament* (Halle: 1806–7).

G. H. Wilson, *The Editing of the Hebrew Psalter*, SBL Dissertation Series 76 (Chico: Scholars Press 1985).

E. J. Young, *Thy Word is Truth. Some Thoughts on the Biblical Doctrine of Inspiration* (London: The Banner of Truth Trust 1963).

Notes

CHAPTER 1: *What is the Bible?*

1. For details of the Bibles referred to see the Bibliography. The Bibles mentioned do not, of course, exhaust the number of translations available, but are taken as representative.

2. For a recent discussion of the early history of the conflict see M. Müller, *The First Bible of the Church. A Plea for the Septuagint*, JSOTSS 206 (Sheffield: Sheffield Academic Press 1996).

3. H.-P. Rüger, 'Apokryphen I', *TRE* 3, pp. 294–5.

4. See further S. L. Greenslade, 'English Versions of the Bible, 1525–1611', in *Cambridge History of the Bible*, vol. 3: *The West from the Reformation to the Present Day* (Cambridge: Cambridge University Press 1963), pp. 141–74.

5. F. F. Bruce, *The English Bible* (London: Methuen 1963), p. 66. A. C. Partridge, *English Biblical Translation* (London: André Deutsch 1973), p. 77 notes that the Geneva Bible included the Prayer of Manasseh among the canonical books of the Old Testament, positioning it between 2 Chronicles and Ezra.

6. Professor David Loades, in a private communication, informs me that Thomas Matthew was an actual person and not a fictitious name. Whatever role he may have played in the production of Matthew's Bible, the main work was done by John Rogers.

7. The Parallel Apocrypha, ed. J. R. Kohlenberger III (New York: Oxford University Press 1997), contains introductions by scholars representing Catholic, Orthodox, Episcopal, Protestant and Evangelical traditions regarding the status and definition of the Apocrypha.

8. The Bible. *Authorized King James Version, with the Apocrypha*, World Classics (Oxford: Oxford University Press 1997).

9. Bruce, *The English Bible*, pp. 127–8.

10. An extensive list of such obsolete words can be found in A. W. F. Blunt et al., *Helps to the Study of the Bible* (London: Oxford University Press, 2nd edn n.d.), pp. 124–34.

11. E. A. Nida, *Toward a Science of Translating, with Special Reference to Principles and*

Procedures involved in Bible Translating (Leiden: E. J. Brill 1964); E. A. Nida and
C. R. Taber, *The Theory and Practice of Translation*, Helps for Translators, vol. VIII
(Leiden: E. J. Brill 1969).

12. For example, in Genesis 1 humankind are created after the animals and are
created male and female. In Genesis 2 the man is created first, then the animals
and, finally, woman is created out of the rib of the man.

13. These can be seen in the useful reprint of Luther's 1545 Bible, *D. Martin
Luther. Die gantze Heilige Schrifft* (Munich: Deutscher Taschenbuch Verlag 1974,
3 vols).

14. This can be checked from the recent modern-spelling edition of Tyndale's
New Testament, ed. D. Daniell (New Haven: Yale University Press 1989).

15. For these details and other information about editions of Bibles see T. H.
Horne, *An Introduction to the Critical Study and Knowledge of the Holy Scriptures* (vol.
II, London: 1825), pp. 763–73.

16. A. S. Peake (ed.), *Peake's Commentary on the Bible* (London: Thomas Nelson
1919).

CHAPTER 2: *How Biblical Writers Wrote*

1. I owe this example to W. R. Smith's *The Old Testament in the Jewish Church*
(London: A. & C. Black, 3rd edn 1926), p. 104. In the text I have followed
Smith's format, substituting the RSV translation.

2. See E. Tov, 'The Composition of 1 Samuel 16–18 in the Light of the Septuagint
Version', in Tigay (ed.), *Empirical Models for Biblical Criticism*, pp. 96–130.

3. See S. R. Driver, *Introduction to the Literature of the Old Testament* (Edinburgh: T.
& T. Clark, 9th edn 1913), p. 14 for a source division of the Flood narrative,
and pp. 131–5 for a list of expressions characteristic of the P(riestly) source.

4. That the notion of the text in its final form is not free from difficulty was
demonstrated above with regard to Jeremiah 27. Is the 'final form' of the text
the shorter Greek version which is Scripture for the Eastern Orthodox churches,
or the longer Hebrew text that is translated in English Bibles?

5. See J. H. Tigay, 'The Evolution of the Pentateuchal Narratives in the Light
of the Evolution of the *Gilgamesh Epic*', in Tigay (ed.), *Empirical Models*, pp. 21–
52.

6. I have taken this example from the reprint of G. F. Moore's article 'Tatian's
Diatessaron and the analysis of the Pentateuch', in Tigay (ed.), *Empirical Models*,
pp. 243–56. The original article appeared in *JBL* 9 (1890), pp. 201–15. In
reproducing Moore's quotation from the *Diatessaron*, I have substituted the RSV.

7. See most recently P. Gerlitz, 'Pseudonymität I', *TRE* XXVII (1977), pp. 659–

62. Gerlitz points out that pseudonymity is a universal and especially religious phenomenon in the ancient world. He connects it with what he calls 'irrationality', although it would be better in my view to say that pseudonymity exhibits a different rationality from a modern rationality that takes for granted printing and the idea of intellectual property that can be owned and used commercially.

8. For Ephesians see A. T. Lincoln, *Ephesians*, Word Biblical Commentary 42 (Dallas: Word Books 1990), pp. lix–lxxii; for Colossians see J. D. G. Dunn, *The Epistles to the Colossians and to Philemon*, New International Greek Testament Commentary (Grand Rapids: Eerdmans 1996), pp. 35–9. Lincoln and Dunn can fairly be described as moderately conservative critical scholars.

9. For what follows see H. R. Balz, 'Anonymität und Pseudepigraphie im Urchristentum', in *ZTK* 66 (1969), pp. 403–36.

10. E. E. Urbach, *The Sages – Their Concepts and Beliefs* (Jerusalem: Magnes Press 1975), p. 300.

11. Lincoln, *Ephesians*, p. lxix.

12. B. Kienast, 'Bibliothekswesen I/1', in *TRE* 6, p. 410.

13. E. Plümacher 'Bibliothekswesen II', *TRE* 6, p. 413.

14. See G. H. Wilson, *The Editing of the Hebrew Psalter*, SBL Dissertation Series 76 (Chico: Scholars Press 1985), pp. 124–5.

15. E. J. Epp, 'Textual Criticism (NT)', in *The Anchor Bible Dictionary*, vol. 6, pp. 420–21.

CHAPTER 3: *The Making of the Old Testament*

1. For more details see E. M. Meyers and J. W. Rogerson, 'The Old Testament World', in *CCB* (Cambridge: Cambridge University Press 1997), pp. 32–161.

2. In particular, the occupation of Canaan under Joshua is now seen to have been a comparatively peaceful process of occupation of those parts of Canaan that were not inhabited. The Israelites were probably not the only group involved in the occupation, and the stories of Joshua's battles may reflect conflicts among settlers rather than wars of occupation. See further *CCB*, pp. 97–116.

3. But see G. Auld, *Kings without Privilege: David and Moses in the Story of the Bible's Kings* (Edinburgh: T. & T. Clark 1994) for the view that a common source was being used.

4. See further J. Rogerson, P. Davies, *OTW* (Cambridge: Cambridge University Press, Englewood Cliffs: Prentice-Hall 1989), pp. 233–42.

5. In the Moabite Stone, Mesha king of Moab (*c.* 830 BCE) claims to have destroyed the entire population of Nebo after taking it from the Israelites. See Pritchard (ed.), *ANET*, p. 320.

6. See further Rogerson and Davies, *OTW*, pp. 274–309, and *CCB*, pp. 161–228.

7. See Pritchard (ed.), *ANET*, pp. 421–5.

8. See further 'Job' and 'Job's Comforters', in D. C. Jeffrey (ed.), *A Dictionary of Biblical Tradition in English Literature* (Grand Rapids: Eerdmans 1992), pp. 403–5.

9. See *CCB*, p. 253 for further details on this point.

10. See further Rogerson and Davies, *OTW*, pp. 310–22.

CHAPTER 4: *The Making of the Apocrypha*

1. This statement is not quite accurate! 1 and 2 Esdras appear in Protestant Apocryphas between the Old and New Testaments but do not appear in any major Catholic English translations. What appear in some Catholic translations as 1 and 2 Esdras are the Old Testament books of Ezra and Nehemiah. The Apocryphal 1 Esdras has some similarity to Ezra and Nehemiah. The Apocryphal 2 Esdras is an apocalyptic work.

2. Apparently, some editions of the Great Bible (1539) and Bishop Becke's edition of Taverner's Old Testament (1551) included 3 Maccabees.

3. For the sake of ease of comparison the order in the NRSV is followed. The Greek Bible has a different order from that given here, with the four Books of Maccabees together, for example.

4. Again, some slight variation must be noted. In the Septuagint, the Story of Susanna appears as a separate book before Daniel, and Bel and the Dragon is thus chapter 13 of Daniel. See further note 7 below.

5. See further L. L. Grabbe, *Judaism from Cyrus to Hadrian*, vol. 1: *The Persian and Greek Periods* (Minneapolis: Fortress Press 1992), pp. 246–99.

6. See Pritchard (ed.), *ANET*, pp. 427–30.

7. In Bibles where the additions appear as separate sections in the Apocrypha (e.g. the AV, RV, RSV, NRSV, NEB, REB), they are numbered verses 1–27 and 28–68.

8. The most recent general book on the subject is by James C. Vanderkam, *The Dead Sea Scrolls Today* (London: SPCK, Grand Rapids: Eerdmans 1994).

9. The translation is that of G. Vermes, *The Complete Dead Sea Scrolls in English* (London: Allen Lane, The Penguin Press 1997), p. 484.

10. Ibid., p. 10.

11. The difficulties in the consensus view are discussed by Philip Davies, 'Was there Really a Qumran Community?', in *Currents in Research* 3 (1995), pp. 9–35.

12. See Vermes, *The Complete Dead Sea Scrolls*, pp. 583–4, where he notes that the

Copper Scroll's principal editor, J. T. Milik, dated it to 100 CE, and thus later than the other scrolls and fragments. Vermes also notes that other scholars have connected the Copper Scroll with the Essenes (the presumed Qumran Community) because they believe that other material in Cave 3 can be connected with the community. See the list of contents of Cave 3, p. 604.

13. Davies, 'Was there Really a Qumran Community?', p. 15.

CHAPTER 5: *The Making of the New Testament*

1. The literature on the matters discussed in this chapter is vast and technical, and much of it is in German. I have not, therefore, tried to note the discussions in the way that I have done in other chapters. Readers who wish to explore matters further are referred to the Bibliographical Essay on the New Testament in *CCB*, pp. 576–83.

2. For full discussion see Dunn, *Colossians*, pp. 83–104.

3. J. Stevenson, *A New Eusebius* (London: SPCK 1957), p. 52.

4. Tacitus, *Annals*, XV.44.2–8: 'Christus . . . suffered the extreme penalty during the reign of Tiberius at the hand of one of our procurators, Pontius Pilatus', quoted in Stevenson, *A New Eusebius*, p. 2.

5. J. K. Elliott, 'Manuscripts, the Codex and the Canon', in *JSNT* 63 (1996), p. 107.

6. Ibid.

7. Ibid., p. 108. For a different interpretation in which Mark is the lion and John the eagle see the quotation from Irenaeus in Stevenson, *A New Eusebius*, p. 122.

CHAPTER 6: *The Canon of the Bible*

1. For a recent and illuminating discussion see J. Barton, *The Spirit and the Letter. Studies in the Biblical Canon* (London: SPCK 1997).

2. The 39 Articles of Religion are printed as an appendix to the Book of Common Prayer.

3. See F. Robinson, 'Knowledge, its Transmission, and the Making of Muslim Societies', in F. Robinson (ed.), *The Cambridge Illustrated History of the Islamic World* (Cambridge: Cambridge University Press 1996), pp. 210–11; N. Robinson, *Discovering the Qur'an. A Contemporary Approach to a Veiled Text* (London: SCM Press 1996), p. 286; G. Barthel, K. Stock, *Lexikon Arabische Welt* (Darmstadt: Wissenschaftliche Buchgesellschaft 1994), pp. 350–52. Apparently, there *are* some variations in manuscripts of the Qur'an but they are not considered to be important. A radical revisionist view of the rise of Islam that rejects the traditional account of the production of the Qur'an has been proposed by P. Crone and M. Cook, *Hagarism. The Making of the Islamic World* (Cambridge: Cambridge University Press 1977): it is reviewed by Robinson, *Discovering the Qur'an*, pp. 47–59.

4. For a brief outline of ambivalent Anglican attitudes to the Apocrypha see M. C. Callaway, 'The Apocryphal/Deuterocanonical Books: An Anglican/Episcopal View', in The Parallel Apocrypha, pp. xxxv–xxxix.

5. J. J. Collins, 'The Apocryphal/Deuterocanonical Books: A Catholic View', in The Parallel Apocrypha, p. xxxii.

6. For a recent discussion of 'defiling the hands' see Barton, *The Spirit and the Letter*, pp. 108–17.

7. The discussion about proposed dates is summarized in S. Jellicoe, *The Septuagint and Modern Study* (Oxford: Clarendon Press 1968), pp. 47–50.

8. The identity of the Hesychius referred to by Jerome is a subject on which there are differing opinions among scholars. Jellicoe, *The Septuagint and Modern Study*, pp. 146–8 summarizes these views.

9. See ibid., pp. 134–69 for the quotation and for discussion.

10. Ibid., pp. 215–21.

11. See ibid. for a useful summary, pp. 251–6.

12. I am indebted to Dr D. C. Parker for this information.

CHAPTER 7: *The Study of the Bible*

1. Jeffrey (ed.), *A Dictionary of Biblical Tradition in English Literature*.

2. For a fuller treatment of the points that follow see J. Rogerson, 'An Outline of the History of Old Testament Study', in J. Rogerson (ed.), *Beginning Old Testament Study* (London: SPCK 1983; revised 1998), pp. 6–24. See also J. Rogerson, 'The Old Testament', in J. Rogerson, C. Rowland and B. Lindars, *The Study and Use of the Bible* (Basingstoke: Marshall Pickering, Grand Rapids: Wm. B. Eerdmans Publishing Co. 1988), pp. 1–150.

3. Rashi in *Mikra'ot Gᵉdolot, Nᵉvi'im R'ishonim* (Jerusalem: Shoken 1959), p. 106b. For a convenient summary of the Jewish interpreters cited in this section, see A. Krausz, *Short Digest of Jewish Literature in the Middle Ages* (Sheffield: Naor Publications 1984).

4. A standard translation into English of Maimonides's *The Guide of the Perplexed* is that of S. Pines (Chicago: University of Chicago Press 1963, 2 vols).

5. See David Kimhi, *Perush Rabbi David ben Qimhi 'al Hatorah* (Jerusalem: Mossad Harav Kook 1970), pp. 14, 43–4. The interpretation attributed to Sa'adia is not

in the main text of *Perush Rabbenu Sa'adia Gaon 'al Hatorah* (Jerusalem; Mossad Harav Kook 1963), p. 15, but footnote 3 notes that Abraham Ibn Ezra (1089–1164) asserted that Sa'adia taught that neither the serpent nor the she-ass spoke, but that it was an angel that spoke.

6. See Rogerson in *The Study and Use of the Bible*, pp. 77–87.

7. For more details on the deists and the beginnings of biblical criticism see J. Rogerson, *Old Testament Criticism in the Nineteenth Century. England and Germany* (London: SPCK 1984).

8. W. M. L. de Wette, *Beiträge zur Einleitung in das Alte Testament* (Halle: 1806–7). For more details see J. Rogerson, *W. M. L. de Wette, Founder of Modern Biblical Criticism. An Intellectual Biography*, JSOTSS 126 (Sheffield: Sheffield Academic Press 1992).

9. J. Wellhausen, *Prolegomena zur Geschichte Israels* (Berlin: 1883), English translation, J. S. Black and A. Menzies, *Prolegomena to the History of Israel* (Edinburgh: 1885).

10. J. Ussher, *The Annals of the World* (London: 1658).

11. On the 19th-century controversies see P. Addinall, *Philosophy and Biblical Interpretation. A Study in Nineteenth-century Conflict* (Cambridge: Cambridge University Press 1991); J. R. Moore, *The Post-Darwinian Controversies* (Cambridge: Cambridge University Press 1979).

12. S. R. Driver, *Sermons on Subjects Connected with the Old Testament* (London: 1892); *The Book of Genesis*, Westminster Commentaries (London: Methuen 1904).

13. A. S. Peake, *The Bible. Its Origin, Its Significance and Its Abiding Worth* (London: Hodder & Stoughton 1913).

14. See M.-J. Lagrange, *Père Lagrange. Personal Reflections and Memoirs* (New York: Paulist Press 1985).

15. A useful account from an American perspective is G. P. Fogarty, *American Catholic Biblical Scholarship. A History from the Early Republic to Vatican II* (San Francisco: Harper & Row 1989).

16. See L. Jacobs, *Principles of the Jewish Faith. An Analytical Study* (London: Vallentine, Mitchell 1964), chapter 9 for a discussion of how critical methods can be reconciled with Jewish belief and practice.

17. These details are taken from D. J. Constantelos, 'The Apocryphal/Deutero-canonical Books: An Orthodox View', in The Parallel Apocrypha, pp. xxviii–xxix.

18. For these and other details see the entries in Jeffrey (ed.), *A Dictionary of Biblical Tradition in English Literature*.

19. See R. Smith, *Handel's Oratorios and Eighteenth-Century Thought* (Cambridge: Cambridge University Press 1995).

20. See B. Lindars, 'The New Testament', in Rogerson et al., *The Study and Use of the Bible*, pp. 229–397.

21. See Rogerson, *de Wette*, pp. 27–30.

22. For these subjects see further W. G. Kümmell, *The New Testament. The History of the Investigation of its Problems*, New Testament Library (London: SCM Press 1973); C. Brown, *Jesus in European Protestant Thought 1778–1860*, Studies in Historical Theology 1 (Durham, North Carolina: Labyrinth Press 1985); R. Morgan, *Biblical Interpretation*, Oxford Bible Series (Oxford: Oxford University Press 1988).

23. See B. D. Chilton, *The Temple of Jesus. His Sacrificial Program within a Cultural History of Sacrifice* (Pennsylvania: Pennsylvania State University Press 1992).

24. R. P. C. Hanson, Introduction to *The Pelican Guide to Modern Theology*, vol. 3 by R. Davidson and A. R. C. Leaney (Harmondsworth: Penguin Books 1970), p. 20.

25. These quotations from the Westminster Confession are taken from the Appendix to E. J. Young, *Thy Word is Truth. Some Thoughts on the Biblical Doctrine of Inspiration* (London: The Banner of Truth Trust 1963).

26. See G. M. Marsden, *Fundamentalism and American Culture. The Shaping of Twentieth Century Evangelicalism 1870–1925* (New York: Oxford University Press 1980).

27. For Liberation theologies see G. Gutierrez, *A Theology of Liberation. History, Politics and Salvation* (London: SCM Press 1974); N. K. Gottwald (ed.), *The Bible and Liberation. Political and Social Hermeneutics* (Maryknoll: Orbis Books 1983); G. West, *Biblical Hermeneutics of Liberation. Modes of Reading the Bible in the South African Context* (Pietermaritzburg: Cluster Publications 1991). For various approaches to feminism see A. Y. Collins, *Feminist Perspectives on Biblical Scholarship*, SBL Centennial Publications 10 (Chico: Scholars Press 1985).

28. L. Schottroff, 'Die Güte Gottes und die Solidarität von Menschen. Das Gleichnis von den Arbeitern im Weinberg', in W. Schottroff, W. Stegemann (eds), *Der Gott der kleinen Leute. Sozialgeschichtliche Auslegungen* (Munich: Chr. Kaiser Verlag, Gelnhausen: Burckhardthaus-Laetare Verlag 1979), vol. 2, pp. 71–93.

29. For an outline of feminist treatments of Genesis 1–3 see J. Rogerson, *Genesis 1–11*, Old Testament Guides (Sheffield: Sheffield Academic Press 1991).

30. See L. Schottroff and M.-T. Wacker (eds), *Von der Wurzel getragen. Christlich-feministische Exegese in Auseinandersetzung mit Antijudaismus*, Biblical Interpretation Series 17 (Leiden: E. J. Brill 1996).

31. For a good introduction see R. Alter and F. Kermode, *The Literary Guide to the Bible* (London: Collins 1987).

CHAPTER 8: *The Use of the Bible*

1. For more details on this point see the section 'Legal Texts', in Rogerson and Davies, *OTW*, pp. 233–52.

2. See Urbach, 'The Written Law and the Oral Law', in Urbach, *The Sages*, pp. 286–314 for the rabbinic view. D. Novak, *Law and Theology in Judaism* (New York: Ktav Publishing House 1974) provides an illuminating account of how traditional Jewish law works together with classical Jewish narrative traditions.

3. See the articles 'Ethics' and 'Natural Law', in K. Rahner (ed.), *Encyclopedia of Theology. A Concise Sacramentum Mundi* (London: Burns & Oates 1975).

4. Most modern translations note a textual variant which adds 'things strangled' – another way of expressing the avoidance of blood.

5. The problem is that if the meeting did take place, Paul never seems to refer to it or the decree in his extant letters.

6. A. Clarke, *The New Testament of Our Lord and Saviour Jesus Christ; containing the Text taken from the most correct copies of the present Authorised Translation, including the Marginal Readings and Parallel Texts with a Commentary and Critical Notes designed as a Help to a Better Understanding of the Sacred Writings* (London: 1817), p. 839.

7. See Dunn, *Colossians*, pp. 303–7 for a discussion of various views, including the view that Onesimus was not a slave.

8. See, classically, A. E. J. Rawlinson, *The Gospel According to St Mark*, Westminster Commentaries (London: Methuen 1925), p. 134: 'The Lord . . . appeals behind the Mosaic toleration and regulation of divorce to the primary institution of marriage as such, and deduces from Genesis the ideal of permanent and indissoluble marriage.' Rawlinson later became Bishop of Derby.

9. For a much fuller treatment see Rogerson et al., *The Study and Use of the Bible*.

10. For example the Epistle of Barnabas 10:3, 'Thou shalt not join thyself to men who resemble swine.'

11. See further Rogerson et al., *The Study and Use of the Bible*, pp. 54–6.

12. Ibid., pp. 57–8.

13. Ibid., pp. 70–73.

14. Quoted in D. Katz, *Sabbath and Sectarianism in Seventeenth-Century England*, Brill's Studies in Intellectual History 10 (Leiden: E. J. Brill 1988), p. 4.

15. Ibid.

16. Ibid., chapter V, 'English America'.

17. Quoted in ibid., p. 113.

18. M. Bucer, *De regno Christi*, Library of Christian Classics vol. 19 (London: SCM Press 1959), p. 319. This work was dedicated by Bucer to Edward VI of England.

19. See Rogerson et al., *The Study and Use of the Bible*, pp. 92–3.

20. See the essay by O. Barclay, 'The Nature of Christian Morality', in B. N. Kaye, G. J. Wenham (eds), *Law, Morality and the Bible* (Leicester: Inter-Varsity Press 1978), pp. 125–50.

21. M. Green, 'Homosexuality and the Christian – an overview', in M. Green

et al., *The Church and Homosexuality. A Positive Answer to the Current Debate* (London: Hodder & Stoughton 1980), p. 27.

22. R. Loewe, *The Position of Women in Judaism* (London: SPCK 1966), p. 22.

23. Quoted in Katz, *Sabbath and Sectarianism*, p. 113. Of course, the quotation strictly concerns polyandry. For a modern scholarly conservative view that denies that the Old Testament accepts polygamy see W. C. Kaiser Jr, *Toward Old Testament Ethics* (Grand Rapids: Zondervan 1983).

24. For an account of the debates and problems that arose after 1907 see G. K. A. Bell, *Randall Davidson, Archbishop of Canterbury* (London: Oxford University Press, 3rd edn 1952), pp. 550–57.

25. W. Shakespeare, *The Merchant of Venice* (I.iii), where Shylock says of Antonio:

> I hate him for he is a Christian;
> But more, for that in low simplicity
> He lends out money gratis and brings down
> The rate of usance here with us in Venice.

26. The Koran, translated with notes by N. J. Dawood, Penguin Classics (Harmondsworth: Penguin Books, 5th revised edn 1997), p. 41.

27. On this point generally, and on 'natural morality' in particular, see N. H. G. Robinson, *The Groundwork of Christian Ethics* (London: Collins 1971).

28. Lincoln, *Ephesians*, pp. 392–3.

29. For the whole debate see C. K. Barrett, *The First Epistle to the Corinthians*, Black's New Testament Commentaries (London: A. & C. Black 1968), pp. 187–246.

30. A. D. Lindsay, *The Two Moralities. Our Duty to God and to Society* (London: Eyre & Spottiswoode 1940).

31. Ibid., pp. 109–10.

Index

Figures in italics indicate maps. 'OT' indicates the Old Testament, and 'NT' the New Testament.

READ MORE IN PENGUIN

In every corner of the world, on every subject under the sun, Penguin represents quality and variety – the very best in publishing today.

For complete information about books available from Penguin – including Puffins, Penguin Classics and Arkana – and how to order them, write to us at the appropriate address below. Please note that for copyright reasons the selection of books varies from country to country.

In the United Kingdom: Please write to *Dept. EP, Penguin Books Ltd, Bath Road, Harmondsworth, West Drayton, Middlesex UB7 ODA*

In the United States: Please write to *Consumer Sales, Penguin Putnam Inc., P.O. Box 12289 Dept. B, Newark, New Jersey 07101-5289*. VISA and MasterCard holders call 1-800-788-6262 to order Penguin titles

In Canada: Please write to *Penguin Books Canada Ltd, 10 Alcorn Avenue, Suite 300, Toronto, Ontario M4V 3B2*

In Australia: Please write to *Penguin Books Australia Ltd, P.O. Box 257, Ringwood, Victoria 3134*

In New Zealand: Please write to *Penguin Books (NZ) Ltd, Private Bag 102902, North Shore Mail Centre, Auckland 10*

In India: Please write to *Penguin Books India Pvt Ltd, 11 Community Centre, Panchsheel Park, New Delhi 110017*

In the Netherlands: Please write to *Penguin Books Netherlands bv, Postbus 3507, NL-1001 AH Amsterdam*

In Germany: Please write to *Penguin Books Deutschland GmbH, Metzlerstrasse 26, 60594 Frankfurt am Main*

In Spain: Please write to *Penguin Books S. A., Bravo Murillo 19, 1° B, 28015 Madrid*

In Italy: Please write to *Penguin Italia s.r.l., Via Benedetto Croce 2, 20094 Corsico, Milano*

In France: Please write to *Penguin France, Le Carré Wilson, 62 rue Benjamin Baillaud, 31500 Toulouse*

In Japan: Please write to *Penguin Books Japan Ltd, Kaneko Building, 2-3-25 Koraku, Bunkyo-Ku, Tokyo 112*

In South Africa: Please write to *Penguin Books South Africa (Pty) Ltd, Private Bag X14, Parkview, 2122 Johannesburg*

READ MORE IN PENGUIN

HISTORY

Hope and Glory: Britain 1900–1990 Peter Clarke

'Splendid ... If you want a text book for the century, this is it'
Independent. 'Clarke has written one of the classic works of modern
history. His erudition is encyclopaedic, yet lightly and wittily borne.
He writes memorably, with an eye for the telling detail, an ear for
aphorism, and an instinct for irony' *Sunday Telegraph*

Instruments of Darkness: Witchcraft in England 1550–1750
James Sharpe

'Learned and enthralling ... Time and again, as I read this scrupu-
lously balanced work of scholarship, I was reminded of contemporary
parallels' Jan Morris, *Independent*

A Social History of England Asa Briggs

Asa Briggs's magnificent exploration of English society has been
totally revised and brought right up to the present day. 'A treasure
house of scholarly knowledge ... beautifully written, and full of the
author's love of his country, its people and its landscape' *Sunday
Times*

Hatchepsut: The Female Pharaoh Joyce Tyldesley

Queen – or, as she would prefer to be remembered king – Hatchepsut
was an astonishing woman. Defying tradition, she became the female
embodiment of a male role, dressing in men's clothes and even wearing
a false beard. Joyce Tyldesley's dazzling piece of detection strips away
the myths and restores the female pharaoh to her rightful place.

Fifty Years of Europe: An Album Jan Morris

'A highly insightful kaleidoscopic encyclopedia of European life ...
Jan Morris writes beautifully ... Like a good vintage wine [*Fifty
Years*] has to be sipped and savoured rather than gulped. Then it will
keep warming your soul for many years to come' *Observer*

READ MORE IN PENGUIN

ARCHAEOLOGY

The Penguin Dictionary of Archaeology
Warwick Bray and David Trump

The range of this dictionary is from the earliest prehistory to the civilizations before the rise of classical Greece and Rome. From the Abbevillian handaxe and the god Baal of the Canaanites to the Wisconsin and Würm glaciations of America and Europe, this dictionary concisely describes, in more than 1,600 entries, the sites, cultures, periods, techniques and terms of archaeology.

The Complete Dead Sea Scrolls in English   Geza Vermes

The discovery of the Dead Sea Scrolls in the Judaean desert between 1947 and 1956 transformed our understanding of the Hebrew Bible, early Judaism and the origins of Christianity. 'No translation of the Scrolls is either more readable or more authoritative than that of Vermes' *The Times Higher Education Supplement*

Ancient Iraq   Georges Roux

Newly revised and now in its third edition, *Ancient Iraq* covers the political, cultural and socio-economic history of Mesopotamia from the days of prehistory to the Christian era and somewhat beyond.

Breaking the Maya Code   Michael D. Coe

Over twenty years ago, no one could read the hieroglyphic texts carved on the magnificent Maya temples and palaces; today we can understand almost all of them. The inscriptions reveal a culture obsessed with warfare, dynastic rivalries and ritual blood-letting. 'An entertaining, enlightening and even humorous history of the great searchers after the meaning that lies in the Maya inscriptions' *Observer*

READ MORE IN PENGUIN

RELIGION

The Origin of Satan Elaine Pagels

'Pagels sets out to expose fault lines in the Christian tradition, beginning with the first identification, in the Old Testament, of dissident Jews as personifications of Satan ... Absorbingly, and with balanced insight, she explores this theme of supernatural conflict in its earliest days' *Sunday Times*

A New Handbook of Living Religions
Edited by John R. Hinnells

Comprehensive and informative, this survey of active twentieth-century religions has now been completely revised to include modern developments and recent scholarship. 'Excellent ... This whole book is a joy to read' *The Times Higher Education Supplement*

Sikhism Hew McLeod

A stimulating introduction to Sikh history, doctrine, customs and society. There are about 16 million Sikhs in the world today, 14 million of them living in or near the Punjab. This book explores how their distinctive beliefs emerged from the Hindu background of the times, and examines their ethics, rituals, festivities and ceremonies.

The Historical Figure of Jesus E. P. Sanders

'This book provides a generally convincing picture of the real Jesus, set within the world of Palestinian Judaism, and a practical demonstration of how to distinguish between historical information and theological elaboration in the Gospels' *The Times Literary Supplement*

Islam in the World Malise Ruthven

This informed and informative book places the contemporary Islamic revival in context, providing a fascinating introduction – the first of its kind – to Islamic origins, beliefs, history, geography, politics and society.